Vidyasagar

Vidyasagar

Reflections on a Notable Life

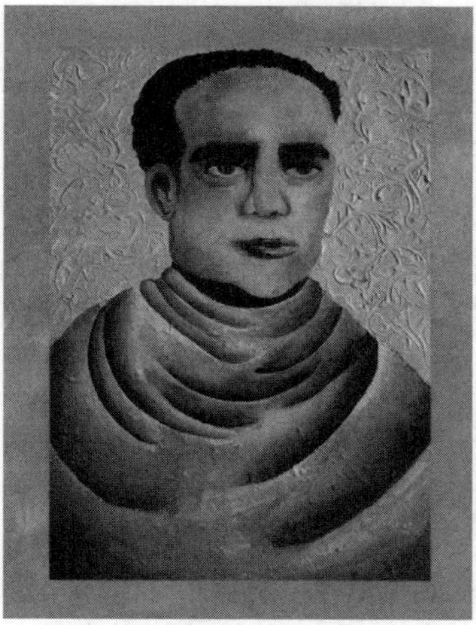

Amiya P. Sen

Orient BlackSwan

VIDYASAGAR: REFLECTIONS ON A NOTABLE LIFE

ORIENT BLACKSWAN PRIVATE LIMITED

Registered Office
3-6-752 Himayatnagar, Hyderabad 500 029, Telangana, India
e-mail: centraloffice@orientblackswan.com

Other Offices
Bengaluru, Chennai, Guwahati, Hyderabad,
Kolkata, Mumbai, New Delhi,
Noida, Patna, Visakhapatnam

First published by Orient Blackswan Private Limited 2021

ISBN 978-93-5442-039-9

Typeset in
Berling LT Std 10.5/12.75
by Le Studio Graphique, Gurgaon 122 007

032912

Printed in India at
Akash Press, New Delhi 110020

Published by
Orient Blackswan Private Limited
3-6-752 Himayatnagar, Hyderabad 500 029, Telangana, India
e-mail: info@orientblackswan.com

For
Rini (Shrobona),
in the hope that she too will,
someday, have a book of her own

Contents

Preface

W*hen in school,* I recall a teacher telling me that the lives of great men and women had to be written afresh every 100 years. To this, she added two reasons by way of explanation. In the first place, this was but a way of re-establishing their greatness, she said, and second, to also interrogate whether time and changing human perspectives required new ways of looking at 'greatness'. Was it not the case that notions of what constituted greatness also changed with time, she had quipped. Those words have stayed with me through every biography that I have so far attempted to write. As it turned out, such advice also eminently suited a historian who is apt to locate a life in its historical context, but also pay adequate attention to deeply personal ways of negotiating that context. There is no denying that the life and work of Pundit Iswarchandra Vidyasagar is best understood in the light of the social and historical environment into which he was born and which vitally shaped some of his core ideas and beliefs. And yet, in the course of working on this biography, it has occurred to me that there were ways in which he also transcended it. On important matters concerning contemporary Hindu society and culture, he held views that often went against received wisdom and was known to act in ways most men of his class would not. Situating him within a certain social class and its distinct behavioural patterns certainly helps, but does not exhaust the range of heuristic possibilities. As some of his contemporaries were quick to point out, Vidyasagar was, in several ways, an idiosyncratic Hindu Bengali.

This biography was written under extraordinary circumstances of the kind that the world has not seen in over 100 years. In this country, the human misery that has followed in the wake of the COVID-19 regime has been depressing and dehumanising, to say the least. While the fortunate among us have had the luxury of complaining about either the self-imposed isolation or enforced captivity, countless more have been forced to spend life in open spaces, painfully separated from their homes and families, disillusioned, dislocated, and disoriented, with only the recurring needs of food and shelter goading them to stay alive and continue to wage their relentless struggle. As I have found from experience, death is a more dramatic but also a simpler event to negotiate than continued human suffering.

In his time, too, Pundit Iswarchandra was a witness to the vagaries of famines and epidemics which ravaged the Bengal countryside and caused great human misery. His personal contribution to the alleviation of such misery and suffering would have been only marginally less than the relief provided by the colonial State. In contemporary Bengal, there were many who were richer than him in personal wealth, but poorer when it came to converting that wealth into selfless charity that could feed the starving, nurse the sick, but above all, show a sense of deep empathy for the deprived and the distressed.

The Bengali mystic, Sri Ramakrishna, once complained before his disciples and devotees that while men could shed bucketfuls of tears upon the death of their wives or family members, they never could shed a single tear while thinking of God. Vidyasagar never revealed an anxiety for God-realisation but could not hold back his tears thinking of the Hindu child-widow who was made to habitually deny herself food and drink; of the pain and the personal indignities that the forsaken Kulin wife suffered at the hands of the polygamous husband; of the famished children who rejoiced at the very thought of some lentils being cooked at home; of the father who faced a jail term for having failed to clear the debts incurred while getting his daughter married; or the poor Santhals who did not know just how to describe a delicacy they had been lovingly fed for the first time in their modest and unassuming lives. Pundit Iswarchanda was both a humanist who saw man as the measure of things and a humanitarian whose heart cried out at the sight of human distress and suffering. It might be wrong to call him a philanthropist for he appears to have acted more out of a sense of compassion and social justice than the public practice of altruism, wherein the call of moral duty was often overlaid with a sense of gratuitous self-importance. In his time, I imagine, there would also have been those who may have equalled his learning, but not his fortitude, nonchalance, and the sense of indomitable manliness.

The idea of writing a biography of Vidyasagar goes back a long time. If I recall correctly, it harks back to the time when I was a young researcher and had occasion to meet Professor K. N. Panikkar at a conference. Even at the time, it struck me that despite our somewhat different ideological leanings, both of us were prompt in showering our praise, affection, and nostalgia for the same man. However, such convergence of pious feelings, even when coming from recognisably different camps, does little to help overlook the fact that Pundit Iswarchandra has to be the only figure from renaissance Bengal whose memory has been vandalised by both the Indian Right and the Left. I also suspect that although equally impressed by the greatness of the man, the premises upon which Professor Panikkar and I rested our arguments were subtly different. If I did read him correctly at the time, Professor Panikkar's appreciation came essentially from the fact that despite belonging to an orthodox Brahmin family, Vidyasagar exhibited enough courage and conviction to upset the world of Brahminical orthodoxy through his several social reform campaigns and disinterestedness in the metaphysical questions raised within the Hindu cultural world. On the face of it, this characterisation cannot be disputed. My own understanding, however, has been to lay greater emphasis on the Pundit's self-understanding as a Brahmin. In this work, I have argued that both his social reform initiatives and educational vision emanated from this self-understanding in a very meaningful sense.

In producing this work, I have been considerably aided and enlightened by recent writings on Vidyasagar, most of which is in the Bengali language. My greatest intellectual debts here are to Professors Ramkrishna Bhattacharya, Paramesh Acharya, and Swapan Basu for their arduous and enduring contributions to the field of Vidyasagar Studies. My way of producing this biography has actually been to get English and Bengali language sources talking to each other in a creative dialogue. I cannot, however, claim with any certainty that I have even reasonably succeeded in this enterprise.

What also sustained me was the inspiration and support from some well-meaning friends and colleagues, who have all contributed to this volume in more ways than they can realise. To my philosopher friend, Malabika Majumdar, I have often acted like a nagging pest. There are several knotty philosophical issues and problems that she has helped me to better understand and resolve. Thankfully, the residual rigours of such painfully dense philosophical disputations were always mitigated by Malabika's enthusiasm for hosting sumptuous lunches.

In the month of February 2020, I was warmly invited to speak on Vidyasagar at three educational institutions in West Bengal: the University of Burdwan, the Women's University at Diamond Harbour (South 24 Paraganas), and Vidyasagar College in Kolkata. I take this opportunity to thank each of the concerned departments and their faculty for extending this kind invitation. My heartfelt thanks to Nandini Bhattacharya, Aparna Bandyopadhyay, and Shekhar Bhowmik, from Burdwan, Diamond Harbour, and Kolkata, respectively, for making it possible for me to test my new-fangled theories, speaking from platforms which they very graciously provided. Happily, this tour of West Bengal also coincided with my becoming acquainted with other distinguished scholars and historians of whom I had heard, but had never met in person. Among these are Professors Geraldine Forbes, Chittaranjan Panda, and his wife, the scholar of Hindu law, Dr Nandini Bhattacharya Panda.

I would be remiss if I failed to mention the kindness and hospitality always extended to me when in Kolkata by Tapati Sengupta, Tapati-di to me. In my reckoning, Tapati-di personally knows about half the people residing in Kolkata and almost everybody in the academic world of West Bengal! It is not hard to imagine how helpful that can be for a floating Probasi scholar like myself.

About a year earlier, I also had the good fortune to make a brief tour of the landmark institution in Kolkata, the Sanskrit College (now also a University), thanks to the then Vice-Chancellor, Professor Paula Banerjee, and Registrar, Dr Arundhati Mukherjee. Simply looking at Vidyasagar's personal desk and the College library, teeming with books and manuscripts, albeit a little dusty and disorderly for want of proper upkeep, was a most gratifying sight. I do wish the Government of West Bengal would give some thought to commemorating the 200th birth anniversary of Pundit Iswarchandra by updating the printed history of the Sanskrit College and more meticulously cataloguing its imposing collection of books and manuscripts.

I do also wish that some kindly and competent soul would think of paying a tribute to the memory of Akshaykumar Dutt, a close friend and collaborator of Vidyasagar, whose 200th birth anniversary also falls this year.

To the best of my knowledge, the last time someone wrote a biography of Vidyasagar in English was way back in 1980. A lot has changed in the past several years. This biography was primarily written for the interested student or laymen who might simply wish to have a feel for the subject without wanting to be drawn into the obfuscating, and sometimes even overbearing, presence of copious notes and citations. I have therefore refrained from using these, but have taken care to indicate a source wherever I considered this important or necessary. I find some relief in confessing that over time, I have come to enjoy writing books which, besides being useful in some ways, also seek to provide some entertainment to the reader.

In 1874, Pundit Iswarchandra was denied entry into the premises of the Asiatic Society on grounds of violating a dress code. In 2019, I was denied participation at a conference on the theme of Vidyasagar and Social Reform in India held at the Asiatic Society, Kolkata, and similarly failed to pass through the gates. I take it, therefore, that this must also have resulted from an undetected violation of some accepted code. However, on each of my previous visits to the Vidyasagar Hall of the Society, I have always made it a point to look admiringly at the portrait of the man whose austere presence and penetrating, yet kindly gaze only made me feel humble. This biography is a tribute in all humility to the scholar, educationist, and social reformer, but above all, a humane soul whose unbounded energy and kindness still continue to touch and to awaken us to a sense of enterprising freedom.

I am delighted that my publishers agreed to use on the title page a portrait of Pundit Iswarchandra painted by a local schoolgirl, Nayantara Sen. I thank Nayantara and her family for acceding to my request that such a portrait be prepared. It is also my fervent feeling that a man who so consistently and passionately pleaded for alleviating the depressing social conditions affecting the Hindu woman and wife, and advocated the cause of female education would have been himself happy at the way he has been thus commemorated by a young girl. Errors of fact or argument, needless to say, are entirely mine.

Amiya P. Sen
Gurgaon

one

Introduction

Where Pundit Iswarchandra Vidyasagar (1820–91) is concerned, quite extraordinarily, the man and his very historical presence may be said to have outlived his work spread over a lifetime. Arguably, his legacy rests not so much on the efforts he made in the fields of public education, pedagogy, language, literature, and social reform as it does on the energetic intentionality and approach that lay behind such work. Apparently, Vidyasagar does not bear a legacy to boast of that is comparable to that associated with some of his notable contemporaries or near contemporaries. Arguably, one reason for that could be that he was not, by instinct, an institution builder. Vidyasagar was not to any of the institutions associated with him what Rammohun Roy (1772–1833) had been to the Brahmo Samaj, Swami Vivekananda (1863–1902) to the Ramakrishna Math and Mission, or Rabindranath Tagore (1861–1941) to Visva Bharati. Although path breaking, bold and commendable in his time, his several enterprises have failed to endure. Some of his important initiatives were subverted or defeated in his own lifetime by social forces contrary to his nature and spirit; some others he gave up prematurely, unable to secure for himself an adequate space and momentum with the help of which these could be taken forward. Towards the second half of his life, he felt himself becoming increasingly isolated and constricted, and his intentions thwarted by opposition and indifference from both the State and civil society. In hindsight, it might even be observed that he had a rather unhappy family life: somewhat indifferent towards his wife, drawn into squabbles and litigation with brothers, and sufficiently upset with the ways of his only son to deny him a share in his property. All of these contributed to make him a lonely man and, for a time, perhaps even a misanthrope.

It is likely, though, that both his contemporaries and posterity misunderstood him, if only because he was, in many ways, different, idiosyncratic, and ahead of his times. To the best of my knowledge, no distinguished figure from nineteenth-century Bengal has been subjected to such contrary ideological pulls as Vidyasagar has been. His earliest biographers read him in quite contrary ways, and in more recent times, both the political Right and the political Left in India have desecrated his statues or images. Ironically enough, notwithstanding his standing as one of the greatest educationists of his time, on both occasions such acts of vandalism were carried out in a locale that was once the site of great intellectual ferment in the history of India and the birth of modern educational institutions. Perhaps this was only because Vidyasagar was himself not given to extremes, distrusting both the radical reformism of an anglicised class of Hindus that could turn both insensitive and irresponsible, and the reactionary social myopia of the Hindu orthodoxy, whose resistance to change bordered on the pathological. Vidyasagar was discomfited by Sibanath Sastri (1847–1919) joining the Brahmo Samaj, not because he disapproved of Brahmo theology or social practices but because of the immense pain and disappointment this brought to his aged father. He might not have agreed, one imagines, with the character Banilal in the famous play *The Persecuted* (1831) by Rev. Krishnamohan Bandopadhyay (1813–85), who proclaimed that the voice of 'truth' rang more loudly than that of the aggrieved father. Quite uniquely, Vidyasagar sought the consent of his parents before launching his campaign to legalise widow marriages, even though the exact sequence of events remains a matter of dispute among his biographers.

On the other hand, with regard to the class of traditional pundits who generally opposed his reformist schemes, he could but express only his disappointment and disdain. Vidyasagar considered such people not only regressive in their social or cultural attitudes, but also bereft of all dignity and self-respect. He once turned down the munificence of the Maharaja of Burdwan on the ground that he belonged to the independent, self-respecting service class created under the aegis of British rule, and that the gratuitous charity (*daan*) that the Maharaja proposed to dispense better suited the 'tulo pundit',[1] the dull, passive, impoverished Brahmin scholar frozen in archaic *chatuspathis*[2] and *tols*.[3] For this reason, too, he might have resented the epithet of 'Brahman Pundit', often disparagingly conferred on the Brahmin scholar who lived off patronage. In his novel *Chandrashekhar* (1875), Bankimchandra Chattopadhyay (1838–94) purposively states that Chandrashekhar was both a Brahmin and a pundit, but not a 'Brahmin Pundit'. I shall presently argue that his self-understanding as a Brahmin conditioned much of Vidyasagar's approach to his social and educational agendas. It was an understanding that was framed with an eye on the Brahmin as the archetype of the ideal scholar and educator, an agent of social change, the source of law as also its authorised interpreter. Apparently, these were also qualities that were important to the colonial ruling class, for whom Vidyasagar's status as an accomplished Brahmin scholar probably outstripped the value of his liberal reformism. It was important that liberality and the will to change originated in the Brahmin, since that made it more acceptable to both the State and traditional Hindu society.

The civilian Romesh Chandra Dutt (1848–1909) once remarked that he had been visibly moved by Vidyasagar's own descriptions of the grinding poverty which he and his father, Thakurdas Bandopadhyay, had to endure in their early days in colonial Calcutta. Quite possibly, one of the underlying purposes behind portraying such poverty and deprivation was to highlight the fact that even such depressing poverty did not take away from the power of endurance, fiery independence, and the righteous will of the ideal Brahmin. Such qualities supported the Brahmin in his claims to a certain social standing and ritual purity. Sri Ramakrishna Paramahamsa (1836–86) once recalled how his father, Khudiram, was a widely respected figure in the village since, despite struggling with poverty, he scrupulously spurned the munificence of wealthy but ritually inferior Sudra patrons.

As an educationist, Vidyasagar ended his career in some exasperation, alleging lack of support from the government and lack of enthusiasm in the public. This is all the more critical since, unlike Bhudeb Mukhopadhyay (1827–94), the other great educationist of the time, Vidyasagar was more an administrator than the author of some innovative discourse in the field of public education. Directly or indirectly, the Pundit alleged that his labours as an educationist had not been suitably rewarded, and that he had been overlooked for promotion to a higher office in favour of an Englishman. This only discreetly stopped short of alleging that the injustice meted out to him followed from notions of racial superiority. More importantly, though, recurring indecision and the lack of timely support from the government floundered his educational schemes and pushed him into a position of acute financial distress, albeit temporarily. His schemes for extending female education in Bengal were similarly affected by the untimely death of his friend and collaborator, John Drinkwater Bethune (1801–51). Given both the lack of enthusiasm and financial support inofficial quarters and the mounting unease in orthodox Hindu circles, a good number of female schools that he had opened in rural Bengal soon languished. Vidyasagar worked for roughly seven years as Principal, Sanskrit College, and his assuming this office in 1851 coincided with important changes to the curriculum, a new educational vision, as well as methods of teaching.[4] This rejuvenated an institution that was being adversely affected by competition from English-medium schools and, no less importantly, it provided quality education at a price that the average Hindu parent of the time could well afford. And yet, such changes that he had once boldly carried out now have only historical value. A classical Sanskrit education is not what the Indian youth seeks today.

His social reform campaigns, on which he staked both his energies and personal fortune, also ended in depressing failures. The attempt to popularise widow marriages among upper-caste Hindus, even in the teeth of rabid opposition and guarded threats to life, produced tardy results; far fewer widows were married in Bengal compared to Maharashtra or coastal Andhra, notwithstanding the fact that Bengal had escaped the wrath of Hindu spiritual leaders like the Shankaracharya who summarily excommunicated enterprising social reformers. His attempt to legally end multiple marriages among *kulin* Brahmin males was thwarted by the combination of an already cautious colonial ruling class and an indigenous opposition which included one-time friends and co-workers. Within Hindu Bengali society itself, this contributed to produce a controversy of a highly personalised character in which, somewhat surprisingly, opposing camps resorted to the use of abusive and indecorous language. In Vidyasagar's defence, though, it might be said that the man possessed the rare gift of combining wit with biting polemics. This was not a quality that Rammohun Roy, also drawn into protracted controversy, revealed. The gradual decline of polygamous practices ultimately resulted not from legislative intervention, but from changes in the political economy, the dissemination of modern education, and a rising social conscience, as some of Vidyasagar's contemporaries and critics had themselves correctly predicted.

Tagore rightly considered Vidyasagar the father of the modern Bengali prose, evident in his several school textbooks, reformist tracts, and Bengali adaptations from Sanskrit classics. By comparison, there was very little creative literature that Vidyasagar himself produced, and some contemporaries faulted him for precisely this reason. Vidyasagar has to be the only eminent literary figure of nineteenth-century Bengal who was not driven by a purely literary zeal. This sets him apart from the contemporary poet Michael Madhusudan Dutt (1824–73) or the novelist Bankimchandra Chattopadhyay (1838–94). He was more a worker than a thinker, and his novelty lay in the realisation that an adequately modernised vernacular, more than literary creativity itself, could be more instrumental in building a new knowledge system based on the advanced scientific and philosophical discourse of the contemporary West. Vidyasagar would have no doubt realised that a translation from one language to another was not always also a translation of ideas. For the latter to happen, the sinews of a language had to be strengthened and its powers of absorption and adaptability augmented. Only this could facilitate the propagation of an innovative moral pedagogy that was vital to the new ordering of social life. Vidyasagar usually spoke a colloquial Bengali but wrote in an elegant prose style, using an epistemic framework that was socially useful and sparklingly secular. This opened up his literary production to even the non-Hindu communities in Bengal. Apparently, his primers and textbooks were in use among Muslims as well in areas at quite some distance from Calcutta. Some discrepancies in his textbook *Bodhodoy* (first published in 1851) first caught the attention of a Mohammed Riyazuddin Ahmed, a Muslim member of a Reading Club located in village Rupsa in Tripura, who then alerted the author. Acknowledging this thankfully, Vidyasagar had the error corrected in the seventy-ninth edition (1883) of the work. The emphasis on building up and modernising the vernacular proved especially important for a politically subjected nation struggling to find self-expression. Perhaps this also made his works somewhat dated. Vidyasagar's creations did not have the power to transcend time as the works of Bankim or Rabindranath did, nor perhaps were they meant to.

What, then, are we left with once we take away from a man his failed campaigns or aborted enterprises? The man himself: a man defined by an undying zeal, a resolute will, and boundless energy, who allowed no degree of adversity or opposition to deter him from the social goals he had set for himself. Tagore himself was to put this very well when he said that it was not his justly famous compassion or even his extraordinary erudition that made Vidyasagar stand out as a man, but his unconquerable virility and manliness. Pundit Iswarchandra was honest enough to admit defeat and disillusionment when these could no longer be denied, and he also freely admitted his errors in judging the qualities of honesty, integrity or empathy in his countrymen. Importantly, though, he never paused to question the underlying purpose or the intrinsic importance of that which he had set out to do. As a child, he was known to be stubborn and as an adult, self-righteous and arrogant. It was common knowledge in late nineteenth-century Bengal that Vidyasagar could brook no opposition or interference, and there is also considerable truth in the allegation that he could never work felicitously as a member of some team. In every case, he chose to work within the rules he himself set, or within the space that he had assigned to himself. In the course of his public life, he was to join but soon tender his resignation from numerous bodies, alleging acute differences of perception and functioning. With the government, which continued to consult him on important matters of public policy or specific issues concerning the Hindu community, he often had reason to express more disagreement than agreement. And yet, all of this only combined to create in him a man quite untypical of the times, and very unlike the average, upper-caste Hindu of his class. At this point, it would only be appropriate to cite once again Tagore's reading of the man amidst his social environment:

> The average Bengali exhibited a lot of enthusiasm and faith but not the will to make these actionable: he fussed over work without actually attempting to perform such work. The Bengali took pride in emulating his English superiors and was delighted when patronisingly acknowledged by them. But what thrilled him most was his own cleverness with the use of vacuous words. (Tagore 2002; translation mine)

Evidently, the persona of Vidyasagar departs in several ways from such characterisation of the typical upper-caste, educated

Bengali *bhadralok* of the time. He was rarely seen in public and never delivered speeches, not even to promote widow marriages among Hindus, which, by his own admission, was the prime objective in his life. He preferred to act rather than write, and always thought of actions that would countermand and correct some previous action of his gone wrong. One of his pupils, the scholar and literary figure Krishnakamal Bhattacharya (1840–1932), gives us to believe that Vidyasagar's reputation and social standing among his countrymen were largely derived from the social and professional importance accorded to him by his English superiors. Indeed, with very few exceptions, people in the highest bureaucratic offices, including successive Lt. Governors of Bengal, befriended him and sought his advice on several matters. While Bhattacharya's observation is not off the mark, we need also to pause and ask if such camaraderie was not born of the fact that Englishmen too found in him qualities they expected to find in themselves. One of his close friends, Dr F. J. Mouat, Secretary to the Council of Education under the Bengal government, found in Vidyasagar a man of remarkable energy and decision-making powers such as he had rarely found in other Bengalis. Perhaps Vidyasagar's popularity with the officialdom and the respect that he earned from the English ruling class came from the fact that he chose to socialise with them on terms of equality. Several extant biographies of the man are replete with anecdotes—that have now become a part of social memory—of how he answered rudeness and incivility from an English official with an audacious discourtesy. By some odd coincidence, another contemporary who happily befriended British superiors and won some admiration from them was also an educationist by profession: Bhudeb Mukhopadhyay.

Pundit Iswarchandra lacked an attractive demeanour. Contemporaries have written repeatedly about his diminutive frame, invariably draped in coarse *dhoti* and *chadar*, wearing locally made slippers, with an oversized head and false teeth, and the forehead closely shaved, giving him the look of an 'Odiya menial'.[5] There are hilarious stories in circulation of how women, young and old, who had eagerly awaited his arrival at some public event were sorely disappointed to find that the man for whom they had weathered extreme heat, dust, and discomfort turned out to be visually indistinguishable from an ignoble *chaprasi*. Some among the educated were disillusioned to find that even as a Brahmin and distinguished educationist, he bore no resemblance to the fair and portly Bhudeb Mukhopadhyay, who also served the government with distinction. At times, people blindly judged him by the many myths, legends, and points of gossip that had been circulating about him. Jogendrakumar Chattopadhyay, the editor of the paper *Hitavadi*, narrates an amusing tale that he had once personally heard from Vidyasagar himself. Once, during an inspection tour of schools in district Hooghly, Vidyasagar broke his journey to be the guest of a local grocer. While he was there, a Brahmin, dressed as a *sanyasi*, also dropped in and began to smoke on his hookah. In the course of conversation, the grocer happened to ask the Brahmin if the current campaign for promoting widow marriage among Hindus had any validity. The question infuriated the Brahmin, who then began pontificating on how a Hindu woman, unlike the Muslim or Christian, could never be married twice. The grocer, not willing to give up so easily, observed that in Calcutta, a Brahmin pundit himself had sanctioned the marriage of Hindu widows. Further infuriated by this rejoinder, the Brahmin lashed out in the following words: 'A Brahman Pundit, you say! That man dines with Europeans, wears boots and a hat, smokes on cheroots and walks with an air of arrogance with his head cocked to one side!'

When asked if he had indeed met this person they called Vidyasagar, the Brahmin promptly retorted that he habitually caught sight of the man at least twice a day, travelling to and from his Badur bagan residence, sporting an impressive moustache and wearing fashionable glasses. At this point, the two men politely asked each other their identity. The Brahmin said that he was from a village in Pandua in north Bengal, but was completely devastated upon learning that he had been speaking to Vidyasagar all the while. 'Which Vidysasagar are you?' he demurely asked, hastily making his exit!

Sri Ramakrishna had once complained before his disciples that men cried bucketfuls of tears on the death of their wives, but did not care to shed even a drop in God-remembrance. Here, one cannot help but remark that Vidyasagar himself was something of an exception. He did weep on the death of his wife, Dinamoyee, who predeceased him, but this came from the sorrow of losing a faithful and long standing companion, not from any sense of sensual attachment to a woman or the effeminacy that Ramakrishna accused all husbands of. It is said that he was in the habit of bursting into tears at the slightest provocation, but such tears were shed neither in God-remembrance nor on account of a separation from a woman or wife. Rather, they were induced by reflection on the harsh tragedy that befell a Hindu child-widow, the pain and the humiliation suffered by the Kulin Brahmin's wife on being deserted by her husband, the suppressed unhappiness of the girl-bride whose childhood, innocence, and playfulness were taken away by premature marriages, and the dehumanising poverty, depravity, and starvation that many a household was forced to endure, especially in times of drought, famine, and virulent epidemics. All his life, Vidyasagar wept for such people, and it was in this that he established his innate humanism and also found the greatest personal solace.

Vidyasagar on the Procrustean Bed: Early Biographies and Conflicting Readings of a Life

Greek mythology speaks of a bandit by the name of Procrustes, who lured unsuspecting travellers into seeking shelter with him. He would then lay them down on an iron bed and once they were asleep, proceed to ensure that the height of his guest conformed to the size of the bed! He performed this act in two ways: in the case of the oversized traveller, he would simply amputate the legs while, with a shorter person, adequately stretch his limbs.

I was reminded of Procrustes and his ways while researching contemporary and later scholarly constructions of Pundit Iswarchandra's life and his manifold activities. Most, if not all, of these accounts have attempted to fit Vidyasagar and his achievements into preconceived frames. Here, it is important to remember that Procrustes laid his guests down on a cast-iron bed which itself could not be altered to fit the guests' size. Likewise, biographers and scholars commenting on the life of Vidyasagar have chosen to use what appears to be iron-clad theories to fit a man and his work into predetermined frames, falling shy of admitting that on many occasions, a close scrutiny of facts belie such fixities. It is of course to Vidyasagar's credit that he has been able to attract such attention from diverse quarters, ranging from the liberal Left to the conservative Right, and stretching across a great expanse of time. A comparable figure from contemporary Bengal, Raja Rammohun Roy, to whom we shall have to make recurring reference, does not appear to have attracted attention as readily. While biographies of Vidyasagar appeared within a few months of his death, Rammohun had to wait close to fifty years for his first (Bengali) biography to appear.

The first biographical sketch of Vidyasagar by his third brother, Sambhuchandra Vidyaratna (1829–1908), and revised by the still younger Ishanchandra appeared within two months of Vidyasagar's death in July 1891 (*Vidyasagar-Jeeboncharit*). An unpublished autobiographical fragment by Vidyasagar was published by his son, Narayanchandra Vidyaratna (1849–1923), in September 1891 (*Vidyasagar-Swarcahita Jeeboni*). Narayanchandra also went on to edit the first set of his Collected Works in 1895. The autobiographical fragment, although valuable in some ways, is an incomplete document, selective in its choices and limiting itself to descriptions of his ancestors and of his early life as a student in the city of Calcutta. It has virtually no information on the days spent at his birthplace, Birsingha, or of his chequered professional life. On the former, we gather some information only from his early biographies and on the latter, mainly from archival sources later explored by researchers. Evidently, the main agenda in the autobiographical fragment was to connect the author to his forebears and to establish his lineage within a class of rural Brahmin scholars. The question of pedigree would have been important to Vidyasagar, especially as he battled orthodox pundits over the twin issues of widow marriage and polygamy, both of which he tried to settle through recourse to Hindu legal texts. The fragment also alludes to the extraordinary strength of body and mind in Vidyasagar's ancestors, qualities that Vidyasagar also expected to find in himself. During his fatal illness in 1890–91, visitors who called on him regularly were to note his extraordinary capacity to endure pain.

Two successive biographies of Pundit Vidyasagar appeared in 1895 within a few months of each other. These were *Vidyasagar*, authored by Chandicharan Bandopadhyay (1858–1916), and *Vidyasagar. Arthat Samalochana Sankalita Iswarchandra Vidyasagarer Jeebon*, authored by Biharilal Sarkar (1855–1921). By his own admission, Biharilal's work had been first serialised in the monthly journal *Janmabhumi*, published from the *Bangabasi Press*. This would suggest that *bhadralok* households in Calcutta had been aware of this biographical work on Vidyasagar even before Chandicharan's work was made publicly available. The latter, however, proved to be relatively more popular. A thousand copies of Chandicharan's first edition were sold out within six months; it was subsequently made prescribed reading for students of Calcutta University, a status never extended to the work by Biharilal.

It is generally accepted that all biographical accounts of Vidyasagar fall into broadly three categories: pure biography; investigative, research-oriented works; and studies quite purposively determined by ideological concerns. However, such a neat categorisation cannot be sustained on closer scrutiny. For one, ideological concerns, whether of a political nature or cultural, permeates nearly every biographical account of Vidyasagar. There have also been authors who have written both on the level of popular, entertaining narratives and investigative research. Here, the name that comes readily to mind is that of Indra Mitra (Arabinda Guha). Mitra's *Karunasagar Vidyasagar* (1969), published by one of the leading publishing houses in West Bengal, underwent its seventh reprint in 2012. Guha followed this up in 1971 with a volume incorporating Vidyasagar's hitherto unpublished letters that have proven valuable to researchers.

The early biographies by Sambhuchandra, Chandicharan, and Biharilal were pioneering works that can claim to be authentic biographies, given the fact that one way or another, all three had access to the private papers of Vidyasagar. Sambhuchandra could also draw upon his personal experiences as a student of the Sanskrit College, Calcutta, to which he and his elder brother Deenabandhu Nyayaratna had been admitted, and of life lived in that colonial city. Of the brothers, he had also had the advantage of being in regular correspondence with Vidyasagar himself in the years to follow. Judging by the nature of this correspondence, it has to be said that this was also the cause of some rift between Sambhuchandra and his eldest brother. Being stationed at Birsingha (the birthplace of Vidyasagar) for most of his life in the company of the extended family, Sambhuchandra was personally drawn into the dynamics of local events or occurrences that both elated and irritated Vidyasagar. It would be only apt to mention here that an issue that caused much discordance between the brothers was the appropriateness of a widow marriage that took place in Birsingha, over which Vidyasagar found himself betrayed by his younger brothers. This event, to which we shall refer again in a subsequent chapter, left Vidyasagar determined never to visit his native village or the extended family again. In 1889, a long letter signed off as 'Birsingha Janani' (Mother Birsingha) and pathetically urging Vidyasagar to return to his native village reached him in Calcutta. It masqueraded as a letter from Bhagavati Devi, the mother, to her eldest son in Calcutta, and romanticised profusely about the Birsingha that once was, where even a peasant could explain the import of a Sanskrit *sloka* to a fellow peasant while winnowing paddy, and how the place had only languished in the absence of its guiding spirit. It specifically mentioned the unfortunate discord between brothers and expressed the wish—which any anxious mother would—that her sons would return to a harmonious fraternal life. Judging from its tone and the disclosure of details about the family, it is tempting to conclude that this might well have been the work of Sambhuchandra or Ishanchandra.

A close knowledge of Vidyasagar's early life in Calcutta enabled Sambhuchandra to dispute some of the dubious claims made by Chandicharan in particular. These are specifically listed in a work of 1896 titled *Bhramanirash* (The Dispelling of Untruth). Some of these errors are plainly factual. Thus, Sambhucharan rightly pointed out that the road accident of 1866 that seriously affected Vidyasagar's health occurred not *en route* from Calcutta to Uttarpara (district Hooghly), but on the return journey. Perhaps it was Chandicharan's Brahmo predispositions that had also led him to claim that Bhagavati Devi, Vidyasagar's mother, was an iconoclast of sorts. Sambhuchandra disabuses us of this presumption, claiming instead that she often prayed to local deities and even organised the autumnal Jagadhatri puja at Birshingha. It is now widely accepted, again on the strength of Sambhuchandra's testimony, that Vidyasagar, in a frantic attempt to respond to his mother's wishes to come to Birsingha, could not have possibly crossed the flooded river Damodar. Modern research has now established that Chandicharan also misled many by his claim that it was the Brahmo missionary Bejoykrishna Goswami (1841–99) who persuaded the 'atheistic' Vidyasagar to include references to God and religion in his school textbook, *Bodhodoy*. However, Sambhuchandra's corrections were not always accurate. For instance, he disputed Biharilal's contention that the gentleman who taught Vidyasagar some English was the Brahmo Rajnarain Basu, alleging that Biharilal had mistaken Rajnarain Gupta for Rajnarain Basu. And yet, we have it on the authority of Basu's autobiography itself that he did teach some English to Vidyasagar.

It is not surprising that in the second edition to his book in 1896, Chandicharan too should have hit back, equally disputing the authenticity of some events or occurrences reported by Sambhuchandra. What is more telling, though, is Chandicharan's accusation that notwithstanding every kindly help and generosity that he received from his older brother, Sambhuchandra was guilty of gross ingratitude, unduly maligning a noble soul for acts that he never committed. It cannot be entirely fortuitous that Sambhuchandra was led to produce a biography of Pandit Taranath Tarkavachaspati (1806–85), once a colleague of Vidyasagar at Sanskrit College, but thereafter his arch opponent over the controversy surrounding the attempt to legally end polygamous marriages.

Chandicharan and Biharilal were themselves considerably aided by Narayanchandra's offering them access to the family papers, but that apart, Biharilal admits to have meticulously researched events and episodes concerning Vidyasagar's professional life. He claims to have done this by turning over the old files of the *Hindoo Patriot,* and frequent visits to the archives at the Sanskrit College and the Asiatic Society. Both these biographies also carry strong ideological undercurrents. Not surprisingly, the Brahmo Chandicharan dedicated his work to Rammohun and expected Vidyasagar to follow the reformist quest begun by Rammohun, especially in relation to questions related to women. Presumably Chandicharan was influenced by the pressing concern that both reformers showed for the social emancipation of Hindu women. For both Rammohun and Vidyasagar, women represented the true proletariat in India, who had to be freed from the chains of enslavement and exploitation. That apart, there was a striking similarity in the methodology that they adopted over reform related to women, resorting to the use of *smriti* or Hindu law books to legitimise their reform campaigns and relying greatly on the printing press to publicise their reformist efforts. Both faced the ire of the Hindu orthodoxy and were drawn into extended polemical battles.

Biharilal, however, spoke from a very different perspective, which was largely conditioned by his long and active association with the Bangabasi press that ran the highly conservative and yet the most popular Bengali daily of the early 1880s. Biharilal had practical experience of running a printing press but, more importantly, he was also instrumental in actually ferrying low-priced Hindu religious classics from door to door, under a publishing scheme initiated by the Bangabasi press. Biharilal held Vidyasagar in great esteem and firmly rebutted any charges of deceit or duplicity in his hero. However, he also believed that no amount of kindness or compassion that his subject had shown in public life could absolve him of the sins accrued from committing certain un-dharmic acts and wantonly hurting Hindu sentiments. Here, his reference was primarily to the widow marriage campaign. When, in 1891, Vidyasagar expressed some reservations against the proposed amendment to the age of consent, Biharilal cheerfully acknowledged it as an act of atonement on the part of a well-meaning but misguided Hindu. In the closing years of the nineteenth century, vitally shaped by a burgeoning Hindu nationalism and a cultural backlash among Hindus, mutually combative postures between 'reformers' and 'revivalists' and the differences of approach or understanding as we find in Chandicharan and Biharilal could be foreseen. Even though he chose to criticise several of Vidysasgar's acts, as for instance his advocacy of female education but more typically, the attempt to legalise the marriage of Hindu widows, Biharilal was otherwise fairly acute in his observations and quite competent as a writer. Contrary to what has sometimes been suggested, his conservatism does not disqualify him as a biographer.

For some reason unknown to us, Sambhuchandra seems to have taken it upon himself to especially controvert many of Chandicharan's claims or assertions related to the life of Vidyasagar. In his *Bhramanirash* of 1896, to which we have earlier referred, there are over fifty such instances. Interestingly enough, he does not equally controvert the work of Biharilal, even when the latter committed the same factual errors. Sambhuchandra remains oblivious to the fact that Biharilal too wrongly refers to Vidyasagar's swimming across a flooded Damodar. However, Biharilal may have also committed relatively fewer errors of fact. In the first edition of his biography, Chandicharan stated that Vidyasagar had five younger brothers when, in fact, he had six. The name missing in this edition was that of Shibchandra. Also, Chandicharan did not list the brothers by age; it is thus that Ishanchandra, who was younger than both Harachandra and Harishchandra, the fourth and fifth brothers, respectively, is seen to precede his older brothers on the list. Such errors were corrected in the second edition of Chandicharan's book. A similar error with genealogy was pointed out by Santoshkumar Adhikari, also a biographer of Vidyasagar. Santoshkumar was the grandson of Vidyasagar's third daughter, Binodini, who was married to Suryakumar Adhikari.[6] In the instance mentioned above, Chandicharan had the name of one of Vidyasagar's sons-in-law wrong.

Sambhuchandra also took Chandicharan Bandopadhyay to task for daring to include in his work a portrait of Vidyasagar's wife, Deenamoyi Devi, among several others. In Sambhuchandra's view, including the photograph of a young married woman went against accepted convention. He was to also express some feeling of revulsion at this work for including the last photograph of the horribly emaciated Vidyasagar, taken at the cremation grounds. Such a photograph evoked only feelings of loathing (*bibhatsya*) and not compassion (*karuna*), Sambhuchandra complained with some bitterness.

Subalchandra Mitra's *Isvar Chandra Vidyasagar. A Story of His Life and Work* (1902), the first biography in English, popularised Vidyasagar beyond ethnic Bengal, but also admitted to have followed the line of criticism laid down by Biharilal. On the age of consent question, for example, Mitra virtually echoes the older work;however, on one level, his argument seems to be that even the genius of Vidyasagar was powerless against the degenerative properties of Kaliyuga that eroded human values and inverted many normative practices. Two other English-language works that have followed suit but remain relatively unpopular are Ananta Kumar Ray's *Vidyasagar: The Great Indian Educationist and Philanthropist* (1921) and Santosh Kumar Adhikari's *Vidyasagar and the Regeneration of Bengal* (1980). Adhikari (d. 2015), as we have noted earlier, was a great-grandson of Vidyasagar, and his book carried some intimate vignettes of the family history not available elsewhere. Of the third major study of Vidyasagar in the English language by Amales Tripathi, *Vidyasagar: The Traditional Modernizer* (1974), I shall briefly speak elsewhere.

Trends in Recent Scholarship

In the 1960s and 1970s, the intellectual agenda before historians and sociologists was to somehow rescue Vidyasagar from the earlier conservative readings of his life and work. In this enterprise, they were considerably influenced by an ideological tilt that occurred in the Indian academia in the 1950s and 1960s towards Left-Liberalism. It thereby became important to project Vidyasagar essentially as an enlightened, rational humanist, free from irrationalities bred by religion and embodying the best ideals of the European Enlightenment. Authors like Benoy Ghose, Badruddin Umar, and Gopal Haldar, all ideologically leaning to the Left, albeit in varying degrees, made much of Chandicharan's claim that left to himself, Vidyasagar would have remained something of an agnostic or an atheist. It is reasonable to say that their enthusiasm now looks quite misplaced. The employment of Marxian methodological tools also led this group of authors to subtly shift from a personality-centred understanding to interrogations of the broader social context. This might explain the remarkable similarity in the titles given to their works by Badruddin Umar and Benoy Ghose. Ghose called his multi-volume study *Vidyasagar O Bangali Samaj* (*Vidyasagar and*

Bengali Society, 1957–59) and Umar, *Iswarchandra Vidyasagar O Unnish Shataker Bangali Samaj* (*Vidyasgar and Bengali Society in the Nineteenth Century*, 1962). Umar, in particular, understood Vidyasagar's life and work as seriously constricted by his own class consciousness, and as quite complicit in the naïve, uncritical acceptance of their social role as a comprador class. There are echoes of this argument too in Gopal Haldar's *Vidyasagar. A Reassessment* (1972). Happily, some degree of Left revisionism, which approached the problem with greater finesse and imagination, has now dispelled the notion that people like Rammohun and Vidyasagar could have willingly functioned as collaborators of the Empire. This internal critique is best manifest in Asok Sen's work (*Iswar Chandra Vidyasagar and His Elusive Milestones*, 1977), which also brings forth greater historical insights and analytical sophistication. Ghose himself, palpably drifting away from Marxism after the 1950s, contested the charge once laid by ultra-Marxist Saroj Acharya (writing in the journal *Deshabrati* under the pseudonym 'Shashanka') that Vidyasagar had consciously sided with the British Indian State against the rebels of 1857. This encouraged people to reinterpret the Left desecration of the Vidyasagar statue in Goldighi in the 1970s as an act of misdirected vandalism.

However, the penchant for markedly shifting our attention from the person Vidyasagar to the broader socio-historical context in which he was situated persisted. Although heuristically helpful, this has also led to a relative neglect of Vidyasagar the man and of his agency and idiosyncrasy. Even in this revisionist Left view, Pundit Iswarchandra continues to surface as a creature of his times, an unwitting captive of his social and cultural predispositions, and unable therefore to transcend his own class limitations. In substance, the thesis suggests that an independent means of production would have *ipso facto* produced the power of unfettered agency in a class that was best equipped to create and act upon this agency. It has been argued that since the rigorous colonialist control over productive forces denied the nascent Indian bourgeoisie both the initiative and the power to transform society, Indians were pulled into performing tasks that had either to be aborted prematurely or else would end in failure. Mostly, the trouble with such formulations is their underlying reductionism, which would have us believe that an independent Indian bourgeoisie, free of colonialist control, would have successfully overcome all forms of conservative resistance to reform. Here, it is important to not overlook the fact that in nineteenth-century Calcutta, opposition to social change was not confined to the traditional literati alone, and a closer look will discover surprising conservatism even among people who otherwise counted themselves among the harbingers of progressive change. Considering the long drawn-out and animated debates over issues like inheritance or fixing the minimum age of marriage among Hindus even in independent India, one would have to say that conservatism can often be divested of a specific class or even a historical setting. In one sense, the conservatism of the *bhadralok* in mid-nineteenth century Bengal could only be tangentially related to the British colonialist presence. Colonialism did not produce this conservatism, although it encouraged and fortified it in devious ways. What also inhibits an effective understanding of some new critical position is the pompousness and opacity with which it is at times expressed. In his otherwise very evocative work, Asok Sen (2016 [1977]) claims that Vidyasagar was a part of

> a middle class which suffered from an unproductive means of livelihood, their lives marked by an absence of intellectual and social forces to work for relevant goals: their spirit of protest never had the corpus of an apposite production economy for adequate social articulation.

Verbosity apart, this argument poses two inherent difficulties. First, going by this argument, we are likely to understand Vidyasagar's educational schemes as being born in some false consciousness. Wasn't Vidyasagar simply naïve in assuming, Sen appears to ask, that the bourgeois moral pedagogy in his school textbooks, admittedly modelled on those in use in the contemporary West, could take root in a soil that could not possibly produce a free bourgeois class itself? In other words, had the man not failed to realise that idealism had to have a basis in tangible materiality? And yet, as it occurs to me, Vidyasagar rested his vision and his efforts not so much on a change in material conditions as on a change in attitudes on the part of his countrymen. An idea had to be first born in the mind, he believed, before it could take social root. This leads me to argue that on one level, Pundit Iswarchandra was more concerned with bringing home instructive ideals and examples than with their practicability. His compilations of biographical sketches of early modern Europeans, as for example in his *Charitaboli* (1836) or *Jeeboncharit* (1849), did not aim at social realism, but what he envisioned as a universally applicable order of values. Here, the usefulness or the intensity of the actions undertaken mattered more than the social and historical context in which they occurred. Ironically enough, it was precisely here that he met with some valid criticism from his countrymen. The contemporary educationist, Bhudeb Mukhopadhyay, doubted that any Hindu schoolboy would agree to kill a cat and then trade its skin for books as Vidyasagar, in his *Jeeboncharit*, showed the Frenchman Valentin Jamery Duval (1695–1775) to have done.

With regard to his social reformism in particular, it might be pertinent to ask if even an independent middle class could play a transformative role in a situation that relied on bringing modernity not so much as an independent historical movement, but as a strategic reinterpretation of tradition. This brings to the forefront larger questions, such as the *modus operandi* that Vidyasagar adopted for effecting social reform. Was the recourse to *shastra* merely a matter of opportunism and strategy for Vidyasagar, or was it also a matter of deeper personal faith? In this context, the critical question that one might also ask is: Why did scriptural sanction, on which Vidyasagar laid such great emphasis, still require the driving force of legislation to make it acceptable and effective? This is an important question to reflect upon since, in hindsight, it is amply clear that the opposition to Vidyasagar's reformism at times separated the question of *shastric* support for reform from that of enacting legislation. Undoubtedly, there were those who disputed the way Vidyasagar interpreted Hindu legal texts, but equally, there were many for whom the opinion of the *shastras* did not matter one way or another. What was in greater dispute was the moral authority of an alien State to overrule a cultural practice that had survived long enough to have practically turned into law. Whether or not Vidyasagar was indeed a 'traditional moderniser', as we are given to understand by scholars like Amales Tripathi, rests on a more nuanced understanding of what both these terms might have meant to Vidyasagar himself. Traditions are indeed capable of modernising and yet, on one level, this remains a thoroughly subjective process that may or may not easily integrate with a larger social consciousness. In the least, one can reasonably say that in the colonial setting of nineteenth-century Bengal, the ideas of both tradition and modernity could have been only selectively appropriated by Pundit Iswarchandra Vidyasagar. A wholesome fusion of the two would have been infinitesimally more difficult.

From about the 1980s, apparently, the passion for producing biographies of Vidyasagar appears to have run dry. Santosh Adhikari's quasi-biographical work of 1980, *Vidyasagar and the Regeneration of Bengal,* was perhaps the last in a long series spanning a period of nearly 100 years. Thereafter, emphasis seems to have increasingly shifted to intensive studies of select aspects of the Pundit's several ideas and projects, be they in the field of education or pedagogy, his relation to Hindu-Brahmanical culture, or his social reform strategies. In the world of English language scholarship, a powerful and productive trend that emerged in these years consciously attempted to make Vidyasagar the subject of social history, a relatively new enterprise in the annals of history writing in India. The methodological tools that such studies employed were also perceptibly different. The two representative contributions in this genre (arriving successively in 1995 and 1996) were authored by Sekhar Bandopadhyay and Sumit Sarkar, respectively.

In his 1995 essay 'Caste, Widow Marriage and the Reform of Popular Culture in Colonial Bengal', Bandopadhyay adopted a sharply feminist approach in addressing the multiple yet thickly enmeshed themes of patriarchy, public control of the private domains of marriage and conjugality, and nineteenth-century reformist discourses affecting social and cultural praxis among various castes. This made Bandopadhyay's essay visibly different from earlier approaches that had employed a predominantly narrative framework and failed to adequately problematise issues. For example, whereas the treatment of Vidyasagar's social reform projects in Ghose's work is impressive with its wealth of information, Bandopadhyay's strength lies in situating his enterprise within the emerging sub-discipline of gender studies. In my reckoning, though, this also creates certain problems. For one, in Bandopadhyay's essay it is hard to separate Vidyasagar's personal sentiments regarding the plight of the Hindu widow from the more generic *bhadralok* strategy of euphemistically giving the name of 'reform' to mounting patriarchal anxieties about socially disciplining the 'wayward' woman. In this view, Vidyasagar is almost consciously implicated in the new patriarchy, for which concern for the suffering woman emanates merely in patronising and paternalistic empathy. Not surprisingly, therefore, Bandopadhyay sees any encouragement given to widow marriages as little more than a carefully controlled move to channelise the 'uncontrolled' sexuality of the widow into the socially legitimate institution of marriage. Bandopadhyay also faults Vidyasagar for making no efforts to 'subvert' or even question the patriarchal order in the course of his social reform campaigns. On the contrary, his approaching the Calcutta *dalapatis* (community leaders) such as Radhakanta Deb of Sovabazar is interpreted as an act of opportunistic sycophancy and submission. In my understanding, Bandopadhyay's reading of the situation stems more from a subtle combination of idealism and predisposition towards a given ideology than from a pragmatically grounded realism. It tends to put too much transformative agency and power in the hands of the individual, placing him in a combative but unequal competition with populous and deeply entrenched conservative sentiments. Quite to the contrary, I am even willing to hazard the guess that in the longer view of things, the effective intercession of a Sudra *dalapati* (Radhakanta) in this matter would have considerably eroded the sanctifying power that Vidyasagar attached to the *shastra*s and to his own standing as a Brahmin legislator. Incidentally, none of the four *dalapati*s who ruled the Hindu community in contemporary Calcutta came to Vidyasagar's rescue, notwithstanding the fact that each of them led rival groups or factions which otherwise disagreed on even petty details. The *dal*s were themselves pretty implicated in factional politics, and had it not been for the ubiquitously conservative sentiment and the pathological resistance to change attached to the issue at hand, there might have been some room for a trade-off. It is important to note that barring Radhakanta himself, no other *dalapati* was approached by an increasingly exasperated Vidyasagar.

In a sense, the rebuff from a *dalapati* only eased Vidyasagar's passage towards seeking State intervention. Arguably, this was in keeping with the annals of Hindu law-making, whereby a royal fiat had the power to overrule all conflicting opinions. It also occurs to me that ultimately, the widow marriage question called for a legal innovation, and not simply the erasure of social opposition. At best, support from the *dalapati*s might have achieved the latter, but not the former. Bandopadhyay also mentions—but does not care to explain—why many more orthodox Hindus and feudal potentates supported Vidyasagar's move to abolish Kulin polygamy than the institution of widow marriage, even though it was the woman and the wife who was the most affected in both cases. After all, as a potentially threatening source of 'unbridled' female sexuality, the abandoned Kulin wife or the marriageable Kulin daughter could not be radically set apart from the widow.

Sarkar's 'Vidyasagar and Brahmanical Society', originally presented as two lectures in December 1996 at the Vidyasagar University, Midnapore, and subsequently reproduced in a couple of anthologies (see Sarkar 1997), takes the writing of social history to new levels. This is a densely argued essay, albeit racy and somewhat diffused in its narrative style. Instead of constructing a central argument, Sarkar weaves a rich tapestry of finely intermeshing ideas and arguments which are difficult to take apart without also identifying the connecting threads that bind the arguments. It is not an essay that a reader without an adequate grounding in the social and cultural history of renascent Bengal will readily understand. The essay, after all, is as much about the ways of the social class to which Vidyasagar belonged as it is about the man himself. Sarkar rightly insists on locating our subject and his work within a materially differentiated *bhadralok*. This is aptly illustrated through the argument that in effect, Vidyasagar's pedagogic experiments were directed not so much at the gilded youth of Calcutta as they were towards the poorer gentry of the *muffassil* and smaller towns. Indeed, this is reminiscent of Bhavanicharan Bandopadhyay's very perceptive reference (in his work *Kalikata Kamalaloy*, 1823) to the layered stratifications within the Hindu *bhadralok,* which included poor but 'respectable' classes. The internal stratification within the *bhadralok,* as Sarkar rightly reminds us, was porous and permeable in nature, which allowed a certain social mobility and freedom of thought and enterprise. This allowed poor but highly charismatic Brahmins like Vidyasagar and Ramakrishna, rooted in rural Bengali culture, to aspire to and ascend in even a social world shaped by urbanism and modern professional learning.

Critical assessments of Vidyasagar's educational thought and pedagogy are undertaken in the writings of Brian A. Hatcher, whose *Idioms of Improvement* (1996) remains a classic, and perhaps the single most important contribution to this field to date. Hatcher persuasively establishes the vital operative differences between the Orientalist and the vernacularist views of culture and educational pedagogy even within a shared locus of 'improvement' (*unnati*). He makes a fascinating study of Vidyasagar's primers and textbooks, which best reveal the process through which a hard-baked bourgeois individualism, borrowed from the contemporary West and valorising human enterprise and labour, are semantically and culturally transformed into their Indian equivalents of *yatna* and *parisrama*, devoted effort and diligence. Such values, furthermore, are seen to bear fruit only when harnessed to the single-minded pursuit of learning. Although a strongly utilitarian and materialistic tone pervaded Vidyasgar's primers, Hatcher's work has the merit of suggesting that at least in some respects, these may have been supplemented by the indigenous *nitishastra* tradition represented by works like the *Hitopadesha* and *Chanakya Slokas*. However, as we shall have occasion to see, Vidyasagar was not always comfortable with the use of such indigenous sources (see Chapter 3), if only because of the Puritanism he imbibed through the contemporary Western discourse. And here, Sarkar makes the fine point that notwithstanding his very persuasive commentary on the moral pedagogy of Vidyasagar, Hatcher still remains trapped within the all too familiar search for 'origins', whereas it would have been more meaningful to investigate the precise social context within which the emphasis on self-disciplining gained ground and social acceptance.

On the subject of Vidyasagar, Brian A. Hatcher now has two more important works to his credit. The first of these, *Iswarchandra Vidyasagar. Hindu Widow Remarriage*, published in 2012, is an extremely useful annotated translation of Vidyasagar's tracts on widow marriage, and scholars of Hindu culture and gender studies who do not read Bengali are bound to enormously profit from it. The other work, *The Life and Afterlife of an Eminent Indian* (2014), although sometimes mistaken for a biography, is actually a close bibliographical survey of studies related to Vidyasagar's life and work. In my reckoning, this makes an excellent companion to a standard modern biography of the man.

Some of us, I imagine, would be quite unfamiliar with the recent Bengali-language scholarship on Vidyasagar, which is otherwise both prolific and prodigious. In 1993, in a ground breaking work (*Samakale Vidyasagar* [*Vidyasagar and His Contemporaries*]), Swapan Basu laboriously dug up a vast volume of archival material to establish just how Vidyasagar and his work were received by his contemporaries. Even though the treatment here is not chronological, as a source-material for reconstructing the social and cultural engagements of Vidyasagar, Basu's work remains indispensable. Going by the range of issues covered or the variety of sources put to use, nothing comparable has followed since. On the question of Vidyasagar's educational thought and enterprise, but even more generally on colonial educational policy, we have reason to recall the impressive researches of Paramesh Acharya. Acharya would be a familiar name to non-Bengali readers, too, for his copious contributions to the study of colonial educational policy that appeared in *The Economic and Political Weekly* in the 1980s with some regularity. Acharya's more grounded studies on Vidyasagar's educational thought and enterprise appear in two volumes published in 2002 and 2011. The first of these, called *Bangali Prabuddha Samajer Seema o Vidyasagar Bitarka* (*The Limits of the Enlightened Bengali Society and the Controversy Surrounding Vidyasagar*), is a collection of essays that originally appeared in various journals, and disabuse us of many commonplace assumptions about just what Vidyasagar's educational objectives might have been. The second work, also a collection of essays titled *Bangalir Shikkha Chinta* (*The Educational Thought of the Bengalis*), is more ambitious, and also examines the post-Vidyasagar era in terms of educational policy.

Ramakrishna Bhattacharya's contribution to Vidyasagar Studies is staggering in its breadth of interest and the incisiveness that he brings to bear when examining select issues connected with the life of Pundit Iswarchandra. Bhattacharya's strength lies in his ability to comment on a wide range of issues, from the quality of Vidyasagar's textbooks to the hermeneutics of social reform, his distinctive understanding of Brahmanical philosophy and culture, and his place within the world of Brahmin pundits. A typical collection of such essays appears in *Vidyasagar: Nana Prosngo* (*Vidyasagar: Miscellaneous Essays*, 2011). To the best of my knowledge, such a broad and critical engagement with Vidyasagar and his work has not been replicated elsewhere, whether in English-language scholarship or Bengali.

Re-characterising Vidyasagar and His Methods of Work

Most biographical accounts of Vidyasagar emphasise his charity and compassion. This is not unwarranted and yet, on one level, represents attempts to sanitise a figure whose personal anguish and exasperations sometimes reached tragic proportions. Bringing out the 'greatness' and some exceptional qualities in men was also a patently Victorian trait in biography writing. Its typical manifestations in colonial Bengal may be seen in the series of biographical sketches that Tagore produced for his '*Charitrapuja*' (literally, *Character Worship*). In the case of Pundit Iswarchandra, however, such readings need to be qualified in at least three aspects. First, Vidyasagar's identity and approach differed significantly from that of Rammohun and, after him, of the Brahmo Samaj. Kissory Chand Mitra (1822–73), a member of the Young Bengal group, saw Rammohun as embodying the spirit of 'theo-philanthropy', a deistic movement that had originated in eighteenth-century France and advocated the idea that service to man was tantamount to the veneration of God. Rammohun's spiritual successor, Maharshi Debendranath Tagore (1817–1905), was fond of reciting the following *sloka*, '*tasmin preetitasya priyakarya sadhanancha eba*' (the veneration of God is accomplished by performing acts dear to Him, that is, service to one's fellow-man). In Vidyasagar's view of philanthropy, however, there was no reference to 'theos', to religion and God. To that extent, he was as much a humanist who took man to be the measure of everything as he was a humanitarian who was moved to care for humanity. Second, inasmuch as it was driven purely by an attempt to alleviate human poverty and suffering and did not have a class dimension, Vidyasagar's concept of charity differed significantly from the Brahmanical concept of *daan*, which was principally directed at a certain class (Brahmins) and aimed at deriving some value from the act, namely *punya* or religious merit. Whether consciously or otherwise, Vidyasagar appears to have followed Manu in believing that charity was the best course of action in benighted Kaliyuga, and yet his intentionality on this issue was markedly different. The noted Bengali scholar of popular science and folklorist, Ramendra Sundar Trivedi (1864–1919), reminds us of how Vidyasagar disagreed with the European concept of charity which, in both intention and effect, only underscored an assertion of the human ego. It was precisely this egoistic assertiveness that had also discomfited Sri Ramakrishna, who did not believe that a pious religious life could be derived from the philanthropic act of building schools and charitable hospitals. While at the Kali temple, the saint warned his devotees, one could not focus solely on feeding beggars while forgetting to pay respect to the Goddess Herself. On one level, this looks somewhat extraordinary since we have here two men arriving at the same conclusion, but from radically different positions. At first sight, there really cannot be valid points of comparison between the deeply pious Hindu devotee Ramakrishna, and a man who, though a Brahmin, often mocked religion, everyday rites and rituals, and conceited religious experts who claimed to truly understand God and religion.

Third, an emphasis on his charity and compassion alone conceals as much as it reveals. It reveals a deeply compassionate man who could not hold himself back at the sight of human depravity and suffering and often went out of his way to help those in distress. And yet the title 'Karunasagar' (ocean of compassion) conferred on him by the poet Madhusudan tends to take away from the other title he rightfully earned at the end of his course of study in the Sanskrit College: 'Vidyasagar'.

Pundit Iswarchandra once confessed before the Ramakrishna devotee and Calcutta schoolteacher, Mahendranath Gupta (1854–1932), that grinding poverty had denied him the opportunity to pursue his studies further. We do also know that Thakurdas, his father, entertained similar feelings about himself, and his first desire upon relocating Iswarchandra in Calcutta was to ensure a classical Sanskrit education for his son so that he, too, could fall back on the traditional calling of his ancestors. The contemporary scholar, Benoy Ghose, takes Knowledge (*bidya*) to be Vidyasagar's true asset, one that he earned purely on the strength of his own merit;'Vidyasagar was a successful trader in knowledge', Ghose concluded. When valorising his acts of charity and compassion, some contemporaries like Madhusudan may have been partly influenced by the magnanimity of Vidyasagar, who often went to the extent of borrowing money from friends and acquaintances in order to rescue another friend in acute distress, with some financially damaging consequences for himself.

The other aspect that has been relatively neglected is Pandit Iswarchandra's self-understanding as a Brahmin. Even the otherwise brilliant essay by Tagore (*Vidyasagar Charit*, 1895, 1898) neglects to adequately stress this quality in the man that was at once the source of his extraordinary courage and compassion. It is noticeable that Vidyasagar does not really complain about the hard life that he had to face as a young boy, partly because in his perception, even a life of grinding poverty did not erode the sanctity or innate powers of Brahminhood. On the contrary, it was the consistent pursuit of simplicity, self-denial, endurance, moral courage, and the will to turn down gratuitous patronage even in times of distress that truly established an ideal Brahmin in his rightful place. Quite possibly, Vidyasagar's persistent sartorial preference for coarse *dhuti* and *chadar* and unostentatious slippers also underscores this identity of a man nobler in deeds than in appearance. I also suspect that his fondness for walking tirelessly for long stretches was also a means of recovering for himself the qualities of an ideal Brahmin through a self-imposed discipline. What is usually overlooked is the fact that he was also opposed to any form of cruelty shown to man or animal. For part of his life, Vidyasagar would not agree to ride horse-drawn carriages for fear of subjecting an animal to hardships that it could not protest. At no stage in his life was Vidyasagar oblivious to his standing as a Brahmin, and here I would venture to argue that both his reforming zeal and moral pedagogy were, at least in part, also derived from his self-conscious location within the potent agency and institution of the ideal Brahmin. This was the Brahminism that also produced a somewhat condescendingly compassionate view of the world and of our recurring follies and frailties, helplessly caught up as we were in the inexorable cycle of births and deaths. The key to unravelling the mysteries of life was unquestionably held by the Brahmin.

In ethnic Bengal, where texts more than custom were seen to regulate social behaviour and hence governed the processes of social change or legal innovation, a Brahmin like Vidyasagar, reputed for his traditional scholarship and yet committed to things modern, was well-equipped to assume a position of social leadership. He would have been especially valuable to those who did not resent change *per se*, but preferred that the initiative for change remained in the hands of competent Hindus. He would have been equally valuable to those who were convinced of the need for social reordering at a time when it looked increasingly difficult to resist or brush aside the moral and intellectual challenges thrown by the contemporary West. Further, he could also make himself useful to the colonial State, which was keen to live up to a professed rhetoric that underscored its 'enlightened' and 'emancipating' presence. In one of the concluding readings of the draft Widow Marriage Bill in 1856, the Law Member to the Governor General's Council let it be known that even in the face of the most vitriolic opposition, the government would still pass the Bill, if only for the 'sake of the English name'. Vidyasagar was clearly important to the success of the Bill in a province where, hitherto, all major acts of social reform had originated in a Brahmin and on the strength of textual hermeneutics. Through the nineteenth century, Bengal clearly followed the path of social initiatives being seized by the Brahmin and in the interests of a subtly controlled enforcement of a reformed Brahmanism. In Bengal, Brahmanism was rarely contested, one way or the other, by radical challenges originating in the lower social orders. On the contrary, a local Sudra potentate like Radhakanta Deb had the power and resources to defend older habits and practices even against Brahmin-led initiatives, as over the controversy surrounding the abolition of sati. Interestingly enough, this encourages us to separate the greater cumulative power of Brahmanism from the initiatives taken by an individual Brahmin. And yet, it would be important to remember that what a man like Radhakanta essentially contested was not the Brahmin's right *per se* to take social initiatives, but a rupture between the Brahmin and Brahmanism. With both the sati legislation and that concerning widow marriage, reformist moves would have floundered had they not originated in a Brahmin. Arguably, there is a curious parallel here too between the top-down model adopted by Pundit Iswarchandra in matters of social reform and the filtration theory he supported with respect to mass education.

It has been suggested, typically by Gopal Haldar, that for Vidyasagar, the recourse to *shastra*s for effecting social change was essentially a matter of strategy. At first glance, this appears to draw support from the Pundit's own admission that his countrymen were unlikely to respond to humanitarian appeals or to the voice of reason, and that locating support in the *smriti* texts would bring them around sooner to accepting novel changes. Going by preceding history, such a surmise appears neither unreasonable nor unfounded. In early modern Calcutta, it was quite common to secure the arbitration of pundits in matters pertaining to everyday life. When running water in taps was first introduced in the city, learned Brahmin scholars were summoned by a local aristocrat, Raja Kalikrishna Dev Bahadur, to determine if its consumption was ritually polluting for the orthodox Hindu. Pundit Premchandra Tarkabagish (1805–67), one of Vidyasagar's teachers at the Sanskrit College, was so averse to its use that he left Calcutta for Kashi, only to die of cholera in that city. Hindus agreed to consume sacred food (*prasada*) from the Jagannath temple in Puri with their shoes on[7] only after a team comprising three ritual experts pronounced their judgement in its favour. In 1829, the first flour mill was set up on the banks of the Ganges amidst great consternation. Pundit Taranath Tarkavachaspati (of whom we shall soon hear more) excluded both ice and soda-water from the list of food and drink that a Hindu could consume without scruple. In 1836, Madhusudan Gupta (1800–56) was deemed an out caste after dissecting a human cadaver at the Medical College, and was taken back into his community only after he defended the *shastric* validity of his position before a team of pundits.

And yet, it was somewhat naïve of Vidyasagar to believe that the day-to-day life of the contemporary Hindu was still significantly determined by the rule of the *smriti*s. In his own writings against Kulin polygamy, Vidyasagar was to cite how customs had been changing over time, with or without reference to the *shastra*s. But more importantly, he also seems to have taken a dynamic view of Hindu law and legalists, arguing that even Hindu law-givers of old were sensitised to the changing needs of society and flexible enough to suitably alter their prescriptions in keeping with the social or moral transformations occurring within the community. This is the ground on which he chose to base his widow marriage campaign, specifically the text by Parasar, which he argued had adopted the principle of *yugadharma*, or conduct befitting a particular age. This made *Parasar Smriti* alone the authoritative text for Kaliyuga. Later down this work, we shall find him arguing that it was pure expediency that had led Parasar to allow the marriage of widows in degenerative Kaliyuga, since the other options left to the Hindu widow were far more difficult to follow. Admittedly, the recourse to the *shastra*s had been partly thrust upon Vidyasagar by Rammohun's earlier handling of the sati campaign, which drew heavily upon Manu and other works of *smriti*. This was a precedence that could neither be ignored nor negated, and it may be reasonably argued that Rammohun's taking to the path of exegesis perhaps only underscores what Vidyasagar was to later express about *shastra* alone being the effective key to procuring a public consensus on social reform. This makes the recourse to *shastra* attuned more towards social realism than strategy.

While Rammohun relied on a combination of reason, humanitarian appeal, and scriptural sanction, with Vidyasagar, 'reason' increasingly took a backseat. On one level, this was unfortunate. Judging by what appeared in the contemporary Bengali press with some regularity, there are sufficient grounds to believe that a good number of men and women had opted to pay attention to the voice of reason and of securing social justice for the beleaguered woman. In all probability, this movement might have been considerably strengthened by Vidyasagar's willingness to provide rationality greater space within his overall approach or strategy. At times, *shastric* prescriptions appear to have also held him on a tight leash. Vidyasagar sided with patriarchy to the extent of approving a second marriage among men in the interests of securing a progeny, as per the dictates of *shastra*s. He would not accept the suggestion made by a distinguished contemporary that since infertility could affect both men and women, it was unjust of men to marry a second time without medically determining just where the fault lay. He similarly opposed the idea of imposing a deterrent tax on men marrying more than once on the ground that this would violate the ruling of *shastra*s, which encouraged men to remarry, even within the lifetime of the first wife, in case she failed to conceive a child within eight years of marriage and cohabitation. On a personal level, Vidyasagar firmly believed in the sanctity of the *shastra*s, and to that extent, his recourse to *shastric* prescriptions could not have been mere strategy.

The heavy emphasis laid on scriptural sanction when the objective, ultimately, was to secure a change in law may seem puzzling. Vidyasagar would have been quite aware of the fact that in Hindu jurisprudence, a royal fiat had the authority to overrule scriptural ruling. This was the very argument that he himself was to use when resorting to the *Parasar Samhita* in favour of widow marriages. Here, he argued that although Parasar also prescribed *sahamarana* (self-immolation of the widow on the funeral pyre of the husband) as one of the three options open to a widow, this was practically ruled out by law and was hence not actionable. It follows from this that by resorting to the use of *shastras*, Vidyasagar was aiming not to convince his countrymen alone but also the ruling class itself, whose hands, as he would have no doubt realised, would be considerably strengthened by the availability of scriptural support. It is also interesting that his earliest tract relating to woman-related reform, on the ills of early marriages, published only five years earlier in 1850, carries little or no reference to scriptural justification. Did Vidyasagar's thoughts on this question, then, evolve over time and through sundry experiences?

Finally, it could be said that the use of *shastras* proved to be a double-edged sword. On the one hand, it may have helped to convince some sections of Bengali Hindu society and the English ruling classes about the appropriateness of his actions. On the other hand, paradoxically, this also rendered his future tasks more difficult. In the case of India, there was a clear divide between *shastra* and custom; they differed both in their origin and objectives. As Vidyasagar himself was often to assert, the objective of *shastra* was to instruct people on *dharma* or righteous conduct in life. This obligation in turn led law-givers to prescribe duties and obligations of a religious nature, which were expected to produce spiritual benefits. Speaking with the advantage of hindsight, it could be justly argued that this complex equation between *shastra*, *dharma*, and social usages encouraged the orthodoxy, that was pitted against reform, to deliberately misinterpret the reformer's rational and humanitarian interpretations as brazen departures from, or violations of, *dharma*. Predictably, this had a multiplying effect on orthodox Hindus, further intensifying the opposition to Vidyasagar's reformist schemes.

In appealing to his countrymen to support the campaign for the marriage of widows, Vidyasagar adopted a hermeneutic approach that even Rammohun had failed to do. Given his argument that the law-givers of old were not inflexible in their approach and were willing to adapt themselves to changing circumstances, we would have to grant that hermeneutics was an ongoing exercise and that ideas or practices had to be interpreted afresh with advancing time. This is exactly the position that Bankimchandra employed when producing his commentary on the *Bhagavad Gita*. Acharya Sankara was no doubt an extraordinary scholar and a revered name among the Hindus, Bankimchandra admitted, and yet his interpretation of the text was anachronistic and ill-suited to the modern age. This leads me to wonder if Vidyasagar too could have ventured into the task of suitably producing modern commentaries on older Hindu social codes. Was it simply humility, diffidence, or a realistic assessment of the situation at hand that prevented him from undertaking this exercise?

I am not entirely convinced by the argument sometimes made to the effect that Vidyasagar's reformist tracts were in substance no different from the *vyavastha*s or rulings on sundry matters that Brahmin scholars were known to have often delivered in the past. This argument needs to be qualified in at least four ways. First, *vyavastha*s were not driven by an innovative reformist zeal, which was clearly the case with Vidyasagar. Second, more often than not, *vyavastha*s were meant to address specific problems affecting an individual or a group of individuals, and not issues affecting the Hindu community as a whole. The kind of resolutions that Brahmins offered, some of which we have mentioned in passing above, addressed specific caste groups, often the Brahmin or else the Sudra. Third, such *vyavastha*s were limited in circulation and were not always propagated in the public sphere. Apart from being a reformer, Vidyasagar also saw himself as a publicist for whom the print media and public spaces were of vital operative importance. Fourth, Vidyasagar's tracts always carried a rational and humanitarian appeal, however weak at times. Leaving aside earlier writings by Rammohun, this was something unique and unprecedented in the chronicles of social change in India.

Notes

1. A *tulo pundit* would be a Brahmin scholar whose main vocation was to run a *tol*. This would be a pundit different from the Brahmin scholars who were patronised by big landowners and royalty.
2. *Chatuspathis* were places of indigenous traditional learning.
3. *Tols* were institutions of traditional, Sanskritic learning open only to boys form the upper castes, predominantly Brahmins.
4. This matter will be taken up in detail in Chapter 3 on education.
5. 'Odiya menial' was a characterisation commonly used by the nineteenth-century Bengali *bhadralok* for the common Odiya worker, petty shopkeeper, or *palki* bearers, etc., who had come as migrants to the city of Calcutta.
6. Oddly, Sambhuchandra commits the error of calling this daughter Saratkumari. Saratkumari, married to Kartikchandra Chattopadhyay, was his fourth daughter
7. Accepting and consuming *prasada* without taking one's shoes off is considered ritually polluting and disrespectful to the God/Goddess. This is comparable to taking off one's shoes or slippers when entering orthodox Hindu homes, or with covering one's head with a hat or scarf when entering a mosque or gurudwara.

two

A Luminous Life Lived in Full

I*swarchandra Bandopadhyay (Vidyasagar)* was born on 26 September 1820 at village Birsingha, then located in district Hoogly, Bengal. It was later made a part of district Midnapore, adjoining Odisha, under the administration of George Campbell, Lt. Governor of Bengal between the years 1872 and 1874. In later life, Vidyasagar would often quip about how this administrative change largely explained why most people mistook him for an Odiya by looks, birth, and upbringing.

A useful description of Vidyasagar's ancestry can be found in the autobiographical fragment he left behind, which was subsequently published in 1891 by Narayanchandra Bandopadhyay, his son. Brian A. Hatcher, an acknowledged authority on the life and work of Vidyasagar, has rightly pointed out some defining qualities about this fragment. First, it remains an incomplete account, omitting many significant aspects of his early life. We know very little of Vidyasagar's life spent in his native village, Birsingha. On this aspect, our information comes mainly through the labours of professional scholars and researchers. Neither Sambhuchandra nor Santosh Adhikari, who were members of his family, has been of much help here. Second, Vidyasagar's account pays more attention to the initial journey from Birsingha to Calcutta than to his life as a student in the colonial city. Perhaps this is only natural, given the ways in which this journey changed the course of his life. As borne out by the story that has now become household legend in Bengal, it was on this journey that the prodigious gifts of the boy were first demonstrated. By merely looking at the milestones planted by the roadside, the 8-year-old boy taught himself the first lessons in English numerals. Third, it says practically nothing about his married or domestic life. Fourth, the autobiography focuses more on Vidyasagar's ancestors than it does on himself. But even within this history, the account is weighted in favour of a particular man, his paternal grandfather Ramjoy Tarkabhushan. It has sometimes been argued, as for example by Hatcher himself, that for Vidyasagar, the narrative on his ancestors was really to underscore his own pedigree and intellectual lineage. Indeed, highlighting his birth in a family of pundits might have helped him to better meet the challenges thrown by his several pundit opponents in the successive controversies surrounding widow marriages and polygamy. On the other hand, neither Ramjoy Tarkabhushan nor Thakurdas Bandopadhyay, his father, were scholars, even though Vidyasagar himself used the expression '*sanskritvyavasai*' (traders in Sanskrit) to describe his ancestral family.

If at all Vidyasagar's primary intention was to establish his *locus standi* as a Brahmin scholar, he might have more justly referred to Bhuvaneswar Vidyalankar of village Banamalipur, his paternal great-grandfather; Umapati Tarkasiddhanta of village Birsingha, his father's maternal grandfather; Panchanan Vidyabagish of village Patul, his mother's maternal grandfather; and Ramkanta Tarkabagish of village Goghat, his own maternal grandfather, all of whom were established pundits of the Khanakul-Krishnanangar area. This area claimed to have rivalled even Nabadwip as a centre of learning. We know from the researches of Benoy Ghose that Umapati Tarkasiddhanta was a famed grammarian who impressed visiting scholars from Nabadwip, and that Panchanan Tarkabagish was a scholar of *smriti* and Ramkanta Tarkabagish, who ran a *chatuspathi*, had earned the honorific title of Tarkabagish at the young age of twenty-one or twenty-two. Ramkanta was also dedicated to tantric *sadhana* and it is reliably learnt that the pursuit of extremely esoteric practices performed with the aid of human cadavers (*shavasadhana*) contributed to an increasing insanity in the man at one point in time, from which he could never fully recover. Within the course of the studies he completed at Sanskrit College, Vidyasagar himself appears to have specialised in *vyakaran* (Grammar) and *smriti* (Hindu law). But of his illustrious forebears in these fields, he says very little.

When describing his grandfather, Ramjoy, Vidyasagar focused on his qualities as a man and an upright Brahmin. In this account, his grandfather appears to be strong in both body and mind, which he exhibited by fearlessly traversing a dacoit-infested area on his own, carrying only an iron staff. Incidentally, the iron staff came in especially handy when once, while passing through a thicket, he was confronted by an angry bear which mauled him badly. Notwithstanding his serious injuries, Ramjoy fiercely beat the animal to death; he was to carry the wounds inflicted by the bear for a long time. More importantly, Ramjoy was fiercely independent and, as it turned out, also drawn to a spiritual life. Sometime after his marriage to Durga Devi, domestic squabbles between himself and his brothers forced him to leave home and set out on a long pilgrimage trail in north India lasting several years. He returned just on the eve of the birth of his eldest grandson in 1820, dressed as a Hindu mendicant, and would not have been identified by the villagers but for his youngest daughter, Annapurna, who promptly recognised her father despite his unfamiliar guise of a *sanyasi*. Reportedly, by the time he returned from his pilgrimage, both his sons Thakurdas and Kalidas had been married and his eldest daughter-in-law, Bhagawati Devi, was pregnant with child. Extant biographies report that his return was prompted by a prophecy that spoke of a prodigious child about to be born in his family. Ramjoy appears to have played an important part in his grandson's life, at least in terms of public memory. It was he who jokingly described his grandson as a 'bull calf' even as he was born, hinting at the stubbornness to which many more were to testify in the years to come. If legends are to be believed, it was also he who predicted that the child would stammer. All his life, Vidyasagar avoided public speaking, even though he was a great conversationalist and could enliven any gossip in the company of his friends and acquaintances. Anandakrishna Basu, the grandson of Radhakanta Deb, tells us that whenever he visited the Deb family at Sovabazar, he spent as much as six to seven hours spinning narratives that were instructively anecdotal, enchantingly humorous, and greatly entertaining. It is said that he could even force the highly anglicised barrister, Womesh Chunder Bonnerji (1844–1906), to temporarily suspend his 'civilised' habits. Bonnerji was otherwise known to even blow his nose in the 'English way'! Going by contemporary accounts, Vidyasagar also had a presence of mind and a good sense of humour. Once, when the Principal of the Bethune Girls School, Miss Piggott, wanted to terminate the services of a pundit for an offence he may not have really committed, the hapless pundit asked Vidyasagar if he could mediate. At the review committee that sat in judgment over the case, Vidyasagar tried hard to convince his English superiors of the innocence of the man. However, upon discovering that he was fast losing ground, he blurted out: 'Okay, have him sacked if you must appease a lady!' Reportedly, the Englishmen present had a hearty laugh at this, and the pundit retained his job.

The attention that Vidyasagar focused on the life and career of his grandfather stemmed from another reason that ought not to be overlooked. This was to do with the mental strength and fortitude of the man who preferred to remain independent and not accept the support or patronage of others, even in times of distress. Upon his return to his native village Banamalipur, Ramjoy could not settle down on account of the continuing persecution that his wife suffered at the hands of her brothers-in-law and their wives. He was forced to settle down at Birsingha, where his wife had temporarily sought shelter with her parents. On the other hand, he would not accept the munificence of the local landlord, who offered him rent-free land on which to construct a modest dwelling house. As long as he lived, Ramjoy paid an annual rent of Rs 9 and 5 annas. His grandson, Iswarchandra, was to similarly refuse gifts from some of the biggest landlords in Bengal, including the Maharaja of Burdwan. In 1867, the *Hindu Patriot* appealed for public contributions to clear a debt of about Rs 82,000 that Pundit Iswarchandra had reportedly incurred from supporting widow marriages and running schools at personal cost. Vidyasagar promptly turned this down, saying that he would much rather clear his own debts. The pundit's public reputation and credibility as an honest and conscientious man was such that many creditors were prepared to advance a loan to a person merely on the strength of his recommendation. On his recommendation, the rajas of Paikpara once agreed to advance a sum of Rs 1 lakh to a person without insisting on any collateral security. Vidyasagar himself was often forced to borrow money from royalty and respectable gentry. The list included Rani Swarnamoyee of Kasimbazar and the rajas of Nadia, Paikpara, Bhagyakul, and Dighapatia. On his death, he left behind no debts for his successors, although many still owed him money.

What the autobiography also glosses over is Ramjoy's quite irresponsibly forsaking his wife, Durga Devi, and their children to their own fates when he left home. By all accounts, this placed the family under great distress. Sambhuchandra informs us that Ramsundar Bhattacharya, the son of Umapati Tarkasiddhanta, who took over the reins of the family from an old and infirm father, turned out to be a henpecked husband and readily gave in to his wife's wishes to force Durga Devi to leave home. Unable to win the sympathy of either her own brothers or members of her husband's family, Durga Devi was forced to fall back for help on her father, Umapati Tarkasiddhanta, who somehow managed to secure for her a small hut of her own on the fringes of the village. Here, she eked out a miserable existence, barely surviving from selling home-spun thread at the local cotton market at Khirpai. This continued till her eldest son Thakurdas was about fourteen or fifteen years old, and ready to supplement the family income. The tendency to somehow overlook the blemishes in his ancestors surfaced in Vidyasagar at other times too. It is indeed odd that the man who consistently promoted female education never attempted to educate his own wife, reportedly on the wishes of his father. In a modern play based on the life of Vidyasagar (*Vidyasagar*, 1948), the eminent Bengali literary figure Balaichand Mukhopadhyay, who wrote under the pen name Banaphool (1899–1979), somewhat twisted this around by suggesting that Vidyasagar had indeed suggested to his wife, Dinamayee, that she educate herself; however, it was her reticence or conservatism that led her to turn him down.

Early Travails in Colonial Calcutta

Sambhuchandra gives us to believe that before setting out for Calcutta, Thakurdas had acquired a passing familiarity with the Bengali language and elementary accounting. These were to hold him in good stead in his initial days in Calcutta. Judging by Vidyasagar's own account, Thakurdas always bemoaned the fact that he himself had been unable to secure a higher education, and it was indeed his wish that he spend a lifetime imparting Sanskrit instruction back home in his village. Even when it was decided to move Iswarchandra from Birsingha to Calcutta for higher education, it had been Thakurdas's wish that his son take to a professional Sanskrit education and eventually establish himself as a pundit, running an independent *tol* or *chatuspathi*. For this reason, Vidyasagar notes, Thakurdas was opposed to the idea of admitting his son to a school imparting English education, which at the time was otherwise in great demand. The Hindu College, established in 1817 by some orthodox Hindus in Calcutta, points to the distinction that even this class made between English as a culturally alien and alienating language—as it tended to encourage the questioning of traditional social and cultural values—and its immense professional and vocational prospects. The idea of English-language instruction had also been supported by Rammohun Roy in his famous Appeal of 1823 to Governor-General Amherst, in which he had opposed the idea of State spending on Oriental learning. The difference was that while the Hindu orthodox viewed Western education as primarily a means of securing employment for Indians, Rammohun viewed it as an intellectually and socially liberating force. Regardless of the reasons behind it, even a rudimentary knowledge of the English language became something of a social statement at the time. In the late 1820s, Nitai Sen and Advaita Sen, two boys studying at Arratoon Petre's school in central Calcutta, were greatly respected in their locality, even though they spoke only ungrammatical English. In the case of Vidyasagar, however, English-language instruction was simply impractical and unaffordable since the institution best equipped to deliver it, the Hindu College, charged a monthly fee of Rs 5. Thakurdas' monthly earnings, even at its peak, was about Rs 10. Hence, within five days of his arriving in Calcutta, sometime in early November 1828, Iswarchandra was admitted to a *pathshala* located at Burrabazar in north Calcutta. It was here that Thakurdas himself had once been hosted by one Bhagavatcharan Singha, who was known to his father, Ramjoy Tarkabhushan.

In Calcutta, the person to first host Thakurdas, also at the behest of Ramjoy, was a traditional Brahmin scholar by the name of Sabharam Vachaspati, who imparted to the boy his first lessons in Sanskrit grammar. Interestingly, however, Ramjoy had insisted that his son obtain instruction in English, which was seen to help in securing some form of employment easily. For a time, this was arranged through the offices of a shipping agent, who agreed to instruct Thakurdas every morning and evening. As it turned out, the arrangements with his English instructor proved to be too taxing and ruined Thakurdas's health. By the time he returned from his evening classes, his hosts would have already had their meal, leaving Thakurdas to go hungry every night. This continued for a while until the boy's emaciated condition caught the attention of his teacher, who volunteered to host the young

Thakurdas on the condition that he cook his own meals, as was only expected of a Brahmin when hosted by a non-Brahmin. Sadly, this arrangement too proved acutely discomforting since the agent had extremely irregular hours of work. This meant that Thakurdas had again to go without food on the days his host could not return home at mealtimes. It was on one such day, when a famished and fatigued Thakurdas approached an old woman for some water to drink, that a remarkable incident occurred. The old lady, herself a petty shopkeeper, was quick to realise that the Brahmin boy had not eaten all day, and fed him some yogurt and parched rice soaked in molasses. She also very graciously offered the boy an open invitation to call on her any other day when such a situation recurred. Vidyasagar's biographers have cited this as one of two incidents that may have visibly shaped his life, particularly vis-à-vis his respect and concern for women. The other incident relates to the family of his early hosts in Calcutta. Vidyasagar was to very nostalgically, and with great feeling, recall the kindness he received from the women of this family, in particular the widowed daughter of Bhagavatcharan Singha of Burrabazar, Raimoni.

Sambhuchandra tells us that for about a year following this incident, Thakurdas was appointed guardian to the widow and orphaned children of an affluent relative of Sabharam Vachaspati. This made it possible for him to remit some money home to his mother Durga Devi, whose misery now began to ease somewhat. Vachaspati, upon learning that Thakurdas had acquired some skills in both English and accounting, introduced him to Bhagvatcharan, possibly a local merchant, who appointed him for clerical work on a monthly salary of Rs 2, besides offering free board and lodging. It was on his host's advice that Thakurdas sent for his brother Kalidas to Calcutta, so that together they might further augment the family income. Upon Kalidas' arrival, Thakurdas took to trading in bell-metal utensils and, for a time, even made some profits. This enterprise, however, was short-lived since Kalidas proved to be quite incompetent in handling his responsibilities and Bhagavatcharan's son, Jagatdurlabh

Singha, insisted that Thakurdas return to his old calling. In 1813, Thakurdas, then aged about twenty, was married to Bhagavati Devi, daughter of Ramkanta Tarkabagish (Chattopadhyay). Their eldest son, Iswarchandra, was born roughly seven years later, in 1820.

Six more sons and three daughters were born to Thakurdas and Bhagavati Devi. Of the daughters, we know practically nothing. Of the sons, Harachandra and Harishchandra died of cholera at a very young age. We have no information on Sibchandra and very little on Ishanchandra, barring the fact that he took it upon himself to revise Sambhuchandra's biography of Vidyasagar. Deenabandhu and Sambhuchandra were also admitted as students to Sanskrit College, and passed out with some distinction. Deenabandhu served for a time at Fort William College in Calcutta and was later elevated to the post of Deputy Magistrate at Barisal on Vidyasagar's recommendation. He subsequently resigned his job and spent his last years teaching in his village and practising Homoeopathy. Deenabandhu predeceased Vidyasagar by a few years. Sambhuchandra never took to any professional career, preferring to spend his life at Birsingha in the company of the extended family, aided by the financial support provided by his eldest brother.

A Gifted Student at the Sanskrit College

Pandit Iswarchandra's journey from Birsingha to Calcutta was undertaken on foot, partly in view of the fact that travellers on the river route were often waylaid by dacoits. Since the 8-year-old boy could not be expected to walk all the way, Thakurdas chose to take along with him a domestic help by the name of Anandaram Guti, who carried the boy on his shoulders for much of the way. Apparently, Thakurdas was too frail a man to do this himself. On one of their subsequent travels between Birsingha and Calcutta, Thakurdas, without Anandaram to accompany him, found it especially difficult to carry the boy on his person.

In exasperation, he would at times beat the boy or else tempt him with offers to buy juicy watermelons. On this particular journey, Iswarchandra developed painful blisters on his feet from walking, which then forced the party to travel down the river Hooghly on a ferry connecting Baidyabati (district Hooghly) and Burrabazar in Calcutta.

While at Birsingha, Vidyasagar had been placed under the care of a Brahmin *gurumohashoy* by the name of Kalikanta Chattopadhayay. In Sambhuchandra's account, it was Thakurdas who personally arranged for his relocation from village Goruti, which was close to Srirampur (district Hooghly), to Birsingha, where he also established a *pathshala*. Reportedly, Thakurdas' fortunes had looked up following the birth of his eldest son, and he was keen to ensure that the child received the benefit of a proper education. Kalikanta took good care of his student, Iswarchandra. It was also he who suggested to Thakurdas that the gifted boy be moved to Calcutta for higher studies. He even accompanied the party which first set out for that city in the early days of November 1828.

The *pathshala* in Calcutta to which Vidyasagar was first admitted was run by a man of the Subarnabanik caste by the name of Shivcharan Mallik. This institution had a teacher called Swarupchandra Das who, in Vidyasagar's own testimony, proved to be an even better teacher than Kalikanta Chattopadhyay. Vidyasagar spent about three months in the *pathshala* before being afflicted by blood dysentery. Forced to return to Birsingha to regain his health, he could come back to Calcutta only by June 1829, when he was admitted to the *vyakaran* (Grammar) Class of the Government Sanskrit College.

The decision to join the Sanskrit College was dictated by a combination of several factors. First, Thakurdas happened to be acquainted with Pandit Gangadhar Tarkabagish, who taught that class in the Sanskrit College. Tarkabagish prevailed upon Thakurdas by advancing two persuasive arguments. The Sanskrit College, as he pointed out, was a respectable, State-funded institution catering to the advancement of traditional

Sanskrit learning. But more practically, it offered its students two professional choices: they could either turn into scholars and pundits who ran their own *tols* independently, or they could be employed with the government in the capacity of Judge-Pundit, an official who advised British judges on the finer points concerning Hindu law. That this was a reasonably lucrative office is proved by the fact that at least two students of the Sanskrit College who were closely connected with the life of Vidyasagar later served in this capacity themselves: his friend and co-author, Madanmohan Tarkalankar (1817–58), and Srishchandra Vidyaratna (?), the first man to marry a widow under the Widow Marriage Act of 1856. Second, a similar recommendation was offered by a close relative, Madhusudan Vachaspati, who was then a student at the College. Third, we should not overlook the important fact that at the time, Sanskrit College charged no fees, which undoubtedly proved to be a matter of some relief for Thakurdas. It is somewhat ironic, though, that his son, Iswarchandra, was to bring about sweeping changes in the way the College was run, which included charging students both a token entrance fee and fees that were charged regularly on a monthly basis.

The Sanskrit Colleges in Benares and Calcutta were fruits of a distinctive educational and cultural policy commonly known as Orientalism. It aimed to preserve India's traditional institutions and promote Oriental learning. The foundation of both these institutions preceded the victory in 1835 of the so-called Anglicists, which changed matters dramatically by adopting English as the medium of instruction in State-funded institutions. The first of these Sanskrit Colleges was founded at Benares in 1791 and the second at Calcutta in 1824. Benares was a natural choice for a Sanskrit College, given its reputation as both a holy site for the Hindus and a centre of traditional learning and scholarship. The case for Calcutta was not as clearly established. For one, it had serious rivals in Tirhut and Nabadwip, both traditionally known as centres of Hindu learning and philosophical disputation. Further, by the early nineteenth century, the idea of promoting Indian knowledge systems over the Western had its serious detractors even among Indians, as borne out by the case of Rammohun Roy. Horace Hayman Wilson (1786–1860), perhaps the most powerful spokesperson for Orientalism, distrusted Rammohun and the anglicised English-educated youth of Calcutta, and setting up the Sanskrit College in Calcutta itself would have been a major triumph for him and his supporters. However, the body officially dealing with educational policy, the General Committee for Public Instruction, leaned on the side of Calcutta, perhaps also for the practical reason that setting up the College in Calcutta would facilitate the running of the Fort William College already established in that city in 1800. The Fort William College had been primarily set up to train young civilians arriving from England in the local vernaculars (Bengali and Urdu/Hindusthani) and the classical languages (Persian and Sanskrit). It was in this institution that Iswarchandra found his first employment.

The foundation stone of the Sanskrit College, Calcutta, was laid on 1 January 1824 on land belonging to the Scottish philanthropist David Hare, and moved to its new premises only in 1826. It instituted a fifteen-year course of study, charged no fees, and even offered some financial help to poor students and to those arriving in Calcutta from neighbouring districts. After the College started charging fees, a distinction began to be made between 'Pay Pupils' and those who were paid supportive stipends. For most of his life as a student in Sanskrit College, Iswarchandra himself benefited from such financial support. Initially open to Brahmin boys alone, admission to the Sanskrit College was also extended in 1826 to those belonging to the Baidya caste who wished to pursue a course in native medicine. Madhusudan Gupta, the first Indian to perform dissections on a human body in 1836, was first a student at this college and briefly thereafter, also a teacher. When the Calcutta Medical College was established in 1835, classes on medicine in Sanskrit College were discontinued. However, the non-Brahmin

Baidya student was not permitted to go through the entire course of studies, which included the study of *smriti* or *darshan*, reserved for Brahmins alone. Presumably, this arrangement continued even after Vidyasagar extended the right of admission to Kayastha boys in 1851.

Pandit Iswarchandra spent three years in the *vyakaran* Class (1829–31), during which time he was exposed to the rigours of the *Mugdabodh* text. He found this text especially difficult to master, which over time led to his resolve to simplify the study of Sanskrit grammar. A preliminary introduction to a different approach to the study of Sanskrit grammar appeared in his *Sanskrit Vyakaraner Upakramanika* (1851), followed by a new grammar text called *Vyakaran Kaumudi* (in four parts, 1853–62). Beginning in 1831, his academic performance also won him a monthly stipend of Rs 5, which at one point in time was raised to Rs 8 per month. All through his career as a student of Sanskrit College, Vidyasagar continued to be handsomely rewarded not only for his brilliant performance at the annual examinations, but also for the quality of his prose and poetic compositions. He was also famed for his good handwriting. In the long run, such pecuniary benefits allowed him to persuade Thakurdas to retire to Birsingha where, as per his longstanding desire, he bought some land with the intention of starting a *chatuspathi*.

In 1827, Sanskrit College authorities had provided for the teaching of English and although at this time this was optional, it was expected that students of the *vyakaran* class would spend some time on English lessons. It is not known exactly how long Vidyasagar devoted himself to the study of the English language; on the other hand, we can reasonably assume that his knowledge of English remained incomplete and imperfect as English classes at the Sanskrit College were discontinued in 1835. The space for English-language teaching in Sanskrit College was always a contested one. On 30 April 1831, some students had complained to the authorities that local priests had disallowed them to carry out priestly functions so long as they continued pursuing the study of English. By 1839, however, students were also to petition the government for the resumption of English classes. English-language teaching was resumed at the Sanskrit College in 1842, and was considerably fortified after Pundit Iswarchandra took over as its Principal. Sometime after he had passed out of Sanskrit College, Vidyasagar was to seriously seek private instruction in both English and Hindi on the advice of some English friends and co-workers. Among his English instructors were Durgacharan Bandopadhyay (1819–70), father of the nationalist leader Surendranath, and Anandakrishna Basu, from whom he took lessons in Shakespeare. His academic progress thereafter was swift, and he passed every examination with distinction. Between 1833 and 1835, he studied Sanskrit Literature (*sahitya*), spent a year in the Rhetoric (*alankar*) Class (1836), and two years in the *vedanta* Class (1836–37). Between 1838 and 1839, he took instructions in *smriti* or Hindu Law, at the end of which he appeared in and successfully cleared the Hindu Law Committee Examination that qualified him to serve in the capacity of a Judge-Pundit. There is reason to believe that a career in law did not attract him, since he turned down the advice of Sir James Colville (who eventually joined the Viceroy's Council as Law Member) to set up a legal practice. The example of his friend Dwarkanath Mitter (1836–74), eminent legal scholar and jurist, showed him that a legal career left no time for other pursuits. However, the reason for his not accepting the office of Judge-Pundit has more to do with the fact that Thakurdas forbade him to accept the post, which was being offered only in distant Tripura.

The last leg of his studies was spent in mastering *nyaya* (in 1839) and in all probability, it was also at this time that he took instruction in *jyotish* (Astronomy) from a scholar from the Punjab, Yogodhyan Misra. In all, he spent twelve years and five months at the Sanskrit College. The well-known Bengali literary figure and researcher, Brajendranath Bandopadhyay, has drawn our attention to the fact that Vidyasagar ended his career as a student with two Certificates of Merit, one each from the government and his teachers at the College. Also, contrary to general belief, the title of 'Vidyasagar' was awarded to him not in December 1841 at the end of his formal course of study at the Sanskrit College, but earlier in April 1839, when he had cleared the Law Committee Examination.

Life as a student was extremely daunting for Vidyasagar. For one, living conditions in their host's house were appalling, with the kitchen surrounded by filth and choked drains that bred flies, mosquitoes, and other pests. He was allowed only two hours of sleep at night, between 10 pm and 12 am, and Thakurdas punctually woke him up at the stroke of midnight, upon hearing the hourly gong from the clock at the Armenian Church nearby. He was also beaten up mercilessly when he faltered in his lessons, and at times the beatings were so extreme that Vidyasagar would either temporarily escape to a neighbour's house or await kindly intercessions from his hosts, Jagatdurlabh Singha and his sister Raimoni. The physical assaults that the young Vidyasagar was forced to endure at his father's hands goes a long way in explaining his determination to abolish corporal punishment in his schools.

In the case of Vidyasagar, both the thread ceremony (*Upanayan*) and marriage took place during his life as a student. The former took place in 1831 when he was eleven, and he was married three years later, in 1834, to Dinamayee, daughter of Shatrughna Bhattacharya of village Khirpai.

Early Attempts at Educational Work

Arabinda Guha's collection of the unpublished correspondence of Vidysagar draws our attention to an interesting fact. The *Proceedings of the Council of Education* for 23 August 1842 mentions that a certain 'Iswarchandra' had applied to the Sanskrit College for the post of professor in Ancient Literature and History, but that the man eventually recruited to this post was one Kamalakanta Bhattacharya. Now if this 'Iswarchandra' was indeed the subject of our biography, it would reveal an unknown aspect to his professional career. However, such was Vidyasagar's reputation among both pundits and English officials of the time that he was soon offered employment as *Seristadar* (Head Pundit) in the Bengali Department of Fort William College. This was on the recommendation of Major G. T. Marshal, Secretary to the College. Marshal was also actively associated with the functioning of the Sanskrit College itself, and presumably would have been all too familiar with Iswarchandra's intellectual excellence. The vacancy in the Department had arisen with the death of Pandit Madhusudan Tarkabagish and the authorities at Fort William had no hesitation in appointing Vidyasagar to the post on a monthly salary of Rs 50. It was also Marshal who introduced Vidyasagar to the Secretary attached to the Council of Education in Bengal, Dr F. J. Mouat, who was to become the Pundit's lifelong friend and admirer. At Vidyasagar's Badurbagan residence in Calcutta, the portraits of Marshal and Mouat were among those that hung on the walls of his sitting room. A third was of the philanthropist John Elliot Drinkwater Bethune, of whom we shall speak more presently. Two other prominent portraits were those of Thakurdas Bandopadhyay and Bhagavati Devi.

Impressed with his diligence and dedication to work, Marshal further recommended him to the post of Assistant Secretary to the Sanskrit College in 1846. His recommendation letter found the Pundit to be 'intelligent and free from all bias and unworthy motives'. Having served the Fort William College for a little less than five years, Vidyasagar took over as the Assistant Secretary on an identical salary of Rs 50; the attraction here might have been that he was now back at his *alma mater*. His experiences at Fort William College proved helpful in several ways. For one, having worked in close cooperation with indulgent and appreciative Englishmen, he grew increasingly familiar with the workings of the English mind, something he had not been exposed to as a student of the Sanskrit College. Second, he also used this period to improve his knowledge of English and Hindi. Knowledge of Hindi later enabled him to edit a Hindi version of the older Sanskrit classic, *Betal Panchavimsati*, to which he gave the title, *Betal Pacchisi* (1852). A scrutiny of his official letters in English will reveal that over time, the Pundit acquired a reasonably good command over this language, too, although there is an apocryphal tale about how the Derozian Ramgopal Ghosh (1815–68), who occasionally assisted Vidyasagar with his English correspondence, once jokingly told him that a Brahmin pundit, compulsively vegetarian by habit, could not be expected to match the literary qualities of the beef-eating Englishman! Third, it was during his stay at Fort William College that he seriously studied puranic literature and the philosophical school of *Samkhya*. The former, one imagines, proved useful in his future writings on the widow marriage question; his study of *Samkhya*, on the other hand, may have emboldened him to later speak critically of certain schools of Hindu philosophy. At the time, one imagines, such criticism would have deeply hurt not only the traditional Brahmin scholar, but also all those who counted themselves among practising Hindus. While at the Fort William College, he also authored his first work, *Vasudev Charita* (?), based on the life of Krishna as depicted in the *Bhagavata Purana*. The work, incidentally, was never published, possibly because Marshal considered this far too religiously oriented to be of any interest to English civilians. Significantly enough, Vidyasagar himself did not publish this work either, even after he had established his own press. After the 1840s, none of his books were directly derived from a religious theme or were overtly religious in tone. As we shall have occasion to see, he considered even the epics, the *Ramayana* and the *Mahabharata*, as essentially literary works.

It is quite possible that Vidyasagar accepted the post of Assistant Secretary so that he could use this office to bring about some significant academic and administrative changes in the functioning of the Sanskrit College. Some of these were rooted in his own experiences as a student. As early as 19 September 1846, that is, less than two months after his joining the College, Vidyasagar submitted a note to Rosomoy Dutta (1779–1854),

Secretary to the College, suggesting certain changes in the functioning of the institution. Dutta, however, did not take kindly to this enterprise. Fearing a loss of authority and suspicious too of the good relations that Vidyasagar was known to share with his English superiors, he showed great reluctance to give his junior a hearing or in forwarding the proposals to the Council of Education as he was otherwise obligated to do. Frustrated at such unforeseen difficulties and failing to convince Dutta about the worth of his initiatives, Vidyasagar submitted his resignation from the post of Assistant Secretary in May 1847. Many of his colleagues viewed this as going against the interests of the College. Over a dozen pundits then serving the Sanskrit College, some of whom had been his teachers, submitted a memorial requesting the authorities to not accept the resignation. Upon hearing of Vidyasagar's determination to quit a job that fetched a handsome monthly salary of Rs 50, Dutta is believed to have asked, somewhat mockingly, how the unemployed young man would manage to eke out a living. Vidyasagar retorted that if required, he was prepared to sell vegetables on the streets!

In the months to follow, Vidyasagar channelised his energies into the progressively lucrative field of printing and publishing. That this was an immensely productive field which the Bengali *bhadralok* had successfully taken to is amply evident from Rev. James Long's *A Descriptive Catalogue of Bengali Works*, published in 1855. In collaboration with his friend Madanmohan Tarkalankar, Vidyasagar set up the Sanskrit Press and Book Depository in 1847. The Book Depository functioned as a bookstore where authors and publishers could deposit their books and rely on the Depository to handle sales. The press itself had to be bought on a borrowed sum of Rs 600, but the debt was soon paid off. Here again, his friend G. T. Marshal proved to be of great help. Marshal pledged an order of 100 printed copies of the poet Bharatchandra's *Annadamangal* at Rs 6 each for the Fort William College. However, judging from official documents pertaining to this period, there is reason to believe that this work was edited by Madanmohan Tarkalankar and not Vidyasagar himself. After the former's untimely death in 1858, an unpleasant dispute broke out between members of his family and Vidyasagar. In his biography of Pundit Madanmohan (*Madanmohan Tarkalankarer Jeeboncharit O Tadgrantha Samalocana,* 1872), his son-in-law Yogendranath Vidyabhushan pressed the claim that Vidyasagar had appropriated for himself some works of the late Pundit and even failed to pay up the dues that he owed to his friend and co-worker. Vidyasagar successfully disputed most of Vidyabhushan's allegations, but on the question of editing the *Annadamangal,* he preferred to remain silent. However, it is also known that he took Marshal's munificence quite seriously. It was Vidyasagar who travelled all the way to Krishnanagar, where the author Bharatchandra had once lived as court poet, to obtain an authentic manuscript copy of the text. The following year, Vidyasagar published *Banglar Itihas*—Part II (History of Bengal), adapted from the last nine chapters of John Clark Marshman's *Outline of the History of Bengal* (1838). This launched him on the future path of producing an entire range of greatly popular school textbooks.

Some two years after he quit the Sanskrit College, Vidyasagar was inducted into the Fort William College once again, in this instance as Head Writer and Treasurer on a salary of Rs 80 per month. For this, he had to furnish a security of Rs 5,000. It so happened that the man whom he succeeded was none other than Durgacharan Bandopadhyay, one of his teachers of English. Durgacharan had been increasingly drawn to a life of a medical practitioner, and resigned his post in 1849. In September 1849, the Sanskrit Press published Vidyasagar's *Jeeboncharit,* which included short biographical sketches of eminent European men and for which Vidyasagar relied on the multi-volume works of the Scottish brothers, Robert and William Chambers.

That month, his only son, named Narayanchandra, was born to him.

Soon afterwards, the post of professor of literature fell vacant in the Sanskrit College and Rosomoy Dutta was himself keen that Vidyasagar be appointed to this post. Perhaps Dutta's sense of the matter was that it would be safer to handle Vidyasgar in a purely teaching capacity than in the administrative. Vidyasagar, however, refused to be drawn into this plan and strongly recommended that his friend, Pundit Madanmohan, then teaching at Krishnanagar College, be offered the post. The chain of events that followed makes it amply clear that Vidyasagar's heart was still set on the idea of carrying out educational reforms. In November 1850, when Madanmohan Tarkalankar left the Sanskrit College to take up the post of Judge-Pundit at Murshidabad, Vidyasagar agreed to take over that position on condition that the government would eventually elevate him to the position of Principal, Sanskrit College. He worked till January 1851 as a professor of *Sahitya*.

It is not clear if the idea of creating the office of the Principal, Sanskrit College, originated entirely in Vidyasagar himself, but this suited the government's plans eminently. The Council of Education, writing to the Bengal government, noted with some displeasure the fact of Rosomoy Dutta's frequent absences from work, and his attending more to his private calling than to the needs of the College. It was further noted that he knew no Sanskrit and was hence incapable of contributing to the academic improvement of the institution. Given the need of the hour, the Council could not think of anyone more suitable than Pundit Iswarchandra, and hoped that he would prove as vital to the interests of the Sanskrit College as the recently appointed Principal of the Calcutta Madrasah, Dr Aloys Sprenger, whose excellent command over Arabic had proved valuable to that institution. The government did not fail to also take note of the fact that Pundit Iswarchandra had already demonstrated his abiding interest in curriculum-building and moral pedagogy for schoolboys through the publication of *Banglar Itihas* and the *Jeeboncharit*. The Council concluded by saying that the creation of the new post would not entail any extra expenditure since the posts of the Secretary and Assistant Secretary, which between them had been drawing a salary of Rs 150, could now be merged into that of the Principal, who would draw exactly the same sum. Vidyasagar joined the Sanskrit College as its first Principal on 22 January 1851. On his recommendation, his friend Rajkrishna Bandopadhyay succeeded him to the post of Head Writer and Treasurer at the Fort William College.

By March 1854, roughly three years after Vidyasagar had taken over as Principal, there were 370 students in all on the rolls of the Sanskrit College, comprising 200 Brahmins, twenty-eight Baidyas, and forty-two Kayasthas. Between 1850 and 1854, Pundit Iswarchandra devoted himself to the task of carrying out educational reforms, bringing about both structural innovation in the functioning of the institution and a thorough revision of the curriculum. These came in the form of official 'Notes and Correspondence' stretching from April 1850 to February 1854. Between them, these Notes covered the following areas: revision of curriculum, strengthening of English-language teaching, emphasis on evolving a modern vernacular, reform of examination systems, and the question of whether to permit boys of non-Brahmin castes to also be admitted to the Sanskrit College. Inasmuch as these reflect his educational thoughts, they will be taken up elsewhere (see Chapter 3). On the last issue, Vidyasagar showed some social flexibility by allowing Kayastha boys to be admitted to the College in 1851 and boys from other 'respectable classes' in 1854, although only nominally. His argument here was that even Sudras were not debarred from a Sanskrit education *per se*; what they might not study, however, was *sruti* or esoteric knowledge. *Prima facie*, this may not appear as liberal as the position earlier adopted by Rammohun, which had opened up even the *sruti* to both women and Sudras. On the question of admitting non-Brahmin boys, Vidyasagar again revealed a mix of liberality and conservatism. When, in 1855, Shyamacharan Sen, a man of the Subarnabanik caste, traditionally traders in gold and jewellery, appealed for the admission of boys of his caste to the Sanskrit College, Vidyasagar turned this down, stating that the caste was very lowly placed in the ritual order and he feared that their induction would both offend the Hindu orthodox and materially affect the reputation of the College. That same year, when a Normal School for the training of teachers was instituted at the Sanskrit College, only teachers from upper castes were initially recruited.

However, such decisions also reflected some pragmatic realism and a gradualist approach to change. Vidyasagar's willingness to allow Kayastha boys to be admitted to the Sanskrit College had come in the face of opposition from three prominent Pundits then serving the College, Jaynarayan Tarkapanchan, Bharatchandra Shiromani, and Premchandra Tarkabagish, who also happened to be among his erstwhile teachers. Subsequently, even though an order of December 1854 opened up the prospect of entering the Sanskrit College for all 'respectable' castes, this appears to have been implemented only around 1863. Up to that point in time, the College admitted only Brahmins, Baidyas, Kayasthas, and the nine intermediary castes placed immediately below these, known by the collective name of *Nabasakh* (literally, nine branches). In the Annual Report submitted by E. B. Cowell, Vidyasagar's successor in office, there appear at least twenty students who would have been summarily denied admission prior to 1854. Of these, as many as thirteen were from the Subarnabanik caste, three each from the Tantis (weavers) and Gopas (pastoralists/agriculturalists), and one from the Kaivarta (farmers, fishermen) caste. In Vidyasagar's time and even for some time thereafter, the ratio of non-Brahmin to Brahmin students was roughly 1:2. The year 1864 was an exceptional year; as many as forty-three students out of a total of fifty-seven were non-Brahmins. Evidently, the demand for Sanskrit studies remained higher among Brahmins compared to all other castes taken together. This was only natural, given the fact that even the higher caste groups within non-Brahmins, such as Baidyas and Kayasthas, could not have taken to teaching in *tols* and *chatuspathis* or presided over as pundits in aristocratic households.

Other important interventions that occurred in this period were changes carried out to the College calendar through the introduction of vacations, keeping the College closed on

Sundays and other public holidays in lieu of the earlier practice of following the Hindu calendar, regulating the entry and exit of students and staff of the College during working hours, recruiting young and competent teachers, and introducing an admission charge of Rs 2 and a monthly tuition fee of Rs 1. This, as we have noted earlier, was not uniformly applied to all since there were some who enjoyed stipends, either on grounds of financial need or personal merit. On 31 March 1855, only thirty-nine students at the Sanskrit College were 'pay pupils', that is, they were charged monthly fees. All of the above changes were carried out between the years 1851 and 1854.

Apparently, even though he was able to effect far-reaching administrative and educational changes in the functioning of Sanskrit College, Vidyasagar was unable to appreciably alter the work environment under which teaching was conducted, or the methods of teaching adopted. In a work published in 1853, that is, after Vidyasagar had taken over as Principal, the daily routine at the College was described thus by a visitor:

> On any ordinary day, the visitor will see, on a table, in the midst of a small room, one of the professors sitting in Oriental fashion, after the manner of tailors ... around the table are squatted a number of dirty looking youth ... the majority are dozing and well they may for, it is sleepy work—the same verses nasally intoned by one another with unvarying monotony and doubtless with similar errors. The professor seldom speaks for he too is dozing on the table, awaiting the bell that is to release him to liberty and dinner. (Capper 1853)

But even his limited success in bringing about structural changes in the Sanskrit College considerably enhanced its financial solvency and public reputation. Absenteeism among students dropped, as did the recurring migration to other schools. The student strength of the college had been steadily going up even before Vidyasagar joined as Principal. Standing at a meagre 115 in 1824, it rose to 299 in 1851. In 1854, the government, happy with this state of affairs, doubled the Principal's monthly salary, which henceforth stood at Rs 300. Some of the changes that the Pundit had earlier contemplated but could not bring about at this stage in his educational career were later realised by the 1870s, once he had given up his duties at the Sanskrit College and was able to run his own educational institutions.

Promoting Vernacular Primary Education

Vidyasagar's contribution to the field of education, however, is not limited to the Sanskrit College alone. Equally important are his efforts to promote vernacular education among Hindu boys and girls, especially in rural Bengal. As is well-known, a good number of the works he authored targeted this field, and it is also with this object in mind that he introduced important curriculum changes in the Sanskrit College itself. In his own vision, apart from imparting a Sanskrit education, this College was to also act like a 'nursery' for producing a new crop of competent teachers who commanded the knowledge of an improved vernacular.

In modern Bengal, the idea of seriously promoting primary vernacular education among the masses took off from William Adam's report on the state of education in early colonial Bengal, submitted to the government between 1836–38. Europeans, in fact, had taken the earliest steps to set up rural *pathshalas*, as for instance Robert May in Chinsura (district Hooghly) and Captain Charles Stewart in Burdwan. By 1824, Charles Lushington, an evangelist attached to the Church Missionary Society, was running eight schools in the Kidderpore area in Calcutta. A notable attempt on the part of Hindus themselves in this direction was the *Tattwabodhini Pathshala*, launched by the *Tattwabodhini Sabha* (founded 1839), initially set up in Calcutta but later forced to move to Bansberia (district Hooghly) in view of the growing competition from English-medium schools. Around 1844, Governor-General Henry Hardinge (1785–1836), also enthused by the idea of spreading elementary education among the people, opened about 101 schools (hereafter called the Hardinge Schools) in the province of Bengal, then including Bihar and Odisha. Considering the geographical extent of the province in question and its population, this was a noble but grossly inadequate effort. We would also have to reckon with the fact that in terms of the number of primary, state-funded schools, Bengal remained at a comparative disadvantage. Government spending on primary schools in this province was lower compared to Bombay, the North-Western Provinces, and the Punjab. In 1845, that is, even after Hardinge's plans had been launched, Bengal had fewer schools in proportion to its population compared to the Bombay and Madras Presidencies. An official circular published in 1868 (*Note on the State of Education in Bengal during 1866–67*) found Bengal to be the province with the 'most marked contrasts: a small number of students taught language and philosophy of the West at government expense and chasing universities while there are mass schools where students are taught to scratch letters on the dust'. We have little information on the progress or functioning of these 'Hardinge schools', but by the early 1850s, the Government of India was forced to take fresh initiatives, following the phenomenal success of the Vernacular (*halaqbandi*) schools opened in the North-Western Provinces by Lt. Governor James Thomason between 1843 and 1853. On 4 November 1853, the Government of India directed the Bengal government to seriously adopt Thomason's model for establishing rural schools in Bengal. Sir Frederick James Halliday (1806–1901), Bengal's first Lt. Governor, responded enthusiastically in his Note of 16 November 1854 which, incidentally, cited with approbation the educational work of Vidyasagar. Halliday's rejoinder, in fact, closely followed Vidyasagar's own Minute, titled *Notes on Vernacular Education*, of 7 February 1854, in which the following main points had been listed:

1. The existing *pathshala*s were quite useless and not conducive to the growth of quality education.

2. Even though the propagation of primary education was of the utmost necessity in rural Bengal, it would not do to give the boys a superficial education. On the contrary, they had to be exposed to a more comprehensive knowledge system that went beyond basic literacy or computation skills. The revised curriculum had to be drawn upon subjects like arithmetic, geometry, natural philosophy, history, and geography.
3. That each of these schools would require at least two teachers to begin with and eventually be supervised by a Head Pundit. Teachers had to be paid a reasonably attractive salary ranging from Rs 20 to 30, depending upon their skills or proficiency.
4. Although there existed some standard school textbooks for disseminating education (and here Vidyasagar cited his own textbooks published by the Sanskrit Press, such as the multi-volume *Shishusikha*, *Pashwabali*, *Banglar Itihas*, *Jeebon Charit*, and *Charupath* by his friend, Akshaykumar Dutta), competent authors had to be further encouraged to produce more.
5. The new schools should be confined to only four districts for the time being (Hooghly, Burdwan, Nadia, and Midnapore), and the government should ensure that there did not exist any competing English-medium school and college in the vicinity.
6. That the government should create the post of Inspectors of Schools under the supervision of the Principal, Sanskrit College.
7. That a Model School be started at the Sanskrit College itself for the training of teachers.

The government agreed in principle with all these points. In May 1855, Vidyasagar was given the additional charge of Assistant Inspector of Schools for south Bengal, covering the four designated districts. This fetched him an additional remuneration of Rs 200 per month, raising his total monthly salary to Rs 500. A Normal School with two sections, an upper and a lower, were started in the Sanskrit College by July 1855. Its function was to prepare qualified teachers in the vernacular, who could then be suitably employed in district schools. In the early 1860s, the Model School had about ninety-four pupils on its rolls, of whom fifty-four qualified for employment as teachers. Other than supervising government-aided schools, Vidyasagar also launched private schools of his own. In 1853, he opened a boy's school at his native village, Birsingha, entirely at his own expense. The school charged no fees, fed about thirty boys daily, and supplied free stationery to another 300. In the mid-1850s, it had about 160 boys on its rolls. Vidyasagar also personally met the salaries of about six to seven teachers attached to this school. This school was to be badly hit by the cholera epidemic of 1868 and temporarily closed down in 1875, when the dilapidated school building had to be abandoned. It resumed functioning only by 1890.

By January 1856, Vidyasagar was also able to open five schools in each of the four districts on a monthly expense of Rs 50 for each school. These were designated as Vernacular Model Schools and were expected to promote the quality of teaching and curriculum improvement in other aided schools running locally. In November that year, his post was re-designated as Special Inspector of Schools.

The issue of female education, however, was a more vexed one, since popularising it also meant negotiating the conservatism of contemporary Hindu society. Female literacy was not unknown in Hindu society, as was evident from the reports submitted by Adam, who demonstrated that this existed in two very different strata of Hindu society—the landed aristocracy and the ritually defiled castes among Bengal Vaishnavas. With the first group, literacy developed from certain functional needs: thus, women in zamindari families were imparted certain basic skills so that they could manage their estates even upon the untimely death of their husbands. With the other class, literacy was encouraged so that women could read Vaishnava religious classics. In early nineteenth-century Calcutta, there was a class of Vaishnava females called 'Ma Gossains', who were engaged by respectable families to impart some literacy to young girls of the *zenana*. The Derozian Pearychand Mitra (1814–83) tells us that even in the 1820s, he had noted that his mother and grandmother were able to read texts. At the time, it was also known that the women of the Sovabazar Raj family, the Tagores, and the Posta Raj family had women who could read and write. In 1822, Pandit Gourmohan Vidyalankar, associated with the Calcutta School Book Society, produced a primer for girls with encouragement from the conservative leader, Raja Radhakanta Dev (1783–1867). Pandit Gourmohan believed that the practice of keeping girls illiterate was opposed to Hindu *nitishastra* (moral codes). Even more extraordinary was his claim that the woman was four times as intelligent as the man, and hence qualified all the more for education. Another girl's school was set up in Calcutta in 1834 with patronage from the philanthropist Raja Baidyanath Roy (d. 1859). Radhakanta himself is known to have founded a school for girls, and had even arranged for the students of the Female Juvenile School, run by Christian missionaries, to be examined at his place. In the field of female education, too, the early intervention of missionaries proved important. We know that in 1818, Hannah Marshman, the wife of Joshua Marshman, had set up a female school at Serampore. By the 1820s, at least two other similar organisations, the Ladies Society and the Calcutta Diocesan Committee, were running schools for girls. There is also some evidence to suggest that in places, it was an accepted practice to send girls below the age of nine or ten to *pathshalas*, accompanied by their brothers or male cousins.

However, the idea of educating women was also met with keen resistance. Reportedly, people were more averse to the idea of female schools than to female education itself. This fear arose in the fact that girls would be exposed to the public gaze on their way to school, and from the presence of male teachers in schools. Mary Carpenter (1807–77), the British philanthropist and reformer who had personally known Rammohun Roy and visited India thrice on her social missions, alleged that the Hindu upper class was totally unconcerned about the condition of women, and that the seclusion practised in upper-class society actually had a pernicious effect on the lower classes too. As early as 1811, William Ward had noticed how the orthodox Hindus feared that literacy would make women conceited and even lead to their forming criminal connections and writing love-letters. It is equally important to remember that with advancing Hindu cultural nationalism in the late nineteenth century, the Hindu woman also became the symbol of indigenous resistance to alien ways of life. Western education, it was alleged, had evolved a new breed of women who had fallen easy prey to the new consumerism and were averse to performing household chores, thereby taxing the husband's already paltry clerical salary. By the 1870s, there was to be a backtracking on the question of women's education even within the reformist Brahmo Samaj, as exemplified by Keshabchandra Sen (1838–84). Keshabchandra opposed the idea of higher education for women that would entail the teaching of mathematics, philosophy, and science to girls. Significantly enough, this change in attitude occurred after his return from a short tour of England in 1870. Rather than further liberalise his thoughts on women's education or, more generally, on gender relations, exposure to Western ways of life had only served to strengthen his conservative instincts. The Western-educated Kashiprosad Ghosh (1809–73), who ran the weekly paper *Hindu Intelligencer*, also had reservations on the question of female education.

Such conservatism stands in some contrast to the position of Rammohun Roy, who, in his second tract on Sati (*Sahamaran Bishaye Pravartak O Nivrataker Samvad*, 1819), had bemoaned how Hindu women had never been permitted the education that would have truly enabled them to develop their innate gifts or qualities. For both Rammohun and Vidyasagar, women represented the true proletariat in India who had to be rescued from the thrall of ignorance and oppression. Vidyasagar's efforts in the field of woman-related reform have been dealt with in additional detail later (see Chapter 4). Suffice to say here that on the question of furthering women's education, his great zeal and interest were eventually to meet with sour disappointment.

In Calcutta itself, female education took a great stride forward with the intervention of John Elliot Drinkwater Bethune, sometime Law Member in the Viceroy's Council. Bethune was greatly motivated by the call for female education and, in 1849, he gave the Calcutta Female School that had been set up earlier a new name: *Hindu Balika Vidyalaya*. After his untimely death in 1851, it was renamed in his honour as the Bethune School. In this enterprise, Bethune was ably supported by two distinguished students of Derozio, Ramgopal Ghosh and Dakshinaranjan Mukherjee, and by Iswarchandra Vidyasagar, then serving in Fort William College. In 1851, Vidyasagar was appointed Secretary to the School, a position he maintained until 1869. Since orthodox Hindu objections stemmed more from the fear of putting young girls in public view than to their acquiring some basic education, Vidyasagar arranged for the transportation of girls who had been admitted to the school in a private horse-drawn carriage. On both sides of the carriage was inscribed a verse from Mahanirvan Tantra advising fathers to bring up the girl child with care and to provide her with education. The College even offered to transport girls free of cost to the school and back in case their parents could not afford a carriage or a palanquin. Pandit Madanmohan Tarkalankar, Vidyasagar's friend and co-worker, promptly admitted both his daughters, Kundamala and Bhuvanmala, to the Bethune School. This followed from an essay he had written earlier in the *Sarvashubhakari Patrika* in 1850 on the need for promoting female education. The same journal, as we shall see, also carried the first reformist tract from Vidyasagar himself on the evils of child marriage. Another friend and colleague of Vidyasagar at the Sanskrit College, Pundit Taranath Tarkavachaspati, also admitted his daughter, Jnanada, to the Bethune School.

However, the educational career of girls at the Bethune School, as elsewhere, proved to be extremely unstable and erratic. By one estimate, in 1849 the number of girls admitted was fifty-four, of which twenty-nine withdrew by the end of the year. By 1868, as reported in the feminist journal *Bamabodhini Patrika*, the number of girls on the rolls of the College had risen marginally to thirty. From contemporary reports, we also know that only girls from 'respectable' families were admitted to the school. This practice of limiting admission to upper-caste girls also had its negative aspects. Vidyasagar's *Report* on the status of the Bethune School on 29 July 1865 mentions forty-five girls being admitted that year, of whom thirty-seven withdrew, the 'majority taken away in marriage'. Sister Nivedita (1867–1911), who also ran a girls' school in north Calcutta, was to note how her plans were defeated by the common practice of early marriages among upper-caste girls. Only exceptionally would the husband's family allow the bride to continue with her education post-marriage. What is remarkable, though, is the steady induction of girls from the marginalised castes into the School. An official report for 1861 reveals that in that year, the school had five students each from the Karmakar (blacksmiths) and Gop castes (pastoralists/farmers), fifteen from the Telis (oil pressers), sixteen from the Tantubay (weavers), three from the Modaks (confectioners), and nine from the Subarnabaniks (goldsmiths). The three upper castes of Brahmins, Baidyas, and Kaysathas accounted for twenty-six students, of whom fourteen were from the Kayastha caste.

With some encouragement from Lt. Governor Halliday, Vidyasagar now undertook the task of starting new female schools. The first such school was inaugurated at Jougram (district Burdwan) in May 1857. This was followed by thirty-five more schools in the space of the next six months: twenty in district Hooghly, eleven in Burdwan, three in Midnapore, and one in Nadia. The total sum spent on these was Rs 845 and the number of students enrolled, about 1,300. Vidyasagar's enthusiasm, however, was soon to be dampened by the refusal of the Government of India to financially commit itself any further to the cause of female education. Its position here was that the government could only support local initiatives, and not assume the entire responsibility of meeting the recurring costs all by itself. Arguably, in the days immediately following the uprising of 1857, the government's financial resources had been stretched to its limit, with caution and conservatism being the watchwords everywhere. In September 1858, only a month after Vidyasagar had retired from public service, School Inspector Henry Woodrow, writing to the Director of Public Instruction, said: 'The rule now observed in Bengal is that an Inspector of Schools who wishes to see native females instructed must pay for his schools himself.' Despite intercessions from the Bengal administration, the imperial government decided to increasingly withdraw from the project, forcing Vidyasagar to shut down his female schools. At the time, he owed his teachers arrears of pay to the tune of Rs 3,439, which, however, the Government of India eventually paid up. Sadly, the ill-effects of the government's withdrawing itself from the field of female education were also aggravated by the callousness and lack of initiative on the part of the local population. Schools were allowed to deteriorate for lack of both pupils and teachers even when they received aid from the government. In March 1859, E. Lodge, Vidyasagar's successor in office as the Inspector of Schools for South Bengal, had the following to report on the status of one of the schools he visited, then running at a monthly cost of Rs 32, borne entirely by the government: '... not a girl, boy, nor Pundit was in attendance and a blackboard was the only indication of a school that I could discover.'

Elsewhere, he also noticed how the girls 'all held their spelling books before them but only one or two knew how to open or to hold them. The third best scholar attempted to read the book inverted.'

Incidentally, Lodge was to also observe the 'bitter hostility' he found in some local officials against Vidyasagar and his schemes.

One redeeming feature, though, in which the Pundit may have taken some personal comfort was that the girl's school which he had opened at Birsingha continued to do well. In 1864–65, Inspector Lodge himself described it as the 'best aided school'. He also reported meeting one of the Pundit's daughters there, whom he described as the 'most favoured girl I have ever met with in any of the aided schools'.

Hereafter, attempts to promote female education proceeded only sporadically. Notwithstanding the rebuff from the government, Vidyasagar opened a voluntary agency by the name of *Nari Shiksha Pratisthan,* which the rajas of Paikpara supported, and to which the then Lt. Governor, Cecil Beadon, himself committed a monthly sum of Rs 55. Nothing further is known of the *Pratisthan*. In the meantime, the activities of the Bethune School engaged Vidyasagar and, for a time, there was excitement in the air in view of the expected arrival of Mary Carpenter on her first visit to India in 1866. Carpenter had been greatly impressed with the life and labours of Vidyasagar and was keen to meet him. She eventually met the Pundit through the mediation of the then Director of Public Instruction, William Stephen Atkinson. As it turned out, the two also differed sharply over one important question: whether or not to set up a Normal School at Bethune School on the lines of the Sanskrit College. Carpenter considered this fundamentally important to the future success of Bethune School, and in this, she was supported by some Brahmo leaders, chiefly Keshabchandra Sen and Dwijendranath Tagore (1840–1926), the eldest son of Maharshi Debendranath. A meeting to consider this question was convened on the premises of the Brahmo Samaj, to which Vidyasagar objected. In part, his objection was that the organisers, whether from a sectarian motive or otherwise, had shied away from inviting Hindu men of wealth and eminence in contemporary Calcutta, who might have substantively contributed to advancing the project. But more importantly, he disagreed with the idea of setting up a Normal School at Bethune with the hope of training competent female teachers. Writing to Lt. Governor William Grey on 1 October 1867, Vidyasagar pointed to certain practical social problems that he feared would thwart any such move. In the first place, given the fact that Hindus were reluctant to allow even young girls of ten or eleven to attend school, it was simply inconceivable, he argued, that they would agree to send adults. The only class of women who might be found willing would be widows, which in itself would raise suspicion. Even if their competence was not in doubt, their very presence was likely to be socially objectionable. In all probability, Vidyasagar was hinting at what had transpired at the Dacca Normal School earlier, where it was discovered that the majority of female teachers were widowed Vaishnavas of 'disreputable castes'. Undoubtedly, in airing such objections, Vidyasagar was only giving expression to certain social realities which he understood rather well. In 1867, the government decided to side with Miss Carpenter and a Normal School was indeed set up in the premises of the Bethune School. However, as Vidyasagar had predicted, it failed to procure trainee teachers and was closed on the orders of Lt. Governor George Campbell in 1872.

Mary Carpenter's visit also coincided with an unsavory incident that affected Pandit Iswarchandra's life. In 1866, while returning from an inspection tour of schools, the carriage carrying Vidyasagar overturned while negotiating a sharp turn, causing serious internal damage to its occupant. Incidentally, it was Miss Carpenter's prompt and careful nursing that brought the Pundit some temporary relief. By all accounts, the accident seriously affected his health thereafter, and is believed to have even hastened his death.

The pursuit of his educational goals eventually brought Vidyasagar on a collision course with some government officials. The first of these was Gordon Young, an English civilian who was appointed the first Director of Public Instruction for Bengal under changes introduced by the Wood's Dispatch of 1854. Young was not an imposing or overbearing man, and some of his objections to Pundit Iswarchandra's ways of working at the Sanskrit College were quite just and reasonable. For one, he took exception to the way Vidyasagar would recruit teachers without publicly advertising vacancies. This, as he rightly found, was contrary to established rules, and yet Young was gracious enough to ultimately accept these appointments. Young also objected to the fact that the Pundit's school textbooks, published by the Sanskrit Press, were priced rather high, compared to those published by the Calcutta School Book Society or the Vernacular Literature Society. However, when asked to lower the price of these books, Vidyasagar declined to comply. Differences between the two are reported to have also arisen in 1857 with both soldiers and the civilian population rising in revolt against the government. Until about the late 1960s, it was widely believed in the Left circles of West Bengal that Vidyasagar had colluded with the colonial government and voluntarily handed over the premises of Sanskrit College to the authorities, which were then used for quartering British troops. In 1970, this led to Vidyasagar's bust, which had been originally set up in 1899 at College Square, being decapitated. This version has since been contested by Benoy Ghose, after he progressively moved away from the Left. Two other biographers, Ananta Kumar Ray and Santosh Kumar Adhikari, have presented their own versions which vary somewhat in details. The latter claims that Young did not consult Vidyasagar over the issue of quartering troops, provoking the Pundit to write a letter of protest on 11 August 1857. The exact chain of events is difficult to establish, although in the present state of our knowledge, it is possible to state two things quite clearly: first, that the Sanskrit College had to temporarily move to rented premises close by, and second, that this incident did accentuate the distrust that Young and Vidyasagar had been developing for each other.

It is tempting to speculate that the recurring disappointments or unpleasantness that Vidyasagar had to face in his role as an Inspector of Schools might have blown over, or at least been partly assuaged, had the government only somehow compensated him by way of professionally rewarding his services. However, growing disagreements with Young only made this unlikely. By August 1857, Vidyasagar had come to believe that his enthusiasm and hard work in the field of education had not been adequately rewarded. In hindsight, it appears that he was expecting the government to promote him to the position of Inspector of Schools in place of Hodgson Pratt, who was proceeding to England on leave. However, by the time he approached the authorities, the Bengal government had already found a successor in Lodge. In the meantime, his health had begun to break down, mainly due to his stormy involvement in the controversy surrounding the widow marriage campaign. It had also begun to increasingly emerge that he had been wilfully passed over in favour of an Englishman. His letter of 27 August 1857 to Halliday clearly indicates his desire to retire from public service. Halliday, who had taken a great liking to the Pundit, tried to stall any rash move on the part of an offended Vidyasagar, but the Pundit's mind was already made up. On 15 September 1857, in a letter to the Bengal government, he clearly confessed that his failing health was only one among several reasons for his seeking premature retirement. Had this been purely on health grounds, Vidyasagar argued, he might have opted to go on a long leave to recuperate. This letter clearly lists two main reasons for his quitting public service: first, the lack of encouragement and cooperation from his superiors in office, and second, his being overlooked for a promotion which he believed he otherwise fully deserved. However, Halliday himself could not be persuaded to accept this point of view, believing that the Pundit had no just cause for grievance. While thanking him for the services rendered to the community, he regretted that the Pundit 'thought fit to make his retirement somewhat ungraciously, especially as he can have no fair reason for dissatisfaction'. A more eloquent tribute came from the Inspector of Schools, Eastern Bengal, Henry Woodrow: 'His (Vidyasagar's) liberality to his countrymen is well known to have been bounded only by his means and he retires from the service of the government, rich in honour but in nothing else.'

At the age of thirty-eight, Pundit Iswarchandra quit his posts of Principal, Sanskrit College, Special Inspector of Schools for South Bengal, and Member, Board of Examiners for Calcutta

University. Although he was made a Fellow of that University back in 1857, he never attended any official meetings in that capacity. *Prima facie*, it does also appear somewhat odd that in 1876, the University of Calcutta chose to confer an honorary doctorate degree on Rev. Krishna Mohan Bandopadhyay, but not on Vidyasagar. In 1883, however, the newly opened Punjab University honoured him by appointing him as Member to the University Senate. On 3 November 1858, Edward Byles Cowell (1826–1903), the scholar who was also to be the first Professor of Sanskrit at Cambridge University, succeeded him as Principal, Sanskrit College.

Life after Sanskrit College

Having worked for no more than ten years in an official position, Vidyasagar was clearly not entitled to a pension and the government did not think of granting him an endowment either. Fortunately for him, the Pundit never reached the level of desperation that might have been the fate of many an unemployed man in Bengal. By one estimate, his annual income at the time varied between Rs 36,000 and Rs 54,000, the bulk of which came from the sale proceeds of his books. Although a Brahmin by birth, Vidyasagar showed great business acumen in handling book-production and the print media which, scholar Paramesh Acharya feels, justifies our calling him the 'Vyabasayi Vidyasagar' (Vidyasagar the Merchant). Acharya tells us that *smriti* classified teachers into three categories, the Guru, the Acharya, and the Upadhyay. Of these, the Upadhyay was the least respectable since he alone made a living by turning learning and knowledge into a commodity. By this definition, Vidyasagar and Taranath Tarkavachaspati, both of whom ran successful business ventures, were modern prototypes of the erstwhile Upadhyays.

Vidyasagar's uniqueness lies in the singular fact that he was printer, publisher, and author, all combined in one. In Chandicharan Bandopadhyay's reckoning, Vidyasagar authored and published fifty-two books in all, of which thirty were in Bengali, seventeen in Sanskrit, and five in English. Some of these books underwent over forty reprints in Vidyasagar's lifetime alone. James Long's Catalogue of 1857 informs us that in that year, a total number of 5,71,670 volumes were published by about forty-six presses located in Bengal. Of these, as many as 84,220 were published by the Sanskrit Press alone, making it the most successful vernacular press at the time. What also secured Vidyasagar a near monopoly in the field of book publishing is the fact that the government gave him the power to eliminate from the reading list books that did not meet his expectations. He is known to have used this power abundantly. He was also responsible for formulating syllabi and fixing reading lists for the students of model schools, the Sanskrit College, and the Normal School. Not surprisingly, a good number of texts adopted by these institutions were authored by him; it is no coincidence that the Sanskrit Press published most of the twenty-seven books in use at the Sanskrit College itself. His business acumen is evident in other instances too. In 1855, when asked to lower the price of his books, Vidyasagar came up with a novel scheme under which the prices of books would be suitably lowered, on condition that the government advanced him a sum of money and agreed to buy back a certain number of copies of the book. Such a scheme could hardly bring losses to the printer and publisher. Even in the field of social reform, his tracts proved to be sensational. Although the widow marriage movement itself had disappointing results in Bengal, Vidyasagar's tracts were an instant success; the second tract on widow marriage had to reprinted within the space of a few months.

Vidyasagar's public activities were diversified even further after he resigned his posts with the government. In November 1858, he collaborated with Dwarkanath Vidyabhushan (1819–86), also from Sanskrit College, to start *Somprakash,* which was to become a leading Bengali daily in late nineteenth-century Bengal. Roughly three years later, he took over the management of the *Hindoo Patriot,* a paper hitherto edited by Harishchandra

Mukhopadhyay (1824–61). The editorship was now entrusted to the veteran public figure Krishnodas Pal (1838–84), with great success. Although he was no longer in public service, the government continued to consult him on various matters concerning the running of educational institutions and on the finer points of Hindu laws related to property, inheritance, and even revenue matters. In 1863, he was appointed a Visitor to *Ward's Institution*, an exclusive body that had been established in 1855 to educate and train the sons of zamindars and suitably prepare them for public life. In 1865, on the request of the government, he submitted a detailed report on the state of its functioning and came to the conclusion that those who had been educated in that exclusive institution were no better than those who were not. In 1870, the government consulted him on the appropriateness of the Hindu Wills Bill, which sought to deny a man the absolute right to gift or alienate his assets in perpetuity. In this instance, Vidyasagar's position was that this would go against Hindu conventions and law; he also used this occasion to observe that the British Indian courts were not always the best judges when it came to adjudicating the finer points of Hindu law. Together with the poet Nabinchandra Sen (1847–1909) and a few others, he started the *Hindu Annuity Fund* in June 1872, which offered a kind of pension scheme for destitute women and widows. However, he soon resigned from the body, submitting a detailed resignation letter on 21 August 1876 that ran into twenty-two foolscap pages. The letter revealed financial irregularities on the part of the Directors and the concerned staff. It was also alleged that Vidyasagar's own efforts to improve the functioning of the institution had been thwarted at every stage by vested interests.

Prima facie, it might be difficult to agree with Subal Mitra's remark that 'in pecuniary point of view, he (Vidyasagar) was nothing but a common man of middle station of life'. And yet, this may not be seriously off the mark, given his prodigious charity that depleted his savings and his uncommon habit of borrowing money from friends and creditors to help another friend in distress. There were many who borrowed money from him, but failed to repay him fully. The most well-known case here is undoubtedly that of the poet Madhusudan Dutta (1824–73), to whom Vidyasagar advanced money repeatedly. On occasions, Dutta showed no urgency to pay up, despite desperate prodding from an acutely embarrassed Vidyasagar. He ultimately managed to clear most, but not all, of his debts through distress sales of his property. But even outside this are numerous tales, some documented, others apocryphal, of his helping a father who was about to be jailed for failing to clear the debt he had incurred on his daughter's marriage; of a bookseller who posed as a needy student, only to sell off in the market the books graciously gifted by the Pundit; of poor women who kept calling on him with appeals for help; of his hosting as many as twenty students in Calcutta at a time when he was not settled in service; opening charitable dispensaries for the treatment of malarial fever during the epidemic of 1859; running free kitchens at Birsingha and other places during the famine of 1866; maintaining a free school for boys in his native village; and carrying clothes and sundry food items to be distributed among poor Santhals at Karmatar, the retreat that he had procured for himself in 1871.

Vidyasagar thought beyond his immediate family and friends when it came to taking care of people. His last Will and Testament provided a monthly pension for Harakali Chaudhuri, a cook who had served him many years, and for Bhuvanmohan Singha, son of Jagatdurlabh Singha, who had been his host at a time of critical need. To fellow scholars like Pandits Rakhal Das Nyayaratna (1829–1914), a distinguished scholar of Nyaya from Bhatpara, and Jaganmohan Tarkalankar (1829–1900), associated with the translation of the *Mahabharata* sponsored by the Burdwan Raj, he paid a monthly stipend for some time. Ironically, those whom he had helped, financially or otherwise, were among his consistent critics, and there is a popular story to the effect that Vidyasagar could easily identify his debtors by the infamy they showered on him. By 1865–66, his mounting debts had driven him to briefly reconsider joining government employment. Evidently, the then Lt. Governor of Bengal, Cecil Beadon (1816–80), would have obliged, but for the fact that Pundit Iswarchandra agreed to work only on certain conditions. When a professorship of Sanskrit came up at the Presidency College, he requested that he be considered for the post, but on a salary comparable to that paid to European teachers. Predictably, the government did not agree to this. In 1869, to raise some money with which to pay his debts, Vidyasagar sold off a part of his shares in the Sanskrit Press and Depository to friends; one of the beneficiaries was his long-time friend and supporter, Rajkrishna Bandopadhyay. The remaining shares were also sold to Rajkrishna in 1885.

One of the enduring memorials to Vidyasagar's efforts as an educationist was the Metropolitan Institution, opened in central Calcutta in 1872 and subsequently renamed Vidyasagar College. The founding of this institution enabled the Pundit to not only practically realise some of his cherished educational ideals, but to also demonstrate the capacity and worthiness of Indian efforts at self-help in the field of education. The faculty of the College was fully Indian and it received no grant from the government. Acharya Prafulla Chandra Ray (1861–1944), chemist, educationist, and entrepreneur, wrote the following in defence of his choosing to study at the institution founded by Vidyasagar:

> More than one reason determined my choice of Vidyasagar College. In the first place, the Metropolitan Institution was a national institution and something we could look upon as our own; in the second place, Surendranath Banerjee, who was almost the god of our idolatry, was professor of English literature and Prasanna Kumar Lahiri, a distinguished pupil of Tawney (of the Presidency College) was professor of poetry.

Undoubtedly, Vidyasagar had a talent for spotting competent teachers and he also paid his teachers handsomely; at the Metropolitan, teachers of even lower classes were paid Rs 50 as against an average monthly pay of Rs 10 elsewhere.

The Metropolitan Institution has a long pre-history. It grew out of an institution called the Calcutta Training School (founded 1859), with which Vidyasagar was associated for a time. Internal squabbles within the Managing Committee led to a group breaking away, and founding the Hindu Metropolitan Institution in 1864. In 1872, Vidyasagar, with assistance from Dwarkanath Mitter and Krishna Das Pal, formed a new Management Committee and took greater control of the school, now renamed the Metropolitan Institution. In 1874, the Calcutta University granted it the status of a second-grade college, enabling it to run the First Arts Course. The following year, the Metropolitan ranked second among all colleges in the F.A. examinations, with Jogendra Chandra Basu topping the merit list, prompting even Registrar Sutcliffe of Calcutta University to remark, 'the Pandit has done wonders!' Vidyasagar rewarded the meritorious boy with a set of Walter Scott's Waverley novels, bound in leather and embossed in gold, taken from his personal library. In 1879, Metropolitan was granted the status of a first-grade college and the B.A. course introduced. It was the first unaided college to be granted that status. Between 1881 and 1892, 498 students of the Metropolitan Institution passed the B.A. degree examination and thirty-three, the M.A. examination. In 1882, a law course was started at this college and 513 students cleared the B.L. examination over the next ten years. A comparison of the student strength in various colleges within Calcutta will reveal the growing popularity of Vidyasagar's venture. In 1876, Presidency College had 310 students, General Assembly's Institution, 118, and Metropolitan, 146. Eight years later, in 1884, Presidency had only 342 students as against Metropolitan's 506. In the 1880s, branches of the college were opened at Shyampukur, Burrabazar, and Bowbazar, and functioned as schools. Vivekananda (then Narendranath Dutt) was recruited for the Bowbazar branch and the well-known Ramakrishna diarist, Mahendranath Gupta, for the Shyampukur branch. Vidyasagar himself spent about a lakh on the new building for the main college (opened in 1887), with money borrowed from the Bhagyakul zamindars.

In Vidyasagar's lifetime, the Metropolitan Institution was noted for certain distinctive features that were a part of the everyday routine. First, all forms of corporal punishment to students were abolished. A teacher at the college lost his job for violating this rule. The second was the introduction of innovative pedagogy. In the interests of maintaining discipline, Vidyasagar would personally undertake surprise visits to the college; additionally, he also arranged for regular feedback from students on the quality of teaching. Two boys from each class were deputed for this purpose, who were to report to him periodically. Finally, he would also adopt confidence-building measures among the students. In 1886, he dismissed Mahendranath Gupta from service when students of the Shyampukur branch performed badly in the annual examination. Vidyasagar read this as Gupta's dereliction of duty, resulting from a growing interest in the religious personality of Ramakrishna of Dakshineswar. And apparently, he had a deep insight into child psychology. Once, on an inspection round, he found a teacher directing a question to a second boy after the student who had been asked earlier failed to answer. In this instance, Vidyasagar had cause to personally intervene. His advice to the concerned teacher was to avoid such methods in class, as these might embarrass the relatively weaker student. A better method, he suggested, was to help him answer the question, with some leads or encouragement from the teacher himself.

In 1884, Vidyasagar appointed one of his sons-in-law, Suryakumar Adhikari, to the post of Principal of the Metropolitan Institution. But the experiment with Suryakumar failed and, for reasons allegedly connected with financial mismanagement, he had to be removed from the post. In 1884, he also undertook a brief tour of northern India to regain his health, but on the whole, his health only deteriorated over time. He was troubled by acute abdominal pain and recurring bouts of asthma. His increasing withdrawal from public life left a mark on his educational institutions. By 1889–90, Metropolitan had been left behind by growing competition from two stars that had newly risen on the horizon: the Ripon College started by Surendranath Banerjee and City College by Anandamohan Bose. In 1890, sixteen of the 129 students appearing for the B.A. examination from Ripon College passed in the first division; for Metropolitan, the number was only seven out of 120. By 1891, the year Vidyasagar passed away, the student strength at Metropolitan had dropped substantially.

Even with its declining popularity, the Metropolitan College encouraged Indian enterprise in the field of higher education. Outside Calcutta, it led to the opening of the Burdwan Raj College (Burdwan) in 1881; Victoria College (Narail) in 1886; Victoria College (Cooch Behar) in 1888; Brojomohun College (Barisal) in 1889; Victoria College (Comilla), also in 1889; and Murarichand College (Sylhet) in 1892. Prior to the launching of the National Education Movement in the Swadeshi years, this had to be the most successful phase of Indian entrepreneurship in the field of education.

The Last Years

In November 1869, Vidyasagar wrote the following to his father:

> For several reasons, I have developed a strong feeling of disenchantment and not even for a moment do I wish to implicate myself any further in any worldly matter. Given the present state of my body and mind, I do not think I shall live long if I were to do otherwise. Hence, I have decided to be at peace and isolate myself from worldly life to the extent possible.... In matters worldly, there cannot be a man more unfortunate than I; I have always tried my utmost to please everyone, but have now come to realise that I have utterly failed to achieve this. The old saying that he who tries to please everyone ends up pleasing none spells a truth that cannot be overlooked. I am fully convinced that of those from whom a worldly man may come to expect some affection or empathy, not a single

> person has volunteered to show such feelings for me in the slightest.... (translation mine)

Letters replicating such feelings were also sent to his mother, wife, brothers, and sisters-in-law. In his letter to his wife, he asked for her forgiveness for any wrong that he might have unwittingly committed towards her, also indicating that this might be the last communication between them.

For the rest of his life, Pundit Iswarchandra did not visit his native village again.

In hindsight, it is possible to connect such feelings of defeat and despondency to several factors. His health, as we have noted, progressively broke down after the Uttarpara mishap of 1866, resulting in recurring bouts of diarrhoea. But even earlier, the widow marriage campaign in which he had invested a great deal of his emotions, energy, and resources had failed to make any substantive progress, causing him great personal disappointment. The year 1856, when the first widow marriage had been held, was justly a time for jubilation, but battling his adversaries even before that momentous event could take place had sapped his vital energies. It was also increasingly clear to him that the campaign to stop polygamous marriages would prove to be more difficult than he had imagined, given the dogged opposition from his countrymen, among whom were some erstwhile friends and colleagues, and the reluctance on the part of the government to engage itself in another act of social legislation. About five months before the first widow marriage was solemnised in December 1856, he complained of acute illness and was advised six weeks of paid medical leave.

In the years preceding 1869, Pundit Iswarchandra had increasingly detached himself from public activity, resigning successively from the Ward's Institution and the Hindu Annuity Fund; in 1869, he resigned from the Bethune School (Management), notwithstanding his great personal attachment to its founder. In 1871, driven by a growing sense of disenchantment and betrayed by family, friends, and creditors, Vidyasagar sought refuge in the remote tribal hinterland of Karmatar, now in district Jamtara, Jharkhand. There, he built a private house with a spacious mango garden, euphemistically calling it the 'Nandan Kanan', a heavenly paradise on earth. He periodically retreated to this paradise, although never for long. Work in Calcutta beckoned him back from time to time, and friends and relatives would also drop in obtrusively, somewhat marring the peace and fragility of the place. It is said that at this time, life's burdens and the pretentious ways of people from his own class had turned Vidyasagar into something of a misanthrope, but this was adequately compensated by the innocence and sincerity of the local Santhals, who frequently and unabashedly called on him for food and other small requirements. He watched them dance and sing and express delight at savouring even the most modest delicacies of the confectioner's art, carried from Burdwan or Calcutta. In several matters, the newly arrived visitor in their midst surprised the Santhals, for unlike other Bengali *bhadralok* stationed in the area, he refused to accept things gratuitously and paid honest wages for work performed, often in excess of what was ordinarily paid. What delighted Vidyasagar himself was his Santhal hosts' happiness in the simplest acts of human reciprocity, a far cry, as it seemed then, from the convoluted world of urban Calcutta.

Sadly, Karmatar did not survive Vidyasagar for long; it was one among Vidyasagar's several assets to be sold off by Narayanchandra to a business family from Calcutta. Judging by a press report published in 2003, the house was already in ruins; its wooden doors and windows had been stolen by local residents and the grounds itself were apparently serving as a camping ground for volunteers from right-wing organisations.

The years immediately preceding 1869 had witnessed Vidyasagar's gradual distancing from the extended family. Most biographers agree that at Birsingha, there was little love lost between the brothers. Reportedly, Vidyasagar blamed this on his brothers, who were rumoured to be henpecked husbands, incapable of maintaining any degree of peace and goodwill within members of the extended family. In 1867, he partitioned the family residence between his brothers, creating independent spaces for each household. Subal Mitra tells us quite disapprovingly that this stemmed from Vidyasagar's 'Western' ways of thinking. It is on the whole true that at least in the urban metropolis of Calcutta, nuclear families were becoming more popular, driven by a new consumerism and greater social and professional competitiveness between siblings, their wives and children, and the never-ending litigation resulting from partition suits. On the other hand, for this phenomenon to have been replicated in a remote part of rural Bengal, some extraordinary circumstances would have been required.

For Vidyasagar, however, there was more trouble brewing on other fronts. In 1868, Deenabandhu, Vidyasagar's younger brother, instituted a suit claiming a share in the Sanskrit Press and Depository, and the matter had to be settled through the mediation of close friends and confidants. Close on the heels of this came another unfortunate incident that permanently ruptured Vidyasagar's links with his native village. Ironically enough, this had to do with a widow marriage, on which the Pundit and his brothers found themselves placed in mutually hostile camps. It so happened that on the repeated request of an influential local family, Vidyasagar agreed to not press for the marriage of one Muchiram Bandopadhyay to a widow. When the marriage did take place in his absence and contrary to his wishes, Vidyasagar felt greatly slighted and decided never to visit his extended family in Birsingha again. In his biography, Sambhuchandra referred to this incident to only highlight what he called the 'cowardice and duplicity' in Vidyasagar: his great enthusiasm for widow marriages on the one hand, and the inexplicable opposition to it on the other.

In hindsight, though, such opposition can be justly interpreted not so much as some reluctance, as a personal affront. From a perusal of his life, it becomes amply clear that Pundit Iswarchandra agreed to work for any cause purely on his own terms, and would brook no dissent or opposition. Also, he rarely forgave his detractors. When Jashodanandan Sarkar, editor of the journal *Samaj Darpan*, alleged that Vidyasagar was hungry for personal fame, the Pundit retaliated by retracting his praise for Sarkar's textbook on grammar, leading to a sharp drop in sales. He terminated the services of his longstanding cook, Harakali Chaudhary (whom we have mentioned above), merely for suggesting that his employer be more discreet when directing his charity. At the Metropolitan Institution, he similarly dismissed not only the teacher who had violated a rule, but also fellow-teachers who had spoken in support of the dismissed teacher out of pure empathy. Vidyasagar and his family narrowly escaped an unpleasant incident comparable to that involving Muchiram Bandopadhyay, and surprisingly, this occurred with respect to his son Naryanachandra's marriage to the widowed Bhavasundari in 1870. When Narayan expressed his desire to marry Bhavasundari, Vidyasagar proudly wrote back to say that this constituted the crowning moment of his life, since people would have only rebuked him if his own son had preferred to marry a virgin. However, we gather from Sambhuchandra that Vidyasagar had himself arranged for Bhavasundari to marry a gentleman stationed in the North-West Provinces, and that preparations for the marriage had reached an advanced stage. This turn of events would no doubt have embarrassed him somewhat, especially because his wife, Dinamayee, was unwilling to have her only son wedded to a girl as old as Bhavasundari. Things reached a critical state when, on the wedding night, no woman from the groom's family was found willing to greet the newly wedded pair and invite them home. Sambhuchandra writes that on this occasion, the saving grace was the 'courageous' Taranath Tarkavachaspati and his wife, who readily came forward to perform this customary ritual. Was it also not unnatural for Vidyasagar to not personally attend the wedding of his only son?

Although the government consulted him on educational matters even after he had relinquished his office at the Sanskrit College, Vidyasagar had more occasions to disagree with the official position than to agree with it. In April 1859, he fought a move originating in Principal Cowell, the Indologist Dr Edward Roer (1805–66), and the Inspector of Schools Henry Woodrow, which mooted two vitally important proposals: first, to discontinue the teaching of *Smriti* and Vedanta at the Sanskrit College, and second, to introduce Sanskrit Studies in English-language schools and colleges. Vidyasagar responded by pointing to the practical utility of studying *Smriti* for purposes of interpreting Hindu law, while he found the study of Vedanta 'unexceptionable' in view of the great importance attached to it by Hindus. He found the idea of teaching Sanskrit at English-medium schools and colleges impracticable, given the fact that such institutions had failed to do justice to even Bengali. Although stalled at the time, the issue was revived in 1872 when the government decided to abolish the post of *Smriti* professor in Sanskrit College. It was rumoured that Pundit Iswarchandra had connived to play a hand in this. When Vidyasagar issued a public statement protesting this charge, Lt. Governor Campbell was offended and ordered the Education Department to take several books by the Pundit off the reading list for schools. In any case, we now know that Campbell had turned out to be a notable exception among Vidyasagar's English superiors. We shall later have occasion to see how the two also differed strongly with respect to educational policy.

In early 1874, there occurred the well-known but unpleasant incident which a popular Bengali daily, the *Sadharani* (of 5 July 1874), was to later immortalise through an editorial called 'Taltalar Chati' (The slippers made in Taltala). This was a reference to the leather slippers that Vidyasagar habitually wore, and which, in this instance, became the subject of a public controversy. The details of what Subalchandra Mitra calls the 'shoe question' are as follows. On 28 January, Pundit Iswarchandra, accompanied by his friend from Benares, the eminent Hindi poet and journalist Harishchandra, and Surendranath, the son of Rajkrishna Bandopadhyay, attempted to enter the Indian Museum and Asiatic Society which, at the time, shared the same premises on Park Street, Calcutta. Here, the visitors met with a rebuff. Harishchandra and Surendranath, being formally dressed in Western clothes, were allowed to enter by the porter, but not Vidyasagar, ostensibly on account of his 'quaint' attire of coarse *dhoti*, *chadar*, and the ignoble slippers. As is only too well-known, the porter could not have been the first to take Vidyasagar for a nondescript Odiya menial; similar perceptions have been recorded by a wide variety of men and women, and are now legend. On being denied entry, Vidyasagar promptly returned to his carriage and later sent a letter of protest to H. F. Bransford, Honorary Secretary to the Indian Museum. The incident created some stir in the press and even the *Englishman*, a paper which could not have been expected to side with 'natives', felt that this called for an apology. Significantly enough, the authorities did not agree with this view, and the complaint was eventually dismissed. Looking back at this incident, it might be reasonable to conclude that it was the underlying racial affront more than the question of complying with an awkward rule that irked Vidyasagar. Once, when he was similarly asked by the gatekeeper to the Burdwan Raj palace to remove his slippers, Vidyasagar had complied without the slightest hesitation. The Maharaja, upon hearing of this, had ordered the concerned gatekeeper to be removed from service, but later reinstated him on Vidyasagar's request. The man had simply been following orders, the Pundit had graciously said.

Did the man whom posterity has subjected to contrary political pulls have political views of his own? There is no reason to doubt that Vidyasagar accepted, in principle, the reigning *bhadralok* discourse on British rule playing a progressive and socially liberating role in India. His tract on the evils of polygamy invokes this widely shared perception in the following words:

> The British nation is neither stupid nor worthless and cowardly. Contrary to what some may believe, they (the British) did not arrive here driven by sheer material greed or to enjoy the fruits of political power. The sole object of their conquest has been to bring about the all-round development of this country. (translation mine)

Prima facie, such observations seem no less naïve than Rammohun's pleading for the extended European colonisation of Indian agriculture or his supporting the movement for free trade. Also, such an invocation is all the more understandable in the context of his attempts to persuade the government to agree to social legislation. In hindsight, it would seem that like many other men of his class, Vidyasagar was unable to clearly separate his patriotism from a persistent belief in the development chronology of the Empire. However, such a contradiction is no less apparent in his contemporary, Taranath Tarkavachaspati, who opposed him on certain vital issues. Pundit Taranath plainly refused to believe that the English had arrived on a noble pilgrimage 'from some distant land beyond the seven seas and ten rivers', and yet he led the Reception Party organised in honour of the visiting Prince of Wales in 1875.

Vidyasagar's patriotism comes through in some of his other writings. In his *Banglar Itihas* (1848), he attributed the military defeats of Siraj-ud-daulah and Mir Kasim primarily to betrayals by men they had naively trusted, and also disputed the British characterisation of Maharaja Nanda Kumar. The revolutionary nationalist Bhupendranath Dutta (1880–1961) reports having once heard his teacher at Midnapore, Jnanendranath Basu, speak about how Vidyasagar exhorted them to carry out an armed struggle under the cover of the dense jungles nearby. In Basu's testimony, such talk would grow so alarmingly seditious that the doors and windows of the room would be promptly shut for fear of being overheard. There is a popular story—although it is by no means verifiable—that once, while watching *Nil Durpan* (1860), a play that evocatively dramatises the oppression carried out by European indigo planters on Indian cultivators, Vidyasagar grew so agitated that he flung his slippers at the actor (Ardhendhu Shekhar Mustafi, 1850–1908) who had very realistically portrayed the role of one such planter.

While we cannot be sure that slippers were indeed hurled at the accomplished actor, Vidyasagar's presence on the occasion was a very likely event, for he was a great patron of the theatre.

He moved away from the Bengali stage only when prostitutes began to be engaged to replace men playing female roles. He is believed to have even rusticated a boy by the name of Bholanath Basu from his Metropolitan Institution for playing the role of the female Vidya in a play based on the poet Bharatchandra's well-known romantic poem, *Vidyasaundar.* Indeed, the Pundit could be quite puritanical in his attitudes. Once, when a young Theosophist with long hair approached him for recommendations for a job, Vidyasagar's first reaction was to jestingly ask him whether he was indeed a man!

In his later years, two other habits became an integral part of his life: building up his personal library and the enthusiastic pursuit of Homoeopathy. His personal library became a cause for wonder, and many contemporaries have expressed surprise that a man should so 'wantonly' invest a great deal of money in simply buying books and storing them. Even as a student, he would invest in manuscripts, which later became a part of the library. His decision to build a separate house for himself at Badurbagan was primarily motivated by the urgent need to find suitable space for his growing personal collection of books and manuscripts. By one estimate, he had in his possession as many as 16,000 volumes in Sanskrit, Bengali, Hindi, and English. This, in all probability, is an exaggerated figure. Going by the detailed list provided in some editions of his Collected Works, it would appear that he had roughly 360 books in the Bengali language, about 285 in Hindi and Sanskrit, and fifteen in English. No separate lists are available for manuscripts. This was not an astonishingly large collection; what impresses us more is the range of subjects covered. Was Vidyasagar able to read or practically put to use a reasonably good part of his personal collection? In his *Kalikata Kamalalay* (1823), a work describing the ways of life in early colonial Calcutta, Bhavanicharan Bandopadhyay (1787–1848) had ridiculed the habit commonly found among the Calcutta *nouveaux riche* to acquire and store books without ever aspiring to read them. Indeed, this is reminiscent of the habits of the merchant-patrons and bankers of sixteenth-century Florence, Milan or Venice. However, it is doubtful if this was true of Vidyasagar himself. The man was not only a bibliophile, but he also took pride in the very act of making a book look aesthetically delightful to himself and to his visitors. This was not a matter which he judged on grounds of prudence or practicality, for with some of his imported volumes, the binding in expensive leather and the embossing in gold which he had especially requested cost more than the printed book itself. In itself, the range of his interests looks staggering, covering literature, grammar, philosophy, religious manuals, and works on Hindu law. Much of this is understandable; what does occasion some surprise is the good number of volumes dedicated to religious subjects, ranging from a collection of Christian psalms to Vaishnava texts and discourses on Brahmoism. At first sight, this does appear intriguing for a man who was commonly believed to be an atheist or, at best, an agnostic.

After Vidyasagar passed away, the library met with an unworthy fate. It was auctioned off by Narayanchandra to the Raja of Lalgola (district Murshidabad) to raise additional money that would clear his debts. In 1914, the Raja graciously donated it to the Bangiya Sahitya Parishat, the Bengal Academy of Letters, where it was opened up for public use.

Vidyasagar pursued the study of Homoeopathy diligently and even managed to convert his friend, Mahendralal Sarkar (1833–1904), the founder of the Indian Science Association and an allopathic physician by profession, to the practice of Homoeopathy. Vidyasagar had been a generous donor to the Indian Science Association, but he especially took it upon himself to convince Dr Sarkar of the merits of Homoeopathy. We do know that in this enterprise, he succeeded. Dr Sarkar was to serve as a Homoeopathic physician to Sri Ramakrishna during the latter's critical illness in 1886, while Vidyasagar successfully and joyously experimented with the Santhals of Karmatar. Interestingly, he observed that Homoeopathic treatment worked more effectively on his Santhal patients, who led an arduous but an unassuming life.

In the closing years of his life, one imagines, Vidyasagar would have also bemoaned the loss of several friends and supporters. Much to his personal disappointment, he survived many of his close friends and relatives, and the list is indeed long. In 1868, he lost the Derozian Ramgopal Ghosh; in 1870, Maharaja Mehtabchand of Burdwan and Dr Durgachacharan Bandopadhyay; in 1871, his mother Bhagavati Devi; in 1873, his eldest son-in-law, Gopalchandra Samajpati; in 1874, the jurist Dwarkanath Mitter; in 1875, fellow educationist Pearycharan Sarkar; in 1876, father Thakurdas Bandopadhyay; and in 1883, his wife, Dinamoyee. Three of his younger brothers, Deenanath Nyayratna, Harachandra, and Harishchandra predeceased him. It also undoubtedly saddened Vidyasagar that in the latter half of his life, acute differences developed between himself and his one-time friends and co-workers. This was true of at least three prominent contemporaries: Pundits Taranath Tarkavachaspati, Madanmohan Tarkalankar, and Dwarkanath Vidyabhushan. It is somewhat ironic that Pundit Iswarchandra had interceded to secure the employment of all three at various stages of his life.

As with certain other things, Vidyasagar had also to suffer estrangement from his only son, Narayanchandra Bandopadhyay. The will that he executed in May 1875 denied his son any inheritance, but fixed a monthly payment of Rs 15 for his daughter-in-law, Bhavasundari Devi. Exactly what led Vidyasagar to take this extreme step is still unclear, although we do know that he described his son as 'self-willed' and as a man 'taken to immoral ways'. From the way Narayanchandra mishandled and eventually ruined several assets of his illustrious father, it would be reasonable to conclude that at some stage in his life, he had indeed been led astray. Chandicharan, who always appreciated the help extended to him by Narayanchandra, would have us believe in the presence of vested interests, which worked hard to keep the father and son apart. What exactly these were, though, he does not care to disclose. Naryanchandra clearly lived beyond his means and had, over time, accumulated huge debts which called for drastic remedial steps. Sambhuchandra and Santoshkumar Adhikari allege that Naryanachandra even bribed his sisters and other close relatives so they would not contest the suit that he had filed challenging his father's last Will and Testament. This apparently paid off since the High Court eventually set aside the clause in Vidyasagar's Will denying his son any share in his property. Sambhuchandra tells us that sheer neglect on the part of Narayanchandra also led, after Vidyasagar's death, to the immensely popular *Bodhodoy* ceasing to be listed among school textbooks. If Sambhuchandra is to be believed, Narayanchandra was also guilty of petty and nefarious acts that were quite unbecoming of a highly educated man. In order to escape paying a monthly sum of Rs 100 for the upkeep of the Bhagavati Vidyalaya, the school in Birsingha named after Bhagavati Devi, and as required under Vidyasagar's Will, Narayanchandra resorted to giving it a new name, 'Thakurdas Bandopadhyay School', claiming that Bhagavati Vidyalaya had ceased to exist. Bhagavati Vidyalaya was brought back to life only in 1896 after a series of recriminating letters had been exchanged between the rival parties. Official documents from the year 1900 reveal that Narayanchandra was still not regular with his obligatory monthly payments.

On the positive side, it has to be said that Narayanchandra did somehow manage to win the affections of his ailing and distraught father, thanks largely to the pleadings of his extremely unhappy mother, Dinamayee Devi. On her deathbed, Pundit Iswarchandra promised his wife that he would forgive their errant son. Biographers record that Vidyasagar, who otherwise chose to stay away from his wife for long periods of time, wept inconsolably on her death. And even after he had disinherited Narayanchandra, the Pundit would occasionally steal glances at his son's portrait hanging from the walls, and shed copious tears of remorse. Such indeed was the man who could quite extraordinarily combine an uncompromising sternness with the most tender outpourings of the heart.

Pundit Iswarchandra has to be one of the few luminaries of British India whose portrait was printed and sold in his lifetime.

In 1859, the *Tattwabodhini Patrika* advertised the sale of posters prepared by N. C. Ghosh & Sons. Such was the respect and reputation attached to the man even in official circles that on the occasion of inaugurating the Calcutta University in 1857, the Chancellor (Governor-General Canning) was flanked by the Lord Bishop of Calcutta to his left and Vidyasagar to his right. In his lifetime, Vidyasagar was publicly honoured several times. He was elected Fellow of the *Royal Asiatic Society of Great Britain* and made a Corresponding Member of the German cultural body, *Deutsche Morgen Landische Geseilscaft*. In 1877, on the occasion of the Delhi Durbar, he was awarded a Certificate of Honour by Sir Richard Temple, Lt. Governor of Bengal, and three years later, the Companions of the Order of the Indian Empire.

Pundit Iswarchandra Vidyasagar passed away in the early hours of the morning of 29 July 1891. In the city of Calcutta itself, most schools stayed closed as a mark of respect, as did booksellers, stockbrokers, and the petty shopkeepers of Radha Bazar. On 27 August, Lt. Governor Charles Elliot presided over a mammoth obituary meeting held at the Calcutta Town Hall. It was also reported that at a gathering of ladies chaired by Kamini Roy, once a student at Bethune College, a handsome sum of Rs 1,390 had been raised by way of donations, and that this sum would be used to institute fellowships for meritorious girls as a special way of honouring the life and work of Vidyasagar.

three

Thoughts on Education

In the second half of the nineteenth century, three teachers and educationists considerably influenced the course of primary and secondary education in Bengal. Other than Pundit Iswarchandra himself, whose voice was indeed the more dominant and professional success even greater, there were also Pearycharan Sarkar (1823–75) and Bhudeb Mukhopadhyay. Pearycharan served the Presidency College and was actively involved with the Temperance movement in Bengal, which was later taken up by Keshabchandra Sen and the Brahmo Samaj. His primer, called *The First Book of Reading for Native Children* (1850), was hugely popular in his time, and even thereafter. He also served as the editor of the *Education Gazette*, a paper started by Bhudeb, and launched the important, albeit short-lived, reformist journals, the *Well Wisher* and *Hitasadhak*. With his untimely death in 1875, Vidyasagar lost a close friend and collaborator in his social and educational campaigns. There are interesting points of similarity between Bhudeb and Vidyasagar, but also sharp contrasts. For one, they were both born into orthodox Brahmin families which prided themselves on the virtues of traditional learning. Bhudeb's father, Pundit Viswanath Tarkabhushan (Mukhopadhyay), was a poor but upright Brahmin who ran a *chatuspathi* in his native village, Chinsura (district Hooghly). Like Vidyasagar, Bhudeb had an active and successful career with the government and was eventually inducted into the Bengal Educational Service, Class I. For several years, he was Inspector of Schools in different provincial educational 'Circles', including Bihar. When in Bihar, he supported the cause of Hindi–Nagari as against Persian. He was also a prolific writer in Bengali, producing school textbooks on history and elementary science, novels, and a wide range of essays that were sociological and ethnographic in nature. The government conferred upon him the C.I.E. three years before the same honour was conferred upon Vidyasagar.

What sets Bhudeb apart from Vidyasagar, though, is the former's open identification with Hindu social and religious culture, and his representing a fairly conservative position within that. In the closing years of his life, he created an endowment of over Rs 1 lakh for the propagation of classical Hindu Studies. While Pundit Iswarchandra remained sceptical about the study or even the relevance of Hindu philosophical traditions, Bhudeb took to the study of Vedanta at Kashi after his retirement in 1883, and was also drawn to the study and practice of Tantra. To honour his father, he eventually opened a *chatuspathi* and a charitable dispensary run by the Viswanath Trust Fund. Again, unlike Vidyasagar, Bhudeb Mukhopadhyay supported the idea of early marriages, the extended Hindu family, and ritual conformity on the part of the ideal Hindu, in defence of which he produced elaborate treatises. We have earlier noted his unhappiness with Vidyasagar's penchant for celebrating European lives to the exclusion of Indians.

The move to take up school education seriously in Bengal was first manifest in the formation of two officially sponsored societies, the *Calcutta School Book Society* (1817) and *Calcutta School Society* (1818). The former was modelled on the *Cheap Book Society* of Dublin and the fact that it preceded the School Society clearly indicates that while contemporary Calcutta and adjoining areas had a reasonably good number of schools, there was a visible lack of quality textbooks to keep them functioning properly. To the School Book Society belongs the distinction of first producing standard textbooks for children at very affordable rates. Between 1817 and 1827, the Society published a total of 78,500 books, of which 48,750 were in the Bengali language alone. With time, there was a proportionately greater emphasis on printing and publishing English-language books. In 1832–33, of the 26,380 books published by the Society, as many as 14,792 were in English alone. This followed from the fact that by 1830, the Calcutta School Book Society had obtained the right to reprint books published by the London Society for the Diffusion of Useful Knowledge. The purpose of the Society had always been two-fold: to prepare as well as to procure quality books for children, and from time to time it approached potential authors with the request to produce suitable schoolbooks. It is also important to remember that the Managing Committee of the Society could successfully persuade influential members of the Calcutta gentry to work for its cause. In 1817–18, for instance, four well-known residents of Calcutta were on its Committee: Radhakanta Deb, Tarinicharan Mitra, Pundit Mritunjay Vidyalankar, and Ramkamal Sen. This made the project of disseminating education easier and socially more acceptable.

The Calcutta School Society had been launched at the behest of established educational workers and influential residents of the city, such as Radhakanta Deb, William Carey, and David Hare. As with the School Book Society, its Managing Committee was mixed in composition; eight of its twenty-four members were Indians. Its objective was to renovate and suitably refurbish old schools and build new ones. In order to bring about greater uniformity in standards and government control over education, the School Society placed all aided schools under four administrative units and set up two Model Schools at Thanthania and Champatala in central Calcutta. In 1834, the two were merged to form the well-known Hare School. The number of primary schools in contemporary Calcutta appears to be uncertain, and different available sources do not appear to agree on the numbers. What is indisputable, though, is that there were *pathshalas* located in and around the area that later grew into the city of Calcutta. Edward Eves noticed them in 1756–57, on the eve of the Battle of Plassey, a fact later confirmed by John Taylor Crawford and William Ward. In the early 1820s, Gourmohan Vidyalankar, himself an author of a primer for females, produced a list of 166 schools in Calcutta, identified area-wise. Most of these were in central and north Calcutta, in the 'Black' part of the town. Another report from the period suggests that in 1824, there were fifty-six schools under the control of the Calcutta School Society alone, with 3,487 students on its rolls. A well-known primary school in contemporary north Calcutta was the Arapuly *pathshala*.

The proliferation of schools and even the availability of printed books did not immediately change matters. It is also known that *pathshala* teachers were greatly reluctant to use books produced by the School Book Society, fearing that these would impart lessons unsuitable for Hindu boys. In 1819, on the invitation of Radhakanta Deb, only seventeen such *gurumohashays* (teachers) showed any inclination to use these books. While the Society was keen to replace handwritten manuals with printed books, the attempt did not succeed at once. The common *pathshala* teacher preferred to go by the manuscript copies of some elementary lessons that he might himself have copied, or else had arranged to have copied by professionals. These were mostly kept in the possession of *gurumohashays*, who guarded them zealously and refused to consult anything other than what they personally possessed. In 1818, Pundit Jaygopal Tarkalankar (1775–1846), who was to later teach both Iswarchandra and Madanmohan Tarkalankar at the Sanskrit College, published the second edition of his *Shikkhasar* (the Essence of Education), which had been written with precisely this class of *gurumohasayas* in mind. It was written with the hope that a printed work would be easier to handle, would better survive humid conditions, and attacks from termites and other pests. It was also hoped that the circulation of such printed works would help standardise the lessons imparted to *pathshala* boys. Pundit Jaygopal had a wealth of experience working for the well-known Serampore missionaries, William Carey, Joshua Marshman, and William Ward, and served on the editorial team of their weekly journal, the *Samachar Darpan*. In this capacity, he had also contributed meaningfully towards simplifying the Sanskrit-laden syntax of the written Bengali of the time. Rev. James Long, who ran rural schools for the children of peasants and artisans at Thakurpukur, southwest of Calcutta, had himself authored a booklet on Bengali handwriting, *Lipidhara* (1816). By the 1820s, the School Book Society collated such works to produce handy English-language manuals for teachers. One such work was J. D. Pearson's *Instructions for Modeling and Conducting Schools* (1827), which was in demand, especially in missionary-run primary schools.

An important feature of the educational practices in early nineteenth-century Bengal was the discernable thrust given in the direction of a secular education and practical vocational training in place of a purely literary education. Interestingly enough, this had the support of some Christian evangelists as well as orthodox Hindus. In his Thakurpukur school, Rev. James Long imparted basic agricultural and artisanal skills, given the fact that most of his students came from the labouring classes. In 1847, Kalikrishna Mitra (1822–91), in collaboration with Pearycharan Sarkar, opened an agricultural college in Barasat (in north 24 Parganas); in 1852, this school had as many as fifty students. Radhakanta Deb, otherwise known to identify with the conservative party, showed a remarkable liberality when it came to advocating educational schemes for Hindu boys. He deemed practical vocational training to constitute the very heart of primary and vernacular education:

> As soon as the people will begin to reap the fruits of a solid vernacular education, agriculture and industrial schools may be established in order to qualify the enlightened masses to become useful members of the society. Nothing should be guarded against more carefully than the insensible introduction of a system whereby, with a smattering of

> English, youths are weaned from the plough, the axe and the loom, to render them ambitions only for clerkships.

It is, however, possible to read this warning in two radically different ways. On the one hand, this underscores the importance of extending modern vocational education to the rural youth in ways that might only profit them occupationally. On the other, this was but an early expression of certain anxieties that were beginning to surface among the urban Calcutta literati. In the first place, they read this as signs of surreptitious, lateral entry by rural intermediary castes into the privileged world of the urban *bhadralok*, a good number of whom came from the socially and ritually superior castes and for whom the purely literary education available at the time in cities like Calcutta was fast becoming more the means to a livelihood than the source of intellectual fulfilment. Second, there was also the covert but growing fear that given the paltry sum that the government was seen to spend on public education, there would have to emerge at some point in time serious competition between investments in the primary-vernacular and the secondary or higher levels of instruction. A 'bread-winning education' was clearly the priority for the community, given the colonial control over the economy.[1] Such education was almost exclusively in the English language, and at least in the early decades of the nineteenth century, even a smattering of English could secure some petty employment under the government or in European mercantile offices. On 5 May 1831, the conservative journal *Samachar Chandrika* reported that about 400–500 students in Calcutta were already receiving instruction in English, but we have more detailed figures from 1834. That year, a total number of 1,858 students were pursuing English education, of whom 338 were from the Hindu College, 300 from the schools run by the Calcutta School Society, and 200 from the schools started by the Scottish Presbyterian, Rev. Alexander Duff.

In 1839, the students of the Sanskrit College themselves placed a memorandum before the authorities, seeking resumption of English classes that had been recently suspended. Vidyasagar's own educational reforms in this College, as we shall presently see, included a thorough restructuring of the English Department, which included employing additional staff and recruiting such teachers who were also equipped to teach Natural Philosophy and Mathematics in English. This was not the kind of education that would have been of any use to the students at schools run by Rev. Long, James Stewart or William Carey. 'The utility of the Sanskrit College depends greatly on the efficient state of the English department,' Vidyasagar was to write on 28 February 1852 to the Secretary, Council of Education, F. J. Mouat. Also, given the nature of the textbooks that Vidyasagar authored and which were widely circulated in Bengal schools, it is reasonable to say that these represented more an effort to propagate secondary education than primary. By the 1870s, even the government was forced to wake up to the fact that in the schools located in ethnic Bengal, it was indeed secondary education that was being paraded as primary. Whenever Vidyasagar spoke of propagating 'mass education', it was not the labouring classes that he meant, but the more 'respectable' sections within both the rural gentry and the urban. Reference to the 'common man' or the 'poor' were really references to the relatively poorer strata within *bhadralok* society, and not the rural artisan or farmer. Further down this chapter, I shall have occasion to argue how Vidyasagar was even to doubt if the labouring poor were at all willing to take to education, or if education had any practical relevance for them. This class dimension to educational enterprise, its social spread, and implications was to vitally inform the vision of *bhadralok* educationists, not excepting Bhudeb and Vidyasagar.

Brian A. Hatcher, who has done some pioneering work on the educational history of mid-nineteenth century Bengal, has drawn up a list of ten school textbooks that were published between 1801 and 1849, that is to say, before Vidyasagar effectively entered the world of authorship and book production. Judging from their titles, all these books deal with elementary speaking and writing skills in the Bengali language, but were also carefully fortified with moral lessons suitable for schoolchildren, drawn both from the indigenous, Brahmanical tradition and the contemporary Western. However, a balance between the two knowledge systems was often hard to come by. In the 1850s, Akshaykumar Dutta's *Bahyabastur Sahit Manav Prakritir Sambandha Vichar* (A Treatise on the Relationship between Human Nature and the External World, 1851) was disapproved as a textbook for school students as it had borrowed heavily from the writings of the Scottish phrenologist, George Combe. For some reason not clear to us, Vidyasagar escaped this fate. Some of his primers and readers too were adapted from similar books in use in contemporary England; others, even when based on classical indigenous sources, carried within them the proclivities of a man deeply influenced by the reigning Western ideas and values, and predisposed to read matters in a certain way. Perhaps Vidyasagar's relatively greater success resulted from a combination of several factors: his standing as a Brahmin, as a gifted Sanskrit scholar, an official who headed the Sanskrit College, as a prolific author of school textbooks, and the relatively greater mastery with Bengali prose, which was more adroitly able to conceal the infusion of a Western moral and literary sensibility.

Also important and impressive is the boldness or conviction with which he made his literary proclamations. In advertisements to his multi-volume work, the *Rijupath* (1851) that were devised as aides to Sanskrit learning, Vidyasagar claimed that the *Ramayana* and the *Mahabharata* were purely literary works, also firmly rejecting the possibility of one 'Vedvyas' having authored all the Puranas. Further down this chapter, we shall examine the ways in which he altered commonly accepted tales from the epics and Sanskrit dramatic works to reach more rational conclusions that were better attuned to the contemporary Western discourse on society and culture, on the productive agency of man and the moral value of human enterprise. The language of his primers was an improved Bengali, but not the language commonly spoken in Hindu Bengali homes. His highly popular primer, the *Barnaparichoy* (1855), is replete with 'tatsam' words derived from Sanskrit, even though it marked a vast improvement upon pre-existing multi-volume primers like the *Shishu Sebadhi* (1840), in use at the Hindu College *pathshala*. When suggesting curriculum reform in the Sanskrit College, Vidyasagar repeatedly asserted that a polished Bengali could not come to those who lacked a Sanskrit education. By all accounts, Vidyasagar himself did not speak that language in his routine, everyday conversations.

Here, it must be noted that in certain vital aspects, Vidyasagar's labours in the field of language reform had been considerably facilitated by his intellectual forebears. Early workers in the field of education with a pronounced leaning towards Orientalism, like Nathaniel Brassey Halhed (1751–1830), Henry Pitts Forster (1766?–1815), and even William Carey (1761–1834) himself, had consciously contributed towards purging the Bengali language of Persian and Arabian influences. Pundit Jaygopal Tarkalankar, of whom we have spoken above, strengthened this move through his twin lexical works, the *Parasik Abdhidan* (1838) and *Bangabhidhan* (?), both of which were directed at replacing Persian words by Sanskritic Bengali. Here is what Pundit Jaygopal recommended:

> It is only appropriate that the genteel should use the language of the genteel alone (*sadhu bhasha*). By using a language that was indecorous and not befitting their social status, they would only make people revile them as they are apt to do to the uncultured. (Translation mine)

When, in the 1870s, Lt. Governor George Campbell encouraged the teaching of Persian and Arabic for Bengali Muslims and attempted to strengthen classical teaching in the *madrasa*s and *maktab*s, this was seen as jeopardising the prospects of furthering education and professional opportunities for the Hindu *bhadralok*.

It cannot be said with any certainty that Vidyasagar carefully scrutinised primers and readers already in existence and tried to build upon these. We do know, however, that some of his work for schoolchildren had already been anticipated, mostly by the team of missionary writers at Serampore. Captain James Stewart's (d. 1833) *Varnamala* (1818), possibly the first printed work to introduce the Bengali alphabet to students, anticipated the Pundit's *Barnaparichay* by almost forty years, and its antiquity may itself explain its progressively falling into disuse by the mid-nineteenth century. Similarly, the *Sarsangraha* (1844) by William Yeats (1792–1845) has much in common with Vidyasagar's *Bodhodoy*, published about seven years later. In the world of Bengali journalism, it was again the missionaries who led the way. As early as 1818, Felix Carey (1786–1822), son of William Carey, had started the first Bengali monthly, the *Digdarshan*. However, when it comes to counting productivity in this field, and especially when sustained over a fairly long period, Vidyasagar faced little competition.

Between the years 1846 and 1869, Pundit Iswarchandra produced as many as twelve primers and readers on which successive generations of Bengali children have since been brought up. Some of these, like the *Bodhodoy* (1851), *Sakuntala* (1854), *Barnaparichay* (1855), and *Sitar Banabas* (1860), were immensely popular and a great commercial success. Between April 1855 and June–July 1856, *Barnaparichay*—Part I alone sold 88,000 copies over eleven editions, and we do also know that *Bodhodoy* underwent multiple reprints in its author's lifetime. Of these, *Jeevancharita* (1849) and *Charitavali* (1856) were biographical compilations; the *Kathamala* (1856) was based on Rev. Thomas James' English translation of *Aesop's Fables*; the *Bodhodoy*, *Akhyanmanjari* (1863), and *Neetibodh* (1851) were moral tales adapted from the writings of the Scottish Chambers brothers and those of Samuel Smiles; *Bhrantivilas* was adapted from Shakespeare's *Comedy of Errors*; *Sakuntala* (1854) was an adaptation of the classic play by Kalidas; and *Sitar Banabas* (1860) was based partly on Bhavabhuti's Sanskrit play, *Uttararamcharita*. The *Jeevancharita* and *Charitavali* included biographical sketches of eminent Europeans such as Copernicus,

Galileo, Newton, Herschel, Grotius, Thomas Jenkins, and William Jones. To this, Vidyasagar thoughtfully appended a glossary of words that the average Indian student would have found new and unfamiliar. However, the intention here was not the mere recounting of lives, but the interpretation of each of these as representing certain instructive lessons in a man's honest attempts to be virtuous and his struggles to conquer all forms of adversity. The fact that these works did not include the lives of Indians irked some contemporaries like Bhudeb Mukhopadhyay. That there were comparable works that had cared enough to include the lives of Indians is also evident from Bhudeb citing the *Charitashtak* (Eight Lives) by one Kashimoy Ghatak. Vidyasagar's brother, Sambhuchandra, was himself to author a similar work called *Charitamala* (A Garland of Lives), which offered biographical sketches of fifteen Indians, including Vidyasagar himself.

The *Barnaparichay* proved to be a template for vernacular primers, introducing the Bengali alphabet and including elementary moral lessons. Its unique feature was its direct and engaging tone when addressing student readers. The *Neetibodh*, written in collaboration with his friend Rajkrishna Bandopadhyay, enjoyed brisk sales too. From a letter that Vidyasagar wrote to the Director of Public Instruction for Bengal, Gordon Young, on 25 March 1859, we know that the book had sold 5,000 copies within six months of its publication, and a further reprint of 10,000 copies was requested. The *Betalpanchavimsati* and *Bangalar Itihas*, as we have earlier noted, were books he had authored when at the Fort William College. Incidentally, these were also the only books that Vidyasagar had written specifically for some institution and under its patronage. Beginning with the *Jeevancharita* in 1849, he opened up his works for all, with resounding commercial success. However, his friend and co-worker Madanmohan Tarkalankar still preferred to go by the older practice of writing at the behest of a particular institution or with a certain kind of readership in mind. For example, his *Shishu Shikkha*—Parts I and II (1849–50) were written for the

Hindu Balika Vidyalaya (later, Bethune School). In order to facilitate the understanding of students, Vidyasagar also invented about seventy-four new Bengali terms and expressions that closely corresponded to the meanings of terms, both technical and non-technical, commonly used in the English language. Chandicharan Bandopadhyay and, following him, Rabindranath Tagore, believed that he was also the first among Bengalis to use punctuation marks in his Bengali prose. This is quite off the mark, however, as modern research has cited multiple instances of these being used earlier in time, as for example in Gourmohan Vidyaratna's female reader, *Stree Shikkha Vidhayak* (1822), and in the journals *Bangadoot* (1829), *Samvad Purnachandroday* (1836), and *Vidyadarshan* (1842). Although relatively less well-known, a work aiming to aid the student of Bengali was the *Sabdamanjari* (1864), which Vidyasagar himself called an *Abhidhan* or Bengali dictionary.

Hatcher's analysis of Vidyasagar's school textbooks rightly emphasises their author's ability to creatively converge what he calls indigenous moral values and bourgeois moral pedagogy. It also draws our attention to the tendency among contemporary scholars to somewhat underplay the indigenous roots of Vidyasagar's moral pedagogy. Hatcher himself cites the case of Soumendranath Sarkar (*Bangali Jeebone Vidyasagar* [Vidyasagar in Bengali Life], 1976), whose arguments are tantamount to suggesting that in his school textbooks, Vidyasagar attempted to vernacularise the values comprising the Ten Commandments themselves. However, a question that may naturally arise here is whether, in his act of translating or transferring the ideas and values of contemporary England, by all means a complex process, Vidyasagar was also sufficiently aware of their 'bourgeois' character or the historical circumstances under which these values had taken root. That characterisation appears to be more a case of hindsight on our part than direct historical cognisance on the part of Vidyasagar himself. What might have struck him directly and with more force is, first, the greater human potentialities or possibilities within the progressive knowledge system of Europe; second, the general quickening of intellectual exchanges between India and Europe that was fomenting a mental revolution of sorts in the Indian intelligentsia; and third, the palpable connections between the human virtues of diligence, sincerity, and securing material prosperity in life. The latter was not altogether absent in the indigenous value system, but had been visibly invigorated through an increasing exposure to ways of life in contemporary Europe. Diligence, perseverance, and good business acumen, even without the benefit of a Western education, had clearly benefited the earlier generation of Bengali entrepreneurs in the fields of comprador trade, shipping, finance, investments in land, and sundry services. It was now Vidyasagar's agenda to demonstrate that the world of learning too could turn into an entrepreneurial world, adding further meaning and value to the lives of the educated Bengali Hindu middle class.

Both Vidyasgar in his *Barnaparichay* and Madanmohan Tarkalankar in his *Shishu Shikkha* suggest the centrality of learning and the tangible relationship between the persistent and arduous pursuit of education and material success in life. But it was Vidyasagar who immortalised this argument in Bengali middle-class life by creating the tropes of Gopal and Rakhal in the first part of the *Barnaparichay*, and those of Navin and Jadav in the second. Rakhal and Jadav are the embodiments of sheer disinterestedness, disobedience, mischief-making, and lethargy; Gopal and Navin, on the contrary, are boys who diligently and responsibly take to the pursuit of the right moral lessons in life. Not everybody agreed with this characterisation of childhood. For one, surprising as this might appear, Vidyasagar himself was closer to the Rakhals of this world in his unbridled energy and spiritedness. Tagore himself thought Bengal could do with a few more of the rebellious Rakhals, who had the power to create their own destiny. By the late nineteenth century, such dissenting and rebellious qualities would have inspired a new self-assertion among middle-class, politicised Bengalis, who may have looked askance at the sheer inertness and docility of a Gopal or Navin.

Swami Vivekananda (1863–1902), although otherwise a great admirer of Pundit Iswarchandra, did not consider the over-disciplined Gopal always the right example to follow for the Bengali schoolboy, and in his *Paribarik Prabandha* (Essays on the Family, 1882), Bhudeb Mukhopadhyay was to argue that what the already enfeebled Bengali Hindu most required were stronger sinews and greater mental courage.

Some of Vidyasagar's other works also came in for criticism. We have earlier noted Bankim's somewhat harsh comment that Vidyasagar was not doing much beyond mere translations and producing school textbooks. Such criticism seems to have persisted over time. In 1941, the Bengali writer and literary critic, Sajani Kanta Das (1900–62), felt that Vidyasagar ought to have devoted his talent to better things than simply manufacturing trivial 'toys' like the *Bodhodoy* and the *Barnaparichay* for children. But there were some who also came to Vidyasagar's defence. In 1888, the *Education Gazette* took exception to the remarks made by Bankim and his journal *Bongodarshan*, slighting the Pundit's literary efforts. Even if he had remained merely a translator and the author of school textbooks, Vidyasagar would still be an object of reverence, the *Gazette* claimed.

Bankimchandra noted two qualities in *Sitar Banabas*: first, the moving away from any matter that looked contrived or unnatural, and second, the somewhat irritating tendency to over-induce a sense of pathos in the reader. Vidyasagar deliberately changed parts of the older story as they appear in both Valmiki's epic *Ramayana* and the play by Bhavabhuti. In his rendering, the story of Sita concludes not with her dramatically and miraculously re-entering the womb of Mother Earth from which she had once taken birth, but by succumbing to the great mental and physical exhaustion inflicted on her, as an ordinary woman was wont to do. On the first of these qualities, Bankim made no specific comment; on the second, he was quite critical. *Sitar Banabas*, in Bankim's view, was an overwrought and unduly melancholic retelling of an all too familiar story, a 'laxative', if you like, that could be trusted to produce tears at will! With the advantage of hindsight, we may say that Bankim was not exceptionally unkind in his observations. The same charge was to be later repeated by an English author, H. Jane Harding, who translated the work in 1904 as *The Exile of Sita*. The translator confessed to have 'softened' at some places 'turns of excessive weeping'. Not surprisingly, given his conservative instincts, the biographer Biharilal Sarkar too found the conclusion to this work quite contrived and unacceptable.

However, later readers may have also enjoyed his creative retellings. Nirad C. Chaudhuri (1897–1999) tells us that in his day, Vidyasagar's retelling of Sakuntala (*Sakuntala*, 1854) was more popular than Kalidas' dramatic work itself, although the younger generation was more drawn to the Bengali rendering of Bana Bhatta's *Kadambari* by Pandit Tarasankar Tarkaratna (d. 1858), Librarian at the Calcutta Sanskrit College. Chaudhuri observed that Tarkaratna's work stirred the romantic imagination in the youth in ways that Vidyasagar's *Sakuntala* did not. Brian A. Hatcher has suggested that Vidyasagar's *Sakuntala* be read together with his launching the campaign in support of widow marriages. In Hatcher's opinion, Vidyasagar's portrayal of the wronged woman, Sakuntala, meaningfully connects with his widow marriage campaign, since it was through this work that the reformer tried to create greater public awareness of the plight of the widow and, more generally, of the human predicament depicted in Kalidas' work. While this is not at all improbable, we must take into consideration three qualifying facts. First, Sakuntala herself was not a widow and her desertion by Dushyanta, one could justly say, has greater resemblance to the fate of the forsaken Kulin wife—which, incidentally, was also a matter that greatly agitated Vidyasagar. Second, evidence suggests that the writing of *Sakuntala* preceded his Widow Marriage tracts by at least a month or two. *Sakuntala* was published in December 1854 and the first of the two Widow Marriage tracts in January 1855. It is generally believed that the verses from the *Parasar Samhita*, on which Vidyasagar based his arguments supporting widow marriages, could have been discovered sometime in 1854, if at all they were discovered. Once this is accepted, the connections drawn between the two would appear to be somewhat tenuous. Admittedly, Vidyasagar might have been mulling over the widow marriage question for at least a year or two previously, and yet his priority by the close of 1854 had to have been the tracts and not the retelling of the Sakuntala story. Perhaps the idea of adapting Kalidas' work goes further back in time than is commonly believed, and was more generally connected to the Woman Question rather than to the specific problems faced by Hindu widows.

Third, Vidyasagar appears oblivious to the fact that a more radical version of the Sakuntala story, at least from the perspective of the protagonist herself, and appearing in the *Mahabharata*, had been toned down in several ways by Kalidas himself. Sakuntala of the *Mahabharata* was a fiercely independent and articulate woman, determined to assert her rights, and was not so much an object of public empathy. Evidently, that is not the Sakuntala that Vidyasagar had in mind when dwelling on the subject of the Hindu widow and her possible marriage. The Hindu widow aspiring to remarry, I would like to argue, could not have been the subversive and questioning Sakuntala of the epic. Conversely, if it was indeed Vidyasagar's intention to connect the Sakuntala saga to the suffering Hindu widow, the choice of the 'softened' Kalidasa version on which to ground his plea would have been deliberate.

Although a great commercial success in Vidyasagar's lifetime, the *Bodhodoy* attracted criticism, especially from the Hindu orthodox. The Bengali satirist Indranath Bandopadhyay (1847–1911) parodied it in the paper *Bangabasi*, and it was even otherwise alleged that the book tried to teach too much. We have earlier noted how, for a time, it removed references to God and religion, which would no doubt have offended most theists cutting across the Hindu and Brahmo camps. I imagine this would have also led many people to puzzle over whether he was, by his inner beliefs or convictions, a Hindu, Brahmo or an agnostic.

Among the accusations that Krishnakamal Bhattacharya levelled at Vidyasagar was that he exhibited a sense of 'literary jealousy'. Some of his contemporaries alleged that he would not even so much as glance at the several complimentary copies of books that he received from young and aspiring authors. It was also rumoured that with the exceptions of Harchandra Ghosh (1817–84), a successful dramatist who also translated Shakespearean plays into Bengali, and his long standing friend, Akshaykumar Dutta, Vidyasagar thought poorly of other contemporary journalists, publishers, and authors. While extending his munificence to the poet Madhusudan Dutt, he disliked the poet's experiments with blank verse, and there is some evidence to suggest that he also disliked the prose of Bankim. His real differences with Bankimchandra, however, arose over issues of social reform and the strategies or methods of work to be adopted in that respect. Bankim's rejoinder to his tract on the evils of polygamy so irked Pundit Iswarchandra that it was not reprinted in the latter's lifetime; and when it was reprinted, it appeared without the 'objectionable' parts. The Sanskrit Press that Vidyasagar ran had a rival in the Purnachandrodaya Press, which is believed to have led him to debunk books by an alumnus of the Sanskrit College, Pundit Muktaram Vidyabagish (d. 1860), who chose to publish with the Purnchandrodaya Press. A further reason for their differences was that during the widow marriage controversy, Pundits Iswarchandra and Muktaram were ranged on opposite sides. In 1857, Vidyasagar disapproved of a geography textbook authored by one Kalidas Maitra. In his book, Kalidas had contested Hindu mythological notions about the origins of the earth, which Vidyasagar reportedly considered objectionable on the grounds that this was opposed to the view put forth in the *shastras*. Quite peeved at this, the publisher Srinath Dey of the Tamohar Press of Serampore wrote the following to the government:

> He (Vidyasagar) says that this is contrary to the *shastras*. Is it desired that school geography should be in consonance with the *shastras*? Should we speak of the six oceans of

> milk, of Benares (being) at the centre of the earth and put the earth itself on tortoise back?

It was not long before the *Englishman* noted that the reasons in this case too were purely personal, since Maitra had earlier written a tract opposing widow marriages (*Pounarbhava Khandanam*). It was also speculated that Maitra's book, if approved as a text, would have undercut the sales of Vidyasagar's own *Bhugolkhagol Varnanam*, published by the Sanskrit Press. This latter possibility can actually be ruled out since this work was published only posthumously in 1892. What remains undisputed, though, is the high price of textbooks published by the Sanskrit Press. Vidyasagar's *Banglar Itihas* cost Rs 2 for a paperback copy, whereas a bound edition of the same work published by the Calcutta School Book Society cost as little as 12 annas. The high prices of books published by the Sanskrit Press had grown into a matter of concern for the government even in 1856. A committee set up that year by the Director of Public Instruction, Gordon Young, found this to be a major obstacle in the successful propagation of education in the so-called 'Model Schools', set up through government aid in the rural districts of Bengal. The high price of the textbooks that the student was expected to procure had proven to be 'a prohibitory tax', the Committee noted. However, the government made such observations without overlooking the inherent merit of the books brought out by Vidyasagar and the Sanskrit Press. 'I grumble about the high prices of the Sanskrit Press,' observed C. T. Buckland in 1858,

> but I freely confess that if any one does deserve to profit by selling his books at a dear price, that person is Iswar Chunder Bidyasagar...he will be remembered as the man who first edited school books of such intrinsic merit and so acceptable to the people as to have raised Bengali publications to a remunerating level.

Notwithstanding any criticism, the *Bodhodoy* was good enough to be translated into Hindi and, along with the *Sakuntala*, also in the Odiya language. Vidyasagar's *Vyakaran Kaumudi* proved to be very useful for Sanskrit teaching, both in contemporary India and abroad.

In the closing years of his life, Vidyasagar had to face charges of deceit and fraud from the family of his friend and co-worker, the long-deceased Madanmohan Tarkalankar. The charges were related to the settlement of profits accruing from the sales of Tarkalankar's *Shishu Shikkha* (3 parts), published by the Sanskrit Press. It was alleged that Tarkalankar's family deserved a more favourable settlement than that arrived at between Vidyasagar and Tarkalankar before the latter's untimely death in 1858. The charges amounted to suggesting that hitherto, Pundit Iswarchandra had been cheating the successors of Madanmohan Tarkalankar by not correctly projecting the dues. Tarkalankar's case was represented by the renowned literary figure, Yogendranath Vidyabhushan (1845–1904), the man who had married Tarkalankar's widowed daughter (Bhuvanmala?). It came as shocking news for Pundit Iswarchandra that Vidyabhushan was contemplating filing a suit to press his claims, but this ultimately had the opposite effect of galvanising him into action. In 1888, he wrote a pamphlet, the *Nishkritilabhprayas* (An attempt to absolve myself of the charges), detailing the circumstances under which such a contestation had come to pass. The *Nishkritilabhprayas,* which was a published document and available in the public domain, tells us a very different story. Here, Vidyasagar's first argument in self-defence was that following the death of Tarkalankar, all dues over which his family had claim had been made over to his widow, and that he had additionally pledged a monthly sum of Rs 10 to be paid for life to his aged and destitute mother, who had no son left to support her. It was this stipend, Vidyasagar takes care to remind us, that enabled her to retire to Kashi and live a long life thereafter.

Second, on the suggestion of Yogendranath Vidyabhushan himself, he had similarly agreed to provide a monthly sum of Rs 10 for Tarkalankar's middle daughter, Kundamala. Third,

Vidyasagar indignantly recalled how Vidyabhushan had similarly maligned him on a previous occasion by claiming that the *Betalpanchavimsati* was actually a work by Madanmohan Tarkalankar, but published under Vidyasagar's name. In this instance, Vidyasagar even cited a letter written in his support by his one-time colleague in Sanskrit College, Pandit Girishchandra Vidyaratna (1822–1903), who categorically denied Yogendranath's claims. Yogendranath, however, would not give up easily and produced a rejoinder in 1890, which he chose to call *Nishkritilabhprayas Bifal* (The failure to absolve oneself). Nothing further is known about this controversy. However, Vidyasagar's Will, drawn up in May 1875, reveals that he had provided for a monthly sum of Rs 8 to Madanmohan's mother, Rs 3 to his sister, and Rs 10 to daughter, Kundamala.

Curricula Reform at the Sanskrit College

Pandit Iswarchandra's engagement with curricula reform at the Sanskrit College spans a fairly long period of about ten years, and touches upon certain vital issues regarding the educational policy followed by the Bengal government at the time. The key to understanding this lies in a close scrutiny of the official correspondence, mainly between him and the Council of Education, but occasionally also with officers of the Bengal government.

The relevant correspondence can be listed as follows:

1. 16 December 1850: Vidyasagar to the Council of Education.
2. 12 April 1852: Vidyasagar's 'Notes on the Sanscrit College'.
3. 16 July 1853: Vidyasagar to the Council of Education.
4. 7 September 1853: Vidyasagar's Rejoinder to the Report submitted by James R. Ballantyne, Superintendent, Benares Sanskrit College, to the Council of Education in mid-1853.

5. 5 October 1853: Demy-Official letter from Vidyasagar to the Council of Education.
6. 2 July 1858: Vidyasagar to the Director of Public Instruction, Bengal.
7. 17 April 1859: Vidyasagar to the Council of Education.
8. 29 September 1859: Vidyasagar to Rivers Thompson, Junior Secretary to the Government of Bengal.

That Pundit Iswarchandra was seriously contemplating structural reforms in the Sanskrit College is evident from his letter of resignation (3 May 1847) from the post of Assistant Secretary. We may recall that the resignation itself had been hastened by a growing sense of frustration, given the inattentive and indifferent attitude of the then Secretary, Rosomoy Dutta. However, that this did not deter his plans and hopes of effecting reform can be determined by the letter that he wrote on 16 December 1850 to F. J. Mouat of the Council of Education, only about ten days after he had rejoined the Sanskrit College as Professor of Literature (*Sahitya*). This letter detailed the required curriculum changes, the vital features of which need to be followed closely.

Broadly speaking, this letter addresses two related needs in the field of Sanskrit Studies imparted at the Sanskrit College. First, there was to be a structural overhauling: the total duration of the course would still remain at fifteen years, but priorities regarding the time spent on certain disciplines were to be suitably altered internally. Second, there was to be a radical change in the nature and number of texts recommended for most disciplines studied in that institution.

The first set of recommendations concerned the 'Junior Department' of the Sanskrit College, comprising the disciplines of grammar (*vyakaran*), literature (*sahitya*), rhetoric (*alankar*), and mathematics (*jyotisha*). In the field of grammatical studies, Vidyasagar recommended that the duration of study be shortened from five to four years, but more importantly, he insisted on replacing particularly difficult texts then in use, such as the *Mugdabodh*, by more intelligible and qualitatively better texts like *Siddhanta Kaumudi* of Bhattoji Dikshita. Quite evidently, his decision on this question had been determined by his own experiences as a student trying to master the extremely difficult *Mugdabodh*. Faltering in his grammar lessons, it may be recalled, had even led to his father, Thakurdas, beating him up mercilessly. For the *alankar* class, he similarly cut short the reading list by about half, recommending only the *Kavya Prakasha* and *Dasarupaka*. However, more far-reaching changes were suggested for the *jyotisha* class where he found the texts in use (Bhaskaracharya's *Beejaganita* and *Lilavati*) 'very meagre', difficult to comprehend, and lacking in 'method'. These, he suggested, should be replaced by treatises on arithmetic, algebra, and geometry, suitably compiled from English-language works. A more ambitious recommendation here was the preparation of a Bengali text on astronomy based on the work of William Herschel and others, which he eventually planned to introduce to vernacular schools in Bengal. It was deemed essential that students of advanced disciplines (of *Nyaya* and *Smriti*) also attend classes on modern mathematics. Finally, the course of study in the Junior Department had to be enriched by introducing the students to 'useful and entertaining' subjects drawn from the educational writings of the Chambers brothers (*Moral Class Book, Rudiments of Knowledge*), miscellaneous subjects (the art of printing, navigation, earthquakes, pyramids, etc.), and moral, natural, and political philosophy. Importantly, such knowledge was to be disseminated through the vernacular, which in turn was to become the vehicle for imbibing useful 'English knowledge'.

For the teaching of *Smriti* and *Nyaya*, Vidyasagar's recommendations were quite sweeping, with far-reaching implications. In this instance, he clearly resorted to two methods: first, judging the quality of an Indian text by its compatibility with European texts on the relevant subject, and second, almost disdainfully dismissing older Indian texts and authors, partly on the basis of his own private judgement but also in the light of contemporary European thinking. With regard to *Smriti* or Hindu law, he recommended that the *smarta* author Raghunandan's *Chaturbingshati Tattwa* be taken off the list of prescribed texts, since it better suited the priestly classes and not pure academics. Such a recommendation had to be based on the presumption that all students of Sanskrit College had the pursuit of higher studies in mind. That at least some of them had limited ambitions and were indeed preparing themselves for the office of a priest is evident from the memorial submitted by students of the *smriti* class to the College authorities on 30 April 1831, complaining of hostility from local priests who threatened to oppose their claims to function as a priest unless they gave up the study of English. We shall presently see how Vidyasagar was to make similar presumptions about his students being willing to buy high-priced, standard editions of English-language texts.

The course of reading prescribed for the *Smriti* class was now limited to four legal texts that dealt with matters like property, adoption, and inheritance under both the *Dayabhaga* and the *Mitakshara* systems. With respect to *Nyaya*, Vidyasagar was the sharpest in his objections, and he chose to also comment quite pejoratively on some of the texts then in use at the Sanskrit College. The *Anumanchintamani* of the famed Gangesha Upadhayay he found anachronistic, and here, he especially took it upon himself to argue that a modern European philosopher like Francis Bacon (1561–1626) would have dismissed it as the 'cobweb of learning'. He similarly rejected the *Anumanadidhiti*, a commentary on Gangesha Upadhaya's work, labelling its author, Raghunath Shiromani, a well-known scholar of *Nyaya* from Nabadwip, as the 'dictator of the modern school of Nyaya' (*Nabya Nyaya*). He found the *Khandana Khanda Kavya* of Sri Harsha to represent only 'muddy metaphysics', and the *Tattwaviveka* of Udayanacharya was dismissed for refuting the agnosticism of the Buddha, and the penchant for replacing this by the idea of a creator God. The elimination of the last two from the course of study is particularly interesting and indicates an element of confusion and indecisiveness on the part of Vidyasagar. Sri Harsha was an Advaita philosopher of c. twelfth century who had refuted the syllogism of *Nyaya*, but eliminating him was not tantamount to eliminating the school of *Advaita Vedanta*, especially since Vidyasagar was prepared to prescribe to his students at the Sanskrit College the fourteenth-century Advaitic text, *Panchadashi* of Vidyaranya. In the chapter to follow, I shall argue that in all probability, Vidyasagar's critique of Vedantic idealism was addressed specifically at Advaita Vedanta, especially in view of its metaphysical mysticism. Is it the case, then, that even within *Advaita*, Vidyasagar's critique was actually directed at specific sub-traditions, as for example the highly idealistic philosophy of Sankaracharya? His refutation of the work by Udayanacharya too looks quite intriguing, especially given the grounds cited. In his own works, there are instances where Vidyasagar himself admitted the idea of a creator God (see the Postscript, this volume).

For the Nyaya department, which he wanted re-designated as *Darshana* (philosophy), Vidyasagar chose to prescribe only four texts: *Samkhya Pravachana, Patanjali Sutra, Pancadashi,* and the *Sarvadarshana Sangraha.* The first three of these represented the *Samkhya, Yoga,* and the *Vedanta* schools, respectively, and the fourth, a summary of all the major schools of Hindu philosophy, but also some dissenting traditions like the Buddhists and the Carvakas. The last text he was to later edit personally;it was subsequently published by the Asiatic Society, Calcutta, in 1858. It is generally believed that the publication of the *Sarvadarshana Samgraha* of Madhavacharya first generated an intellectual interest in the Buddhist and Carvaka systems in modern Bengal. It is also no coincidence that Vidyasagar's underlying purpose behind publicising this text was to offer not so much a convenient summary of the various philosophical systems as it was an attempt to persuade its readers to take cognisance of the way the various Indian philosophical schools had battled to reveal the 'flaws' and 'fallacies' in each other. In hindsight, this appears to have been an unusual move, since his intention otherwise was to get students to employ the study of modern European philosophy to better detect the relative 'inferiority' of the indigenous philosophical traditions. The use of an internally generated critique of Hindu philosophical traditions must have struck him somewhat belatedly.

However, it does appear as though, in recommending the study of the *Sarvadarshanasamgraha* only so that students might be doubly convinced of the fallacies within the indigenous systems, Vidyasagar overlooked an important feature of this book. Had he looked at the issue more closely, it would have dawned on him that argumentatively speaking, Madhavacharya's work was arranged in an ascending order, starting with the agnostic/atheistic Buddhist and Carvaka systems and culminating in Advaita. Interestingly enough, Vidyasagar stuck to the idea of teaching Hindu philosophical systems in the College even though, in his opinion, these failed to match the 'advanced' ideas of modern Europe. In part, this was also a functional necessity for him. To take true cognisance of failings within a certain intellectual system, one had to first know the system well. However, he did not fail to cite in support the fact that philosophical systems like the *Samkhya* and *Vedanta* were also held in high reverence by the Hindus. Such concession to public sentiment was not unique for Vidyasagar. On the other hand, this does not go well with the great disappointment and unhappiness that he had expressed over the power that local custom (*deshachar*) had held over the minds of the people. On the question of effecting social reform, he considered long standing public sentiment the greatest barrier on the path of success. Here, it is difficult to resist the remark that although frustrated by the hold of local custom on the everyday practices of the Hindu and apparently in contravention of the *shastras*, Vidyasagar does not appear to have admitted that both *deshachar* and *shastra* sultimately drew authority and sustenance from the Brahmin himself.

The other major recommendation that needs to be dealt with here, however briefly, concerns the reconstitution of the English department. This department had to be strengthened,

Vidyasagar argued, by the induction of additional staff, but more importantly, by assigning English a greater space within the overall curriculum. English was not to be introduced to the student until he had a sufficiently good knowledge of Sanskrit, which was tantamount to saying that contrary to precedence, this was not to be taught to the student of the grammar class, the class that the student first joined on entering College. Presumably, the idea behind this was that an internal reorganisation of courses would equip the student with the mental maturity needed to make a critical comparison between the Sanskrit knowledge system and the European. English, in fact, was to be introduced only when a student had completed about seven years of study and was to continue through the rest of the course, stretching over the next seven to eight years. Finally, the teaching of English had also to be made compulsory, and those opting to drop out of the English course were to be debarred from taking it up again at some future date.

The letter of December 1850 provides the basic framework to the 'Notes on Sanscrit College' of April 1852 that followed, and which may be taken as the template for Vidyasagar's educational schemes. In the Note, certain core schemes or ideas are emphasised and relatively minor issues made to vary only in detail. On the whole, the purpose it served was to concretise proposals made earlier, which were yoked to a broader vision of matters concerned with framing an educational policy. The list of recommended texts for the disciplines of *Alankar* and *Smriti* was confirmed, albeit with certain modifications. Thus, the *Manusmriti* was now added to the reading list for the law class, comprising *Mitakshara*, *Dayabhaga*, *Vivada Chintamani*, *Dattakmimamsa*, and *Dattakachandrika*. That Vidyasagar was contemplating the creation of a body of legal experts with the knowledge and wherewithal to adjudicate on matters on a pan-Indian scale is evident from the inclusion of both the *Dayabhaga* and *Mitakshara* systems in the course of study. Texts on *Alankar* were similarly limited to only three: *Kavyaprakasha*, *Dasharupaka*, and the *Sahitya Darpana* (select parts). As though to redress an omission in the letter of 1850, *Uttara Mimamsa* (Jaimini) and *Vaisesika* were added to the philosophical schools to be now studied. The Note also makes clear that students of the Sanskrit College were not expected to possess any profound knowledge of these philosophical systems, and evidently, the emphasis again was on functionality and practical usage. Underlying this decision was surely the assumption that even a passing familiarity with these systems would reveal to the intelligent student their inherent flaws and weaknesses. Predictably, the main thrust area was still the revitalisation of English-language teaching.

The Note makes more explicit what the letter of 1850 had only tangentially suggested. First, the teaching of mathematics in Sanskrit was to be discontinued and upon reaching the higher classes, the student was expected to pay greater attention to the learning of that language, now committing himself to devoting twice the length of time in comparison to what he had committed earlier. Second, Vidyasagar argued that such changes would be practicable only through additional recruitment in that department. Vidyasagar pressed for the addition of four 'efficient' teachers qualified to handle the teaching of mathematics in the English language as well as Natural Philosophy and English literature. English was thus to be the vital fulcrum on which rested the dissemination of a modern and practically useful education. The Note clearly admitted that the knowledge of English alone would enable the transference of the 'philosophy of the West into "a native dress"'. Hereafter, Sanskrit education itself was to primarily focus on the teaching of grammar and literature. This only underscores Vidyasagar's new vision that could afford to somewhat neglect disciplines like *Smriti* and *Darshana*. In the new scheme, however, Sanskrit was also to serve another important function, hitherto overlooked: to facilitate the growth of an 'elegant, expressive and idiomatic' Bengali. Rightly or wrongly, Vidyasagar strongly believed that an improved Bengali could emerge only through an appropriate and persistent attention to instruction in Sanskrit.

The Pundit was as aware as anyone else of the financial implications of his scheme for the government, and this made him also consider economy measures. Since the new teachers of English were to be paid a monthly salary ranging from Rs 50–100, Vidyasagar mooted the idea of dispensing with the services of two manuscript copyists who, he felt, carried out no useful functions. To this could be added the savings made from abolishing the post of a teacher hitherto entrusted with the teaching of mathematics in Sanskrit.

On one level, the decision to do away with the work of copying manuscripts seems to be an extraordinary step for an institution like the Sanskrit College, for, notwithstanding the advent of print culture, the College had still to depend on a regular acquisition of manuscripts from various quarters. For producing standard printed versions of texts like *Annadamangal* and the *Sarvadarshanasamgraha*, Vidyasagar had to personally travel to Krishnanagar and Kashi, respectively. During his own days as a student, collecting and housing manuscripts was a sacred duty of traditional pundits, who were often also the source of manuscripts that a student could borrow and take home for study. Once Vidyasgar, who had himself borrowed a manuscript from a teacher (Jaygopal Tarkalankar?), nearly ruined it on the way back home from College. In any case, it is presumptuous to imagine that notwithstanding the growing commercial success, the sanctity of the printed word, or even the changing reading habits of the Bengali literati, the older world of writing and copying manuscripts could be entirely supplanted by the products of the mechanically run printing press.

Sometime in the middle of 1853, the Council of Education, perhaps prompted by the need to assure itself of the correctness of changes that it had agreed to, invited the Scottish Orientalist James Robert Ballantyne (1813–64), then Superintendent of the Sanskrit College in Benares. Dr Ballantyne was requested to carefully review and comment on the system recently introduced at the Calcutta Sanskrit College. The report that Ballantyne duly submitted to the government made some exceedingly interesting observations. For one, it did not think that the two Colleges located respectively in Benares and Calcutta stood comparison by way of educational priorities or praxis when it came to the question of imparting Sanskrit education. Calcutta was already 'inoculated with Anglican feeling', Ballantyne observed. What Superintendent Ballantyne hinted at but hesitated to say openly was that at least in his experience, this was true of the Bengali Hindus as a community, irrespective of their location. He was obviously somewhat unhappy at the fact that not a single Bengali Hindu of Benares had taken to a course in Sanskrit Studies at his College; instead, almost as a rule, they flocked to the English school that stood on the same compound as the College. Understandably enough, Ballantyne had no principled objections to the importance attached to English education even within the framework of Sanskrit Studies. Having produced grammars on Hindi, Marathi, and Braj Bhasha, he was also aware of the importance of the vernacular in any educational scheme. However, as an Orientalist, his penchant was for somehow reconciling Indian thought to the Western, and he might have indeed shocked Vidyasagar by suggesting that the 'truths' of the Western world were only 'developments and expressions of truths, the germs of which lay in the Sanskrit system'. Ballantyne was unhappy with the way some people viewed the two systems as perpetually locked in mutual opposition. Keen to draw points of similarity between the two, his report tried to draw attention to the discernible 'correspondence' between *Vedanta* and *Samkhya* on the one hand, and the philosophy of Bishop Berkeley on the other, as also between Mill's *Logic* and the aphorisms of *Nyaya*. Ballantyne's somewhat romanticist vision also contemplated producing an 'Anglo-Sanskrit education' that would successfully 'interpret the mind of Europe' to India. Under the circumstances, he was naturally apprehensive that Vidyasagar's scheme of placing Sanskrit and Western knowledge systems on parallel tracks might lead the average student to falsely conclude that Truth was 'double'. Ballantyne's convictions lay in the ultimate unity of philosophical thought, even allowing for its cultural differentials, and to this effect, he was prepared to admit the utility of comparative philosophy. For Vidyasagar, on the other hand, any comparisons drawn between the two had to be framed within the overarching purpose of demonstrating the superiority of one over the other. Retrospectively speaking, it might even be said that Ballantyne sometimes took a more realistic view of some matters—as, for instance, when he suggested that students of the Calcutta Sanskrit College could do very well with the abstract that he had prepared of Mill's *Logic* (which had been printed by the NWP Government Press, and was hence considerably cheaper), rather than be forced to purchase the book for themselves.

Ballantyne's report was duly dispatched to Vidyasagar by the Council of Education, inviting his observations or comments, and reached him on 20 August 1853.

In his reply dated 7 September, Pundit Iswarchandra vigorously contested some of the critical suggestions made by Ballantyne, and his observations were, on the whole, quite unreceptive and unfavourable. First, he disagreed with the suggestion that an abstract of Mill's work could substitute for the book in the original. He followed this up with a statement that looks somewhat astonishing even by current standards. His students were 'now in the habit of purchasing standard works at higher prices,' Vidyasagar observed. Assuming that Mill's book did not have an Indian edition at the time and had to be imported, this remark *prima facie* appears to be wildly off the mark. It would be only reasonable to argue that students of the Sanskrit College, the majority of whom would have been persuaded to take admission by the attractively low fees charged by the College, could have ill-afforded such a book; and here, attempts to draw comparisons between Young Bengal's enthusiasm for buying Tom Paine's *Age of Reason* even at a premium price and the average Sanskrit College student buying an imported copy of Mill falls flat. In 1838, speaking before the Society for the Cultivation of General Knowledge, the Derozian Uday Chandra Adya (?) pointed to the sharp decline in the student population (from 200 to 140) in the Sanskrit College once stipends had been withdrawn.

However, Vidyasagar's critique of Ballantyne does not stop there. He readily dismissed the latter's recommendation of chosen texts for the study of *Nyaya* and *Samkhya* (*Tarkasamgraha* and *Tattwasamasa*, respectively) as 'very poor treatises', and this despite knowing that Ballantyne was himself a scholar of *Samkhya*. But his more damaging criticism was reserved for Ballantyne's recommending a perusal of Bishop Berkeley's writings to the student, if only to familiarise him with the reported similarities that this had with Indian idealism. Once introduced to students, the philosophy of Berkeley, Vidyasagar feared, would 'beget more mischief than advantage'. More precisely, his fears lay in the possibility that prejudices in students would be 'redoubled' if they were to find modern European philosophers echoing the thoughts found amongst Indians. Such fears that Pundit Iswarchandra openly expressed have to be read together with his claim that Indian systems of philosophy were far removed from 'Truth'. 'That *Vedanta* and *Samkhya* are false systems of philosophy is no more a matter of dispute,' he asserted with an incredible and inexplicable confidence, as though this were some foregone conclusion. Even at the time, some scholars may have puzzled over how idealistic *Vedanta* and empiricist *Samkhya* could both be wrong at the same time. This was followed up by the comment that 'false as they are (these still) command unbound reverence from Hindus'.

As noted above, the irony here is that such criticism notwithstanding, Vidyasagar was not prepared to discontinue the teaching of these disciplines within the prescribed course of studies at the Sanskrit College. It is entirely possible that on this question, he did not wish to unduly offend or antagonise the Hindu nation. Perhaps he was even willing to support the study of these disciplines out of pure historical interest or from a general sense of rootedness in Brahmanical culture. On the other hand, this only leaves us with the conclusion that he was willing to castigate the Hindu nation for being conniving participants in perpetual falsehood. Of his own social and professional class, the traditional Brahmin pundit, he thought rather poorly, not always justifiably. They were a bigoted and intransigent people who could never be brought around to the side of enlightenment and progress, he alleged. Somewhat strangely, he also blamed this class exclusively for being rooted in the obsolete idea of revelation: strangely because they were not the only class to be so rooted, whether in India or in Europe. It ought to be remembered also that he wrote this before he entered the thick of battle with his pundit adversaries over the widow marriage question. It also occurs to me that when Vidyasagar referred to this class as constituting the 'learned' in India, he was being cynically sarcastic. Bankimchandra, who used a similar expression ('educated') to indicate only the Western-educated, was more forthright and honest in his characterisation.

Vidyasagar was quick to dismiss the idea of bridging India and Europe in the realm of thought; his panacea, rather, was to use the instrumentality of an improved vernacular to progressively bring home a Western modernity that would undermine and replace a reportedly sterile and senile intellectual world and a thoroughly archaic and practically useless thought process by one which could truly educate and enlighten the nascent Hindu middle classes.

His rejoinder to Ballantyne concludes on the note that instead of hopelessly trying to reconcile the 'dying' to prospects of a new life, the government ought to extend the benefit of education to the 'masses' through 'vernacular schools, class books and instructive subjects'. For Vidyasagar, Ballantyne's observations also constituted 'a degree of interference', and he smirked at the possibility of any student in Bengal with a reasonably good knowledge of English and Sanskrit fancying Truth to be 'double'. What comes through in this correspondence is his idea of using Bengali as a link language between Sanskrit and English:

> Leave me to teach Sanskrit for the leading purpose of thoroughly mastering the vernacular and let me superadd

> to it the acquisition of sound knowledge through the medium of the English...and I shall be able to furnish you with a body of young men who will be better qualified by their writings and teachings to disseminate widely among the people sound information than it has been hitherto been possible to accomplish through the instrumentality of the educated elves of any of your colleges, whether English or Oriental. (Letter of 5 October 1853, to the Council of Education)

By this time, Pundit Iswarchandra was clearly hinting at turning the Sanskrit College into a training ground for vernacular teachers. By his own admission, this was indeed 'the darling object' of his wishes. In fact, this was made amply clear in even an earlier letter of 16 July to the Council of Education. The Sanskrit College, it states, was to be 'regarded as the Normal School to meet the increased demand for higher order of Bengali teachers'. It seems to have escaped his attention that this scheme amounted to using a language in a rather instrumental sense. I have earlier argued that for Vidyasagar, the 'masses' were not necessarily constituted of the labouring poor and the spread of vernacular education was not necessarily tantamount to the success of mass education. Further down this chapter, I intend to take up this issue in greater detail.

In 1859, within a year of his retirement from the Sanskrit College, Vidyasagar was confronted by a fresh round of challenges. That year, Cowell, who had succeeded him to the office of the Principal, Sanskrit College, the Indologist Dr Johann Heinrich Eduard Roer (1805?–66), and Henry Woodrow, Inspector of Schools for Bengal, collectively commented on the status of the Sanskrit College. In some ways, the report was quite damaging and Vidyasagar was requested to respond to the comments made therein. Inspector Woodrow had hitherto been somewhat favourably disposed towards the functioning of the Sanskrit College, noting how the pundits of the College had been 'seized with the love of publishing books' and had 'showed a growing interest in European science and literature', alluding no doubt to Vidyasagar himself above all. But in 1859, he also alleged 'indiscipline' in the College and attributed it to its 'native superintendence'. This could have been a reference to Vidyasagar's own days as Principal, but fortunately the charge found no support in Cowell himself. Principal Cowell supported in principle the idea that the Sanskrit College be allowed to continue on its present footing, but also recommended that the chairs of *Smriti* and *Vedanta* be closed down. Quite consistent with views expressed earlier, Vidyasagar found the teaching of these subjects at the Sanskrit College 'unexceptionable', albeit on somewhat dissimilar grounds. The teaching of *Smriti* he defended for its sheer utility as it dealt with important issues in civil law, such as inheritance or adoption. In his reckoning, *Vedanta,* although of a metaphysical character, 'invited no objections on religious grounds'. Here, one cannot help the speculation that the proposal to do away with the *Vedanta* Chair could have arisen partly in Vidyasagar's own objections to it in 1853, and surely, in 1859, the Council of Education itself may have puzzled over the Pundit's defence of a practice he had himself once condemned. In 1859, the real challenge to Vidyasagar's educational visions and plans came from Dr Roer, who suggested that the Sanskrit College be closed down and the teaching of Sanskrit be introduced in government-funded English-medium institutions. For Vidyasagar, the proposal to close down the Sanskrit College posed a tangible threat for two related reasons. First, this could have ushered the death of Sanskrit education itself, at least in the urban metropolis of Calcutta, but equally rendered a crippling blow to the idea of building up an improved vernacular based on the Sanskrit knowledge system. The Pundit welcomed the idea of introducing Sanskrit education in English-medium colleges, but doubted if this would yield practical results, given the fact that such institutions could not handle the teaching of Bengali itself. In this, however, he was not mistaken.

The teaching of Bengali was surprisingly weak in colonial Calcutta and apparently, one persistent problem was the dearth of competent teachers. At the Hindu College itself, the authorities had been constrained to engage the services of a Brahmin who had once served as a cook at the house of Ramkamal Sen, an influential member of the Calcutta gentry who was on the management committee of the College. Uday Chandra Adya of the Hindu College, one of the few Derozians to speak in support of propagating Bengali as the first language, draws a dismal picture of the state of Bengali in Calcutta. Adya was 'astonished' at the way the government was squandering money in institutions like the Sanskrit College, which ultimately failed to produce members who could prove useful to society. He was equally critical of efforts made by the Calcutta *nouveaux riche* to run *pathshala*s from their homes, where allegedly ordinary men with little to no knowledge of Bengali grammar were employed on a monthly salary ranging from Rs 3 to Rs 8. In schools run by missionaries, there was indeed an emphasis on teaching the vernacular, but the task wrongly entrusted again to incompetent men. Schools run by missionaries also paid unduly greater attention to religious instruction, to the neglect of other subjects.'No young man became truly religious by studying at these places,' Adya observed,'after some years, these young men learn their own trade i.e shoe-making, driving carts etc. and later take to drinking, running after other people's wives and generally go astray.' In 1844, an essay in the *Calcutta Review* noted how 'scarcely anything could be lower than the native standard of the vernacular'. Even in the early 1850s, the popular dramatist Ramnarayan Tarkaratna (1822–86), Head Pundit at the Hindu Metropolitan College, had to exhort his students by comparing Bengali to the breast milk fed to the infant by the mother.

In 1854, the Government of Bengal urged the imperial government to seriously take up the issue of expanding the base of vernacular education in rural Bengal. On 16 November, the Under-Secretary to the Government of Bengal wrote to his counterpart in the Government of India, stating that while there were many schools functioning in Bengal, their standard was 'universally low and in unsatisfactory condition'. In a sense, this urgency shown took off not only from the success achieved by the *halaqbandi* primary schools of Lt Governor Thomason in the North-Western Provinces, but also from the interest shown in primary education by imperial officers of the highest rank, such as Lord Hardinge and, thereafter, Lord Mayo. Mayo, who was Viceroy of India between 1869 and 1872, focused his thoughts on conceivable objections to the so-called 'filtration policy' in the field of education. This policy had been adopted by the government a long time ago. In his *Nine Letters on Educational Policy* (1872) addressed to Viceroy Lord Northbrook, Keshabchandra Sen could recall that it had been in operation even as early as 1838. Put simply, it advocated the idea of educating the upper classes before taking to the education of the masses, and was based on the theory that the value of good education moved not laterally but over time, percolating down from the 'high' to the 'low'. In the post-Macaulay era, this was obviously associated with the imperial scheme of creating and consolidating an Indian elite that could be suitably persuaded to accept British colonial rule and its attendant political or economic policies. The rapid acceptance of this scheme among the Indian elite, whether founded on genuine convictions or conniving opportunism, was undoubtedly facilitated by the literary quality of the education progressively introduced into the institutions of higher learning in India.

By the 1860s, however, this had turned into a matter of contention between those individuals who wished to uphold the social differential that such education fostered and those who wished to mitigate it in a meaningful and responsible way. At a meeting of the Bethune Society in 1868, when the Derozian Kissory Chand Mitra (1822–73) strongly urged the government to continue with the downward 'filtration theory' in education, he was opposed by Rev. Lalbihari De (1824–92), an erstwhile student of Rev. Alexander Duff who later converted to Christianity. In their social interests or beliefs, no two men could be further apart than Mitra and De. Kissory Chand serialised a very useful social history of the landed aristocracy in

Bengal for the *Calcutta Review*, and consistently articulated the social and political aspirations of the Western-educated Bengali middle class, drawn principally from the upper castes. Lalbihari, on the other hand, belonged to a caste located on the fringes of the *bhadralok*, and wrote evocatively and empathetically on the vagaries of Bengal peasant life and put together an early collection of Bengali folk tales. On this particular occasion, Lalbihari was to quite cynically observe that the upper-class 'filter' was no ordinary filter, 'but a jar hermetically sealed', which effectively prevented the benefits of education from reaching the lower classes, as had indeed been intended. Importantly, De also drew up a practical scheme by which elementary education could be effectively dispersed without imposing a great financial burden on the government. In his estimate, the Bengal government required about Rs 60 lakh annually for bringing education to the masses, and hoped this would be raised in the following manner. First, he suggested charging a monthly fee of 1 anna per student in schools, which was expected to fetch about Rs 10 lakh annually. To this, he suggested adding an Education Cess, which would bring a further Rs 7 lakh. The rest, he proposed, could be met by the government itself.

It is not known if the government examined this scheme with any seriousness, but in hindsight, it has to be admitted that such a plan for Bengal was flawed in its very fundamentals. For one, the government could not legally enforce an additional rural tax or a cess, given the Permanent Settlement of land in the province. As F. J. Mouat, Secretary to the Council of Education for Bengal, was to note, 'the revenue system of Bengal did not afford, particularly in the subordinate native agency, the great bond between the people and the ruling authorities that exists in the *Tehsildari* system of North Western Provinces'. Not surprisingly, one of the reasons behind Thomason's success in the North-West Provinces had been his very ability to levy an additional tax for the purposes of funding education, the first time any British official was able to do so. In Bengal, by comparison, the zamindars and rural intermediaries strongly resisted this move, but opposition, as we shall presently see, was to also come from the educated middle classes.

In the early 1870s, though, there was a temporary drift of ideas away from such conservatism, and this was connected to the assumption to office almost simultaneously of Lord Mayo as Viceroy and George Campbell as the Lt. Governor of Bengal. W. W. Hunter's biography of Lord Mayo (1892) cites the following statement from the Viceroy:

> I dislike the filtration theory. In Bengal, we are to educate a few hundred Babus at great expense to the state. Many of them are well able to pay for themselves and have no other object on learning than to qualify for government employ. In the meantime, we have done nothing towards extending knowledge to the millions. The Babus will never do it. The more education you give them the more they will keep to themselves and make their increased knowledge a means of tyranny.

Quite evidently, Mayo's critique encouraged Campbell in Bengal to swiftly enhance the budget for elementary education and simultaneously reduce grants to institutions of higher learning, thereby raising a huge protest from the educated middle classes in Calcutta and smaller adjacent towns.

Sir George Campbell was the only Lt. Governor of Bengal with whom Vidyasagar failed to have close personal relations. Between 1854 and 1866, he had befriended three successive Lt. Governors in Halliday, Grant, and Beadon, each of whom treated him with respect and affection and considerably helped him in his professional career. The combination of Mayo and Campbell, however, inhibited his plans. It is equally true that the Pundit's reservations on the government's policy on extending education to the 'masses' originated not in Campbell's policies, but as early as 1859 with Lt. Governor John Peter Grant in office. Such reservations are clearly spelt out in a letter that he wrote on 29 September 1859 to Rivers Thompson, Junior Secretary to the Government of Bengal.

This letter clearly rules out the utility or efficacy of low-budget (the word used was 'cheap') schools for the rural classes. From Vidyasagar's correspondence, it appears as though the government was planning to run schools on an abysmally low budget of Rs 5–7 a month; this is surprising, given the fact that even in 1854, after enquiries made with Rev. James Long, the Bengal government had found a sum of Rs 25 per month to be 'reasonable' (letter dated 16 November 1854 from the Under-Secretary to the Government of Bengal to the Under-Secretary, Government of India). All the same, Vidyasagar found the running of such low-budget schools to be not only impractical, but also unworthy. Evidently, he was discontented with the idea that such schools would introduce to the students merely letter-writing, zamindari, and shopkeeper's accounts modelled on experiments conducted in neighbouring Bihar. More importantly, though, he felt that such a scheme would not be of any practical use to the common people and was likely to be rejected by them. 'Such education, insignificant as it would be, will not extend to the masses,' he argued, 'if by that word is meant the labouring classes; for even now, both in Behar and in Bengal, few if any from these classes are to be found among the pupils of these schools.' Such a scheme was bound to fail, Vidyasagar prophesised, because it provided no practical inducement to rural families, which would not agree to educate their children merely for the sake of knowledge; and here, he resorted to the argument that has haunted educationists even in independent India. The labouring classes would not be motivated to send their children to schools because this came in the way of more productive engagement in labour-intensive economies, where free family labour was an effective way of saving on production costs. Vidyasagar was correct in pointing out that the upper classes too were driven more by the vocational prospects of education than the intellectual changes it might be expected to produce, but remained silent on the matter of deciding if, for the reasons cited, the labouring poor in Bengal villages would be better-off without the benefit of an elementary education altogether. At the least, he might have made a more serious attempt at setting up evening schools for such classes, as had actually been initiated by the Brahmo missionaries, Keshabchandra and Sasipada Banerjee (1840–1925). There was indeed a Night School at Birsingha, but in the late 1850s, touring government Inspectors found it entirely deserted.

The letter of 1859 turned out to be the most emphatic pronouncement on the part of Pundit Iswarchandra in favour of the filtration theory. Disputing the perception that it was time to switch official priorities from the field of higher education to that of instructing the masses, a perception that he alleged had wrongly pervaded official circles both in India and in England, Vidyasagar came to the following conclusion:

> An impression seems to have gained ground, both here and in England, that enough has been done for the education of the higher classes and that attention should now be directed towards the education of the masses.... An enquiry into the matter, however, will show a very different state of things...the best if not the only practicable means of promoting education in Bengal the Government should, in my humble opinion, confine itself to the education of higher classes on a comprehensive scale. By educating one boy in proper style, the Government does more towards real education of the people, than by teaching a hundred children mere reading, writing and a little Arithmetic.

In Vidyasagar's view, the only practical way to successfully bring about mass education was for the government to introduce free schools in villages. Perhaps to justify his position further, Vidyasagar argued how, when it came to talking about mass education, in even a highly civilised country such as England, the poor were no better-off compared to the poor in India. Looking back on his arguments, it appears as though the Pundit's panacea had some basis in his own experiences in running free schools in his native village Birsingha, reportedly with some success. However, committing itself on a scale the Pundit had proposed was not a step that the government was willing to take. Also, it is not unlikely that the Campbell administration had been infiltrated by bureaucrats, who had grown somewhat anxious with the ways of the educated and increasingly articulate Babus.

On assuming office in 1872, Campbell increased the budget for primary education almost five-fold, from Rs 1,30,000 to 5,30,000. This was a bold but extremely necessary step. After all, it was precisely the paucity of funds that had frustrated the plans of one of his like-minded predecessors in office, John Peter Grant. The government's supervision of rural schools was now transferred from the agency of Inspectors hitherto appointed by the Council of Education (and who had little or no knowledge of local conditions) to respective district administrations and regularly constituted school committees. The need for additional funds for primary education was met by cutting down on the costs of higher education. Predictably, the Bengali-language press was soon greatly agitated over the fact that grants had been cut for both Anglo-Vernacular schools and the Sanskrit Colleges in Berhampore and Krishnanagar. The *Bengalee* of 11 January 1873 express edits anguish by proclaiming that in no 'civilised country' had collegiate education been turned into a self-financing project. The implications of Campbell's policy adversely affected the Calcutta Sanskrit College, too. The First Arts Course in the College had to be discontinued. While there were twenty-six undergraduates in this college in 1871, this number was further reduced to twenty-three in a year's time. The services of two teachers of English in that College had also to be terminated. But for the Presidency College, Calcutta, no college in contemporary Bengal now had the resources to properly teach courses in science. What is overlooked, or perhaps not as well-known, is the fact that the Hindu *bhadralok* also took exception to the way the Campbell administration increased grants to *madrasa*s and *maktab*s, and encouraged the teaching of Persian and Arabic in schools run by Bengali Muslims. The Hindu *bhadralok* also greatly resented the transfer of funds from the Krishnanagar College to the Hoogly (later Mohsin) College. This had the effect of reducing the Krishnanagar College to the status of a First Arts College. On the other hand, it substantially increased the funds available to the Hoogly College, which was already benefiting from an endowment instituted by the Muslim philanthropist, Haji Mohsin.

In 1874, Bankimchandra produced an anonymous essay for the *Bongodarshan* in which he very insightfully compared the regimes of Lt. Governor William Grey and his successor in office, George Campbell. The former proved to be more popular among Indians, Bankim observed, because he had three things working in his favour: mediocrity, the ability to run an administration quite mechanically, and the cleverness to not antagonise anybody. Campbell, by comparison, was a conceited but a far more intelligent man, and unlike his predecessor in office, did not have a habit of trying to please everybody. Bankim's empathy clearly lay with Campbell and his pro-tenant policies, even in defiance of the powerful zamindars who opposed the cause of primary education. There were also some other outspoken European officers who supported Campbell, not out of any sense of personal loyalty but from a deeper understanding of the problem at hand. One of them, by the name of H. L. Harrison, commenting on a Note from the then Director of Public Instruction, William Stephen Atkinson (1820–76), said in 1874:

> ...a primary school was one in which the lower classes sent their children without the expectation they will thereby rise to the middle classes .... 'D type' *pathshalas* are frequented by boys of the middle classes who seek to rise through its agency to the middle classes that will at least become *gomasthas, muhurris,* head constables or *gurus* themselves. George Campbell was absolutely right in condemning the system of undesirable expenditure of public money in *secondary education under the garb of primary education*. (emphasis mine)

Here, Harrison's reference to 'D type' *pathshalas* points to the educational experiments carried out by Bhudeb Mukhopadhyay largely in Bihar, with encouragement from Atkinson. By

Vidyasagar's own admission in 1859, this scheme was supported by relatively superior textbooks. As Harrison's Note also makes explicit, such schools were patronised by the rural gentry, who hoped to secure greater professional and social mobility through reformed *pathshalas* than had been possible in Bengal.

By 1874, the *bhadralok* opposition to Campbell's schemes had mounted so high that his continued presence in Bengal became almost an embarrassment for the imperial government. Apparently, he did not find favour with the new Viceroy, Lord Northbrook, and was forced to leave India by April 1874, partly also on account of his ill health. After his departure for England, the irate Bengali press felt extremely gratified at its apparent success. The nationalist leader Surendranath Banerjee claimed that it was the vociferous opposition from Bengalis that had forced Campbell to abort his plans. At the time, it would have been highly indiscreet for any member of the *bhadralok* community to state anything to the contrary.

It is quite evident that the government held Vidyasagar and his educational schemes in high esteem. One reason for this was that it valued his 'liberal' and 'enlightened' opinion on matters connected with his community and with its education. It also appreciated his courage and willingness to confront adversity, his honesty and forthrightness about the opinions and convictions that he held, and the firmness he exhibited in pursuing what he held to be worth the pursuit. The government also concurred with the view that a knowledge of Sanskrit was indeed the foundation of an improved vernacular, and more importantly, that this modern vernacular was potentially capable of being wedded to modern ideas and practical social progress. The government was happy that the Pundit had his eye on a scheme that introduced the student to two seemingly different projects: the pursuit of Sanskrit Studies and the dissemination of a modern English education. Vidyasagar's successor in office, E. B. Cowell, credited him with two 'grand experiments': introducing a much simplified text for the easy learning of Sanskrit grammar (the *Vyakaran Kaumudi*) and making the study of English compulsory in the Sanskrit College. Interestingly enough, the Council of Education held out the hope of introducing elementary Sanskrit someday in even the higher departments of Zilla Schools. The government also acknowledged his standing as a scholar in his own right, with or without his contributions in the field of textbook writing or the spread of rural education. In 1858, C. T. Buckland, Junior Secretary to the Government of Bengal, was to call him the 'best Sanskrit and Bengali scholar in the Presidency', and the man who had 'taken the first place among the educators of his countrymen'. Writing in April 1859, Henry Woodrow, the Inspector of Schools for Eastern Bengal, observed the discernable change in attitude that had occurred in the class of Pundits attached to the Sanskrit College over the past decade or so, and without actually naming him, he attributed this to the radicalising presence of Pundit Iswarchandra:

> The learned Pundits of the Sanskrit College, have, as a body, have been with the love of publishing books [*sic*]. They have at last consented to cast away the *Sesquipedalia Verba*, compounded words a line and a half long and to write in a language that ordinary people may read. Simplicity of diction is now their great object. Only fifteen years ago, the Vernacularist might have been tempted to say, can anything good come out of the Sanskrit College? The Pundits of that College then despised European science and literature as utterly as the Madrussa Moulavis do now. Yet during these fifteen years, they have awoke [*sic*] from slumber of hundreds, rather, of thousands of years, and now again are appearing as the instructors of their countrymen.

Although he had to ultimately confront disappointments, Vidyasagar, at least in his early educational career, was reasonably happy with the changes that he had been able to bring about in the minds of people about taking to a modern education. Observing the progress made by his Model Vernacular Schools in the rural districts, he was to note how even the orthodox Hindus of Krishnanagar, who habitually prided themselves on their traditional learning and scoffed at the working of new schools, had happily agreed to send their own children to these schools. In December 1850, Pundit Iswarchandra had expressed the hope that the Sanskrit College 'will become an asset of pure and profound learning and at the same time, a nursery of improved vernacular literature and of teacher thoroughly qualified to disseminate the literature amongst the masse of their countrymen'. At the time, the government clearly endorsed this vision. The annual General Report on Public Instruction for the year 1855 noted:

> Through knowledge of Sanskrit together with a great command over their own language, Bengali, combined with a considerable amount of useful knowledge acquired through the medium of English will make the pupils of Sanskrit College a most efficient class of contributors to an enlightened Bengali literature.

With the advantage of hindsight, it might be possible to argue that some of the implications of his educational scheme had begun to worry Vidyasagar towards the closing stages of his career in the Sanskrit College. In a report submitted to the Council of Education for the quarter ending January 1857, the Pundit spiritedly tried to dispel the notion that only an English education would qualify boys for employment. This impression, he communicated to the government, should be 'removed' from the minds (of parents) by providing vernacular students with suitable employment, as for instance by nominating them to lower offices within the judicial or revenue departments'. That the Sanskrit College could not limit itself to the recurring production of qualified vernacular teachers alone would have undoubtedly struck Vidyasagar with some force by this time. In an earlier correspondence with Dr Ballantyne, too, he had been forced to press this point quite vigorously. On 27 October 1856, responding to a communication from Gordon Young, he wrote:

> ...it appears ...that the Director of Public Instruction wishes the course of instruction in the Sanskrit College to be restricted as qualifying its pupils for the posts of teachers only and for nothing else.... I find that the original

> intentions of the government for its [Sanskrit College] foundation was the revival of Hindu learning and then an English department was added to it subsequently in order to make it an efficient government institution...(if) the object of the institution is merely to bring up men who will be qualified for the purposes of teachers only and nothing else, I beg to submit that it will be very speedily deserted. Men who send their children to it for general education will immediately withdraw them and others who may be anxious to follow the profession of a teacher will leave the institution because they will prefer a Normal School where they can receive free instruction with a monthly stipend.... I do not comprehend how the course of instruction can be restricted to professional teaching alone. Admitting that the object of the College was merely to bring up teachers, it will be necessary to train up the pupils in such a way as will enable them to impart instruction to others in History, Geography, Mathematics, Natural Philosophy, Moral Philosophy etc. etc. Any person with such qualifications will indeed be fit for a teachership but he will be equally fit for general employment. He may for instance become a clerk, an accountant, a *darogah*, an *amlah* and so on. He can either enter the Presidency College or the College of Civil Engineering ....

From the above, it would certainly appear as though the government had taken the idea of the Sanskrit College as being essentially a 'nursery' for competent teachers more seriously than Vidyasagar himself had intended or visualised. This may lead us to wonder if, contrary to what the Pundit had once imagined, the new crop of young men produced by the Sanskrit College had, rather than acting as interpreters between two traditions, become increasingly caught up in the more material and pressing challenges of securing a livelihood.

By the 1870s, the government had clearly dissociated the efforts of Pundit Iswarchanda from the advancement of primary vernacular education. This would partly explain why the Education Commission of 1882 did not seek his advice and cooperation, instead calling upon the services of Bhudeb

Mukhopadhyay. Vidyasagar's career in framing educational policy ran dry by the 1870s; thereafter, he was forced to turn more to the task of educational administration. Bhudeb, by comparison, continued actively for another decade. Second, on the question of the transference of knowledge from one system to another, there appears to have been a perceptible area of disagreement between the two foremost educationists of nineteenth-century Bengal. In Vidyasgar's case, the preference for switching over from the indigenous knowledge system to the Western was more radical, dramatic, and pronounced. Bhudeb, however, believed the transition ought to be slower and at a steadier pace. His modernism was firmly anchored in the moral and philosophical discourse of the contemporary West, and the transference that he insisted upon was unilateral in nature, flowing from a supposedly superior system to one considered relatively underdeveloped or inferior. Admittedly, he borrowed also from the Brahmanical moral and cultural discourse which constituted the world into which he had been born and which, in some ways, also shaped his thoughts and personality. However, somewhat contrary to what Hatcher has suggested, Vidyasagar's borrowing from this discourse also had its limitations. To some extent, what Hatcher calls 'the vernacularisation of the Brahminical discourse' would have occurred even without the moral pedagogy of his textbooks, in the ordinary playing out of folk-life and everyday socialisation. On the other hand, his attempt to bring this discourse into formal classroom teaching, which was otherwise infused by a Western value system, appears to have posed certain problems for Vidyasagar himself. For one, it reinforced his Puritanism. Here, an instance that comes to mind is his refusing to prescribe the study of *Chanakyasloka*s on the ground that the language was 'indelicate', 'vulgar', and hence unsuitable for schoolboys. And he said so despite admitting that these *sloka*s were hugely popular, even among illiterates. Could it be that such popularity had itself proved to be the cause of some inhibition and discomfort from the perspective of genteel morality?

In Vidyasagar's literary oeuvre, there really was nothing drawn from indigenous sources that paralleled the *Jeeboncharit* or the *Charitabali*, and it is not improbable for some Hindu student in his day to have wondered if there were no Indian lives to celebrate. Arguably, in the Pundit's view, any selection of Indian lives that might have set worthy examples for the Indian student, and from which he could have profited, was beset by two related difficulties. First, in the context of Hindu India, any such selection would have had to reckon with lives that were drawn more towards the pursuit of metaphysics and mysticism, which he was understandably predisposed to avoid at all costs. Vidyasagar, I imagine, would never have thought to commemorate figures such as the Buddha, Adi Sankarcharya, Guru Nanak, Ramprosad Sen, or Chaitanya. Second, it would have quickly dawned upon him that the tradition of writing biographies, or more generally, of historical documentation, was far weaker in India than it was in the West. This posed the practical problem of selecting an adequate number of authentic textual sources to draw upon. However, it would also appear that other contemporary writers had circumvented this problem, partly because they were relatively less enamoured of human qualities considered virtuous in the West, or of Western methods of character-building. The art of biography writing was not unknown even in early modern Bengal, as can be proven by Ramram Basu's biography of Pratapaditya of Jessore (*Raja Pratapaditya Charitam,*1801) and Rajeeblochan Mukhopadhyay's life of Krishnachandra of Nadia (*Maharaj Krishnachandra Rayasya Charitam*, 1805), but these were obviously not the kind of lives that Vidyasagar had in mind. While Vidyasagar adapted from either English or Sanskrit to the vernacular, Bhudeb is known to have translated suitable books written in the Bengali language into Hindi for students in Bihar. Such inter-vernacularity never appealed to Pandit Iswarchandra. Nirad C. Chaudhuri once insightfully observed that between them, Vidyasagar and Tagore represented the two poles within the great cultural ferment that occurred in renaissance Bengal.

While Tagore was an Indian in every respect save his attire, Pundit Iswarchandra was a European in every respect but for his attire. After all, one of the sharpest critiques of colonial educational policy, *Shikkhar Herfer* (1893), was to come from Tagore.

The poet Hemchandra Bandopadhyay (1838–1903) parodied Vidyasagar's experiments in the following lines:

> Fried in English butter this is but a Sanskrit dish,
> Our teachers in *tols* and schools are hereby finish. (translation mine)

Krishnakamal Bhattacharya, to whom we have referred earlier, cast both Vidyasagar's linguistic experiments and his 'improved vernacular' in a subtly satirical vein. Writing to the Principal of the Presidency College, he remarked: 'Vidyasagar's works, replete with long Sanskrit phrases from beginning to end are the most popular, most keenly relished and admiringly appreciated by that part of the public who preserved unchallenged its genuine Bengali taste.' Some of Vidyasagar's successors in office expressed their unhappiness at the changes that had been wrought upon the Sanskrit College previously. The *Sangbad Prabhakar* accused him of unduly anglicising the Sanskrit College, but a more biting note came from one of his successors in office, Pandit Maheschandra Nyayaratna (1836–1906). Nyayaratna, who took over as Principal of Sanskrit College in 1877, noted the following:

> I may even mention that the Sanskrit College itself can by no means claim to impart the deep knowledge of Sanskrit which the *tols* do. The instruction imparted in this institution [Sanskrit College] is more of a philosophical nature. It seeks to give an education embodying both Western and Eastern culture. The *tol*...alone in all its highest departments are best calculated to produce scholars with a deep knowledge of Sanskrit.

It would be relevant also to cite the fact that some Sanskrit pundits refused to be drawn into employment, whether under the government or Indian patrons. Chandranarayan

Nyayapanchanan (d. 1833) was labelled 'Bhritya adhyapak' (servile teacher) by fellow pundits when he joined the Kashi Sanskrit College, and was excommunicated. It was rumoured in some circles that a similar fate had befallen Jaynarayan Tarkapanchanan (1805–72), who had once taught Pundits Iswarchandra, Taranath Tarkavachaspati, and Maheschandra Nyayaratna at the Sanskrit College. Taranath Tarkavachaspati himself and his son, Jeevananda Vidyasagar Bhattacharya (1844–1910), spent a lifetime imparting a Sanskrit education in *tols* and *chatuspathis*, run at their own cost. Pundit Jeevananda, who eventually published as many as 107 Sanskrit classics together with commentaries, consistently rejected lucrative offers of employment at the royal houses of Kashmir and Nepal, preferring to retire to his native village of Ambica-Kalna and carry on with teaching poor Brahmin students. It is also somewhat ironic that the *Siddhanta Kaumudi* of Bhattoiji Dikshita, which Vidyasagar had recommended as a grammar text for his students in Sanskrit College, was published in 1866–67 (together with a commentary, *Sarala*) by the man who most virulently disputed his reading of Hindu *shastra*: Pundit Taranath Tarkavachaspati. Pundit Taranath is best known as Vidyasagar's greatest opponent on the question of polygamous marriages; what is far less known is that the two also differed over the question of whether or not an unchaste widow had any rights to her husband's property. In this instance, Pundit Taranath also had the support of Dwarkanath Mitter, but their views were eventually overruled by a judicial bench. It is indeed somewhat extraordinary that even as a reputed Sanskrit scholar of *smriti*, Pundit Iswarchandra produced nothing resembling exegetical literature. In Chapter 4, I have ventured to argue that he might well have done so with respect to certain Hindu legal texts, which critically determined his social reform campaigns.

Note

1. In Bengal, with the colonial state and government almost fully controlling trade and industry, entry to these fields was severely restricted for Bengalis. An education leading to petty employment under the government or else in European mercantile offices was the only avenue left for the educated middle classes. The situation was relatively different in Bombay, where British conquest came later, and where British colonial interests could not fully displace the entrenched Indian trading communities like the Gujarati Banias, Momins, Bohras or Parsis.

four

Vidyasagar and the Woman Question

Between them, the life and work of Rammohun Roy and Vidyasagar bring out most clearly the centrality of the 'Woman Question' in Bengal. By comparison, the issue of caste, which greatly agitated western and southern India through the nineteenth and early twentieth century, was relatively weaker in ethnic Bengal. Many other Hindu Bengalis of the time wrote copiously on the theme of woman's emancipation, and we also know of several journals run by women and dedicated to women's issues; but somehow public memory in the province—correctly or otherwise—tends to settle on the work carried out by the two figures mentioned above. The reasons for this are not far to seek. First, while many addressed woman-related questions from the press and sundry platforms, only Rammohun and Vidyasagar were deeply implicated in important and enduring legal enactments that amounted to innovations in law and social practice. This, they performed even at some risk to their lives and in the face of vitriolic opposition. By comparison, the prohibition of female infanticide (through the ordinances of 1795 and 1804) was entirely the work of British administrators, in which Indians themselves showed little or no interest. Second, there was something deeply personal and emotional in the way both these reformers related to problems faced by women in general. By the mid-nineteenth century, English-educated *bhadralok* society was moved to seriously consider such issues after they too came to believe, in line with contemporary European thought, that a people could be justly judged on the scale of civilisations by the way they treated their women. To this, Rammohun and Vidyasagar added some new dimensions. Their response was more spontaneous and personalised, and the concern they showed for women appears to have emerged as much from genuine respect as from empathy or compassion. This was not simply compassion born of patriarchal condescension or even a mechanical sense of social justice. Rammohun would leave his desk and stand up to greet a woman who entered his room, and Vidyasagar was almost instantly moved to tears at the very sight of a suffering woman or upon hearing of a woman being inhumanely treated. Vidyasagar's statement that promoting the marriage of Hindu widows was the prime objective of his life speaks to both the sensitivity of the man and his humility.

A concern for reforming the condition of Hindu women pervaded at least forty years of Vidyasagar's life, beginning in 1850 and ending with his death in 1891. During this time, he was associated, albeit with varying degrees of success, with five woman-related issues: premature marriages of girls, female education, the question of widow marriage, the evils of Kulin polygamy, and the controversial age of consent. Of these, the issue of female education has already been dealt with in Chapter 3.

The Ills of Premature Marriage

Significantly, Vidyasagar's first writing on woman-related issues begins with a tract (*Balyabibaher Dosh*, 1850) on the ills of early marriages that appeared in the *Sarvashubhakari Patrika*, the organ of the philanthropic body, Sarvasubhakari Sabha. This journal, as we know, also carried an essay by Vidyasagar's colleague in Sanskrit College, and for a time his business collaborator, Pandit Madanmohan Tarkalankar, on the need for female education. We also know that despite belonging to the class of traditional Brahmin scholars, Pundit Madanmohan had been among the earliest to admit his two daughters to the Hindu Balika Vidyalaya, inaugurated in 1849 by Bethune.

There are four distinctive features of Vidyasagar's tract of 1850. First, it was quick to acknowledge the impact of female education on the larger issue of improving the social status of women in Hindu society. Implicit in this acknowledgement was the belief that it was education that would ultimately bring social and vocational independence to women, thereby also providing them with some dignity and self-respect. Pundit Iswarchandra and reformers of his class have sometimes been faulted for focusing their attention on correctional measures such as getting widows remarried, or ending the indignity of women and wives that resulted from the institution of multiple marriages among upper-caste men. Admittedly, he did not think along the lines of the Brahmo reformer Sasipada Banerjee, who set up a Widow's Home at Barahnagar near Calcutta where destitute widows could be given shelter and obtain vocational training that helped with their future rehabilitation in society. On the other hand, it is important to not overlook the fact that Banerjee's Home had the backing of a reformist organisation, the Brahmo Samaj, which orthodox Hindu society despised but had not the power to control. Even this proved no easy task and, at times, widows had to be literally 'stolen away' from Hindu homes in the dead of night and temporarily entrusted to the care of some helpful family.

Second, the tract clearly connected the issue of premature marriages with the incidence of widow marriages. Given the state of public health in colonial Bengal and the high mortality rate, infant marriages, Vidyasagar realised, could only increase the number of hapless widows. Third, his arguments here made no pointed reference to *shastra* as the guiding power behind change, relying instead on reason and humanitarian appeal. Finally, the Pundit looked at the problem from a modern perspective, and the modernity in his approach may be gleaned from the fact that he considered a happy conjugal life the basis of every successful marriage, a conjugality that grew out of mutual love and respect. 'A mental bonding is the very foundation of love,' he wrote in his tract, *Balyavivaher Dosh*, bemoaning the fact that Hindu girls were married off too soon to properly develop such sentiments or feelings.

A question that has been left unanswered in the various biographical accounts of Vidyasagar is why his appeal to the *shastras* increased over time, while other attendant arguments grew relatively weaker. The answer is not quite apparent from his personal experiences of these years. In hindsight, it would indeed appear as though the tract of 1850 did not catch the public eye very much. There is also no evidence of its being reprinted. Could this be the answer we are seeking? Did the lack of public enthusiasm for the *Balyabibaha* tract force a change in the reformer's approach or strategy?

Vidyasagar would have foreseen the long-term ills of premature marriages even outside any strategic concerns. He himself married an 8-year-old girl, his contemporary Debendranath Tagore, a girl of six, Keshubchandra Sen, a girl of nine, Bankimchandra, a girl of five, and Bhudeb Mukhopadhyay, of about eleven. Barring Bankim, none of these figures have reported a happy conjugal life with a child bride. While the failure to report this is not necessarily a comment against early marriages, the tendency to overlook the gender inequities resulting from such marriages does indicate an innate and compulsive conservatism. Vidyasagar had his eldest daughter, Hemlata, married when she was sixteen, and the one immediately after her, only after fourteen. In these instances, interestingly, he does not appear to have followed the dictates of the *smritis*, especially that of Parasar, on whom he otherwise relied greatly for legitimising widow marriages. What seems to have escaped the attention of scholars and social commentators here is that Parasar was a great champion of early marriages, too, as can be judged from his insistence on observing the *garbhadhan* ceremony, a ritual act that a father was obligated to arrange for before his daughter reached puberty. This resulted in getting daughters married at absurdly tender ages. It was considered an act of great religious merit to gift a daughter in marriage when she was eight (*gauridan*), only because texts like the *Parasar Smriti* condemned the Brahmin who married a girl who had already reached puberty to eternal hell.

Two of the earliest available surveys of the general problems afflicting women in Hindu society are the papers read out in 1839–40 at meetings of the Society for the Acquisition of General Knowledge, a body created by students of the Hindu College, Calcutta. In this instance, the authors, Mahesh Chandra Deb and Krishnamohan Bandopadhayay, were both students of the College. Between 1852 and 1857, a number of Bengali-language journals, such as the *Sangvad Prabhakar, Vividartha Sangraha*, and the *Bangavidyaprakashika*, joined in the criticism of early marriages, with even conservatives like Kashiprosad Ghosh (1809–73), Honorary Presidency Magistrate and a juror at the Supreme Court in Calcutta, writing against it in his *Hindu Intelligencer*. By the 1870s, three literary productions on the subject had gained some popularity: Shyamacharan Sreemani's *Balya Vivaha Natak* (1868), Bhubaneshwar Mitra's *Hindu Vibhaha Samalochana* (1870), and Ramchandra Dutta's *Balya Vivaha Nataka*, also from that year. Strangely, Vidyasagar failed to take note of these interventions; perhaps his silence can be explained by the fact that by this time, he was seriously embroiled in the controversy over widow marriage and in the campaign against Kulin polygamy. In ethnic Bengal, the drive against the early marriage of girls weakened somewhat hereafter and was not revived until 1890–91 when it was joined, although quite unjustifiably, to the question of amending the legal age of consent. On the other hand, it became a major issue with reformers from western India, like the Parsi Behramji Malabari (1853–1912), his biographer, Dayaram Gidumal (1857–1927), and Mahadev Govind Ranade (1842–1901) and his Social Conference. Two works that best represent this trend are *Infant Marriage and Enforced Widowhood* by Malabari (1887) and Gidumal's *The Status of Women in India or a Handbook for Hindu*

Social Reformers (1889). One important issue that separated the Bombay reformers from those in Bengal was the question of legal interventions by the State. Malabari, Gidumal, and Ranade actively championed the role of the State in effecting social legislation. 'The state in its collective capacity represented the power, the wisdom, the mercy and the charity of its best citizens,' Ranade was to famously remark. On the other hand, even Rammohun is known to have advised caution to Governor-General Bentinck over the sati legislation: '... the practice of sati might be suppressed quietly and unobservedly,' he had written, 'by increasing the difficulties and by direct agency of the Police.' In Vidyasagar's Bengal, the moral and social propriety of State intervention was opposed by some prominent Bengalis including Bankimchandra, who targeted the efforts of non-Hindus like Malabari in particular. Evidently, the argument that grew stronger with time was that only the Hindus had the moral and social authority to effect changes in established social praxis.

The Widow Marriage Campaign

The widow marriage campaign in Bengal best brings out the two sides to Vidyasagar, the man and the reformer: his sentimentality and deep compassion, along with an unflinching firmness of purpose. The status of the widow, or more specifically, her right to marry, was a question that had moved upper classes in Bengal at least 100 years before Vidyasagar. And, as evident in Vidyasagar's own time, this often began with the deeply traumatic personal experiences of members of the suffering widow's family. In 1756, Raja Rajballabh, a powerful zamindar of the Dhaka-Vikrampur region, unable to withstand the plight of his young widowed daughter, tried to persuade a team of Brahmin pundits to sanction her marriage. This move was subsequently defeated due to stiff resistance from the more influential feudal potentate, Maharaja Krishnachandra Ray (1710–83) of Nadia. This could well have been a matter of personal rivalry between two powerful figures aspiring for social and political ascendancy, but it so happened that one of them, Krishnachandra, was a Brahmin by birth and Rajballabh, a Baidya. His Brahmin birth fortified Krishnachandra's status as *samajpati*, or one who had the power and authority to control social norms. Raja Krishnachandra used this status to good effect in thwarting Rajballabh's plans. Krishnachandra's displeasure, apart from his objections to the act of widow marriage itself, was against the ritual innovations being attempted at the time by the local Baidyas, hitherto considered an intermediary caste. We gather that in the eighteenth century, they were trying to assume the status of the Vaishya in the *varna* hierarchy. This was evident in the efforts of Rajballabh, who encouraged fellow Baidyas to assume the sacred thread and even to shorten the period of ritual mourning in keeping with the norms followed by Brahmins and other upper castes. For Krishnachandra, this was no less a threat to Brahmanism than the act of introducing widow marriage in Hindu society, and hence he stalled both moves by summoning a rival team of pundits who were persuaded to rule against the attempted innovation.

There is an apocryphal story of how Krishnachandra manipulated the pundits to rule in his favour. It is said that when Rajballabh's team of pundits visited Nadia, they were offered a calf buffalo as part of the culinary arrangements. When the invited Brahmins refused to eat the meat of a buffalo on the grounds of customary prohibitions, Krishnachandra's men were quick to point out that a similar reasoning may equally be applied to the taboo on widow marriages. There is no way of determining the veracity of this story, and yet it does underscore the power of custom (*deshachar*) in practically determining everyday practices, a realisation that progressively dawned on Vidyasagar rather belatedly and took the wind out of his sails. That widow marriage among upper-caste Hindus had long since fallen out of favour was granted by no less a man than Rammohun himself in his work *Pathyapradan* (1823), in which he found the practice contrary to *sadvyabahar*, that is, social ideals set by the 'respectable' and the 'wise'. All the same, Rammohun was truly concerned about the rights accruing to Hindu women, particularly in matters relating to her right to property and inheritance. He discussed this in his work of 1822 called *Modern Encroachments on the Ancient Rights of Females.* The issue of widow marriages also entered the reformist agenda of both the raja and his close followers, however briefly. We know from the *Calcutta Journal* of 3 May 1819 that this had been discussed during a meeting of the Atmiya Sabha, the body of like-minded friends and co-workers that the raja had founded in 1815.

Nothing positive appears to have emerged on this front until about the mid-1830s. Bengal was still being rocked by the controversy surrounding the legal prohibition of sati in 1829 and the movement of conservative resistance building up against it under the leadership of the Dharma Sabha. It is noteworthy that even the State deferred determining public opinion on the issue of widow marriages until 1837, when the Law Commission headed by John Peter Grant sought the opinion of the *Sadar Adalat*s of the three Presidencies. Hitherto, the government's hands had been tied by the fact that under both Halhed's *Code* of 1776 and Colebrooke's *Digest of Hindu Laws*, widow marriages were not deemed legally valid. Predictably, the *Sadar Adalat*s returned a negative verdict, declaring the proposed move to legalise widow marriages to be an imprudent innovation. It was only the Bengali press that kept public interest alive on the issue, albeit sporadically. In the 1830s and 1840s, this also brought forth some new features such as women correspondents writing directly to popular journals, complaining about the plight of the Hindu widow and advocating the idea of widow marriages. This took place in the *Samachar Durpan* of 14 March 1835, which published correspondence from some women of Santipur (district Nadia); in another instance, a widow from Chinsura (district Hooghly) wrote to say that a widowed woman ought to be able to marry just as freely as a widowed man. On 29 April 1837, the journal *Jnanyeshan*, edited by the Derozian

Rasik Krishna Mallik (1810–58), proposed a public meeting to discuss the modalities of widow marriages. In April 1842, the *Bengal Spectator*, a journal also run by Young Bengal, published a long essay titled 'Remarriage of Widows' in support of widow marriage. This essay and the one preceding it in the *Reformer* (25 November 1838), edited by Prasannakumar Tagore (1801–68), both cited the favourable ruling from Parasar. The *Bengal Spectator* is believed to have put this in the following words:

> In 1756, Raja Rajbullubh Roy Bahadoor of Dacca, wishing to have his daughter, who had become a widow, married again, applied to the learned pundits of Dacca, Telinga, Benares, Mithila etc. to communicate to him their opinion on the subject which they unanimously expressed in the following words (here follow the lines from Parasar).

Some scholars doubt whether Young Bengal was actually aware of this ruling, since this takes away from the account of Vidyasagar's close friend, Rajkrishna Bandopadhyay, who claimed to have been a personal witness to the Pundit's dramatic 'discovery' of the verse from Parasar when working late one night sometime either during the closing months of 1853 or in early 1854. On the other hand, it seems unlikely that Vidyasagar, then serving the Fort William College, would not have heard of something this sensational being discussed amongst his colleagues or co-workers. In his *Ramatanu Lahiri O Tatkalin Banga Samaj* (Ramatanu Lahiri and Contemporary Bengali Society, 1903), a valuable social and intellectual history of the period, the Brahmo reformer Sibnath Sastri confirms that the verses from Parasar were indeed first published in the *Bengal Spectator*, although he also admitted that he could not be certain if some pundits like Vidyasagar and Madanmohan Tarkalankar had helped them locate these. That Sastri considered help from Vidyasagar to be even within the realm of possibility puts a new twist on the argument. If at all the Pundit had been aware of the *sloka* from Parasar as early as 1842, what indeed was he doing between such time and 1853–54?

On 11 March 1845, the man to first perform the role of Minister to the Brahmo Samaj, Acharya Ramchandra Vidyavagish (1786–1845), issued a *vyavastha* supporting widow marriage. Brian A. Hatcher would have us believe that this came in response to a query put by William Theobold, Secretary to the British Indian Society. Ideally, the Acharya's *vyavastha* ought to have carried some credibility for he had once taught *smriti* at the Sanskrit College itself. It is not known if the Acharya too had taken recourse to Parasar. If he had not, what did he base his arguments on? And if indeed there were supporting texts other than Parasar, why did Vidyasagar not cite them? Incidentally, Acharya Ramachandra was also to support the move to end polygamous marriages through a series of lectures collectively titled 'Neetidarshan'. This is all the more significant given the fact that in the earlier controversy surrounding sati, he had actually sided with the anti-reform party and against Rammohun. Initially, support also came from the otherwise conservative *Sangbad Prabhakar* (of 25 March 1852), which exhorted young men to courageously take to marrying widows. The *Prabhakar*, however, was to radically change its position in the days to come.

Even before he had published his two successive tracts supporting widow marriage in January and October 1855, respectively, Vidyasagar called on the conservative leader, Raja Radhakanta Deb (1783–1867), the architect of the Dharma Sabha that had fought the sati legislation both in India and in England. This was not an unnatural thing to have done since the Debs of Sovabazar represented one of the most powerful factions (*dals*) in early colonial Calcutta that controlled community life in that city. Apparently Vidyasagar had not, at the time, permanently settled on the idea of social legislation, and was hoping to have his goals met by persuading a *dalapati* (leader of a faction) himself. That the rich and the powerful (in Sri Ramakrishna's evocative language, *bodomanush*) had their own ways of influencing public opinion is evident from Bankim's descriptions in his novel, *Bishbrikha* (1873), which also deals with the issue of clandestine love involving a widow. Interestingly enough, the idea of tactically involving Radhakanta also occurs in a modern play authored by one of Bengal's renowned literary figures, Balaichand Mukhopadhayay (1899–1979) alias 'Bonophool'. In the play (*Vidyasagar*, 1948), a Brahmin pundit suggests that if Radhakanta were favourably inclined, widow marriages would begin to be accepted in no time. In Vidyasagar's own lifetime, this argument was to be echoed quite emphatically by a man of aristocratic origins, Pramathabhushan Deb of Naldanga, Jessore. Writing to the government in January 1885, Deb observed the following:

> In Bengal, society is led by rich men of the upper classes, the mass of the people following in their wake. The priests and the pundits watch which way the wind blows and shape their opinions accordingly. They have no power to ex-communicate or persecute anybody.

In Mukhopadhyay's play, however, Radhakanta himself is shown to argue that the matter was really in the hands of the pundits. Perhaps the raja was personally flexible enough to yield to the merit of Vidyasagar's arguments, for he is known to have appreciated these even in a public meeting. At this meeting, he had patiently listened to opposing parties and concluded it by honouring Vidyasagar with an expensive shawl. However, the Pundit would have been naively mistaken had he taken this to be a sign of support or encouragement, since soon after, the raja similarly honoured Pundit Brojnath Vidyaratna, a *smarta* scholar of Nadia, who led the opposition. Sensing such vacillation in Radhakanta and given his apparent inability to rise above popular sentiment, which at the time was strongly in favour of the conservative party, Vidyasagar finally staked his efforts and reputation on the will of the English ruling class. As it turned out, in Calcutta itself, Vidyasagar's efforts at drawing public support for widow marriages was defeated by the fact that all three powerful *dals* based in the city, led by Radhakanta Deb, Radhamadhab Bandopadhyay, and Ashutosh Deb, respectively, were opposed to it.

The two tracts on widow marriage authored by Vidyasagar differ somewhat in the nature of their enterprise. While the first of these, earlier published in the *Tattwabodhini Patrika* of January 1855, laid out the *shastric* argument in favour of widow marriages, the second, published in October that year, was a rebuttal of scholars who had argued against the legal validity of widow marriages. Not surprisingly, the first book was a runaway success compared to the second; 1,000 copies of this book were sold out within a week of its publication and 3,000 extra copies had to be soon printed. In 1856, Vidyasagar published a partial English translation of the tracts, presumably in the hope of catching the attention of English officials. A combined volume comprising both parts was printed thrice between 1857 and 1872.

Vidyasagar admits to have been elated at the overwhelming public response to his tracts. What he might have overlooked, though, was the shallowness of the excitement and sheer sensationalism that the tracts first elicited, which could easily be mistaken for genuine interest or support. His readers were more curious than motivated, more struck by the novelty of the idea than its reasonableness. What also accounts for their popularity is the fact that the tracts were written in chaste Bengali, which both the traditional pundit and the neo-educated in Bengal could easily comprehend. In the controversy that later followed over polygamy, what partly defeated the opposition was that its rejoinders were written in Sanskrit, which practically limited the readership to the traditional literati in Calcutta and elsewhere.

Perhaps the most important intervention that occurred immediately after Vidyasagar published his two successive tracts was an essay by Pearychand Mitra (1814–83) that appeared in the July–December 1855 issue of the *Calcutta Review*. This was based on Vidyasagar's writings and the draft bill prepared under the supervision of the Law Member, Auckland Colvin. A Derozian by disposition, Pearychand, along with fellow Derozian Radhanath Sikdar (1813–73). had been running the *Masik Patrika* which regularly took up woman-related issues. Pearychand's essay was critically framed and while fully supporting the institution of widow marriage, he also pointed to some vital and hitherto unforeseen problems that lay on the path of prospective reformers.

In substance, Mitra made five points of practical importance. First, he pointed out that there was still no clear definition of what constituted a valid widow marriage, especially since the existing law was opposed to such marriages. Hence, he asked, was the State or the people involved willing to undertake an innovation in law? Even at this stage, Pearychand could sense that operatively, the procedure to be followed in such marriages had to be solemnised by the marrying parties, not the legislature. Second, could a man take a widow as his second wife? Third, could the intending partners marry outside their respective castes? Fourth, Pearychand took a broader view of the whole problem by linking the issue of widow marriages to that of a propitious age for marrying girls. Could a child widow of seven years, he asked, be married off just because she was a widow? Finally, Pearychand also detected an anomaly in the proposed Act. Assuming that the proposal to disinherit the married widow under Section 2 of the proposed Act became law, he feared that this would prove unjust for many. While the widow who married as a Hindu could lose her inheritance upon marrying, given the Lex Loci Act (Civil Disabilities Removal Act) of 1850, the same would not apply to a Hindu who had converted to another faith.

In hindsight, we know that the problems anticipated by Mitra proved to be very realistic in nature. For one, men were indeed found to be marrying widows even when their first wives were living, purely for the sake of the monetary incentive that came with such marriages. At some stage in his campaign, Vidyasagar had to insist on the marrying partners signing a contract that ruled out bigamy. Also, widow marriages rarely coincided with inter-caste marriages; a solitary case reported in 1864 involved Parvati Charan Das, in all probability of the Kayastha caste, with the Brahmin woman Swarnamayee. However, such marriages were relatively more common among Brahmos. The Brahmin

Sasipada Banerjee married a widow from a non-Brahmin caste and even got his niece married to a man belonging to the Sudra *varna*. The issue of favouring the marriage of child widows was actually a vexed one. Quite clearly, it invited far less social opposition, and surely Vidyasagar would have been relatively more successful had he limited his campaign to the marriage of child widows. Only a few months before the passing of the 1856 Act, some pundits in Calcutta had responded favourably to the appeal made by one Shyamacharan Das to get his widowed daughter married. The precondition they insisted on was that the girl had to be a virgin (*akshatayoni*). However, as Dayaram Gidumal was to later point out in 1889, it was not important to marry all girls and, in any case, marriage was not the sole end of a woman's existence. At the time, though, this must have sounded like a forlorn voice, especially in Bengal.

In his tracts, Vidyasagar also insisted that the rites and rituals followed in instances of widow marriage be identical to those followed in the case of virgins. From the point of view of legitimising widow marriages, this is perfectly understandable. On the other hand, it is quite possible that this further offended the orthodoxy and made their opposition even more resolute. Colonial ethnography (as for instance the writings of James Wise on eastern Bengal) does reveal that among castes where widow marriage was known to have been practised, the married widow had to put up with certain restrictions, such as not being allowed to serve food in a community gathering. During his widow marriage campaign in Bombay, Ranade himself advocated two sets of marriage rites: Vedic marriage rites for the virgin widow and a different set for those whose previous marriage had been consummated.

Vidyasagar's own arguments in favour of widow marriages may be summarised as follows:

1. Dharma or righteous conduct in life is determined by *shastra*; hence that which is in conformity with *shastra* has to be *dharmic*.

2. Widow marriage is *dharmic* because *shastra* sanctions it.
3. Widow marriage is valid in Kaliyuga since this is permitted by the sage and law giver, Parasar.
4. Parasar is the special authority for the determining of appropriate rites and usages in Kaliyuga.
5. Parasar offers three courses of action for the widow: *sahamarana* (con-cremation), *brahmacharya* (celibacy), and *vivaha* (marriage).
6. Since *sahamarana* is now prohibited under law, it cannot be practically adopted as a course of action. Effectively, that leaves the widow with two choices: *brahmacharya* and *vivaha*.
7. Now, since living a life of strict celibacy is especially hard in degenerative Kaliyuga, it cannot be the desired or expedient course of action.
8. That renders *vivaha* as the best course of action for the widow.
9. Even though there are objections to widow marriage put forth in certain Puranic texts, such as the *Aditya Purana* and the *Vrihadnaradiya Purana*, these can easily be set aside on the strength of the exegetical principle whereby, in the event of any conflict of opinion between a Purana and Smriti, the latter takes precedence.
10. Under Hindu law, a woman remarried is called *punarbhu* and the offspring born of her, *pounarbhava*. In listing the categories of sons born to a woman, Parasar makes no reference to the category of *pounarbhava* and since Parasar also authorises widow marriages, it must be assumed that he equates the son born to a married widow with a biological offspring (*ourasa*). This makes the son socially acceptable and legally entitled to all inheritance permitted under Hindu law.

Not surprisingly, most of these were subsequently contested and the resulting controversy stretched over a long time. Even some thirty years after the Bill was made into law in 1856,

Vidyasagar continued producing pseudonymous tracts answering his pundit critics. Two of the relatively well-known ones are the *Brojo Bilas* (1884) addressed to Pundit Brojonath Vidyaratna of Nadia, and the *Ratna Parisksha* (1886) addressed to Pundits Bhuvanmohan Vidyaratna, Prasannachandra Nyayaratna, and Madhusudan Smritiratna. A third pseudonymous tract of 1884 was directed at the Hindu Dharma Rakshini Sabha of Jessore (now in Bangladesh).

After several hearings of the Bill, interrupted by numerous petitions and counter-petitions, it was finally passed and thereafter came to be called Act XV of 1856. By one estimate, there were fifty-one petitions in all, twenty-three in favour of the bill and twenty-eight against. However, the ratio between the two in terms of signatories is quite telling. The number of signatures in favour of the bill was 5,192 and those against, a staggering 55,746. There also circulated a huge number of protest pamphlets, some addressed to Vidyasagar himself and others to the interested public. One Gangadhar Kaviratna of Murshidabad alone contributed twenty-two of these. Kaviratna was also to be in the forefront of the opposition to Vidyasagar's tract on polygamy. Even before the Bill had been passed, Pundit Padmalochan Nyayaratna, serving the state of Burdwan, wrote a 192-page pamphlet (*Vidhaba Vivaha Howa Uchit Kina* / Should Widow Marriages be Solemnised?, 1855). The Brahmo Prasannakumar Mukhopadhyay's pamphlet titled *Vidabha Vivaha Prachalita Howa Uchit Nahe* / Widow Marriages Should not be Solemnised) expressed the fear that once passed, the Act would encourage women to murder their husbands and seek paramours of their choice. In 1859, in one of the rare English-language pamphlets (*The Remarriage of Aryan Ladies Refuted*), Jogendranath Tarkchudamani alleged that children born of a widow would turn out to be monstrous. Even the German Orientalist Hemann Brockhaus (1806–77), in an essay he wrote in 1865 honouring Vidyasagar and his work (*Die Werke Des Iswarchandra Vidyasagara*), admitted that he did not agree with the Pundit's line of argument over the widow marriage issue, even though he was touched and overwhelmed by the deep connections he found between contemporary reformist thought in India and the cause of humanity.

In essence, four kinds of objections surfaced during the controversy: those alleging a misinterpretation of *shastra*, those offended at the violation of an established custom, objections to State intervention, and arguments that rested on eschatological concerns. Pandit Panchanan Tarkaratna (1866–1940), a young and accomplished *smriti* scholar from Bhatpara whom Vidyasagar had personally known and admired, was to echo the popular argument that a daughter could not be gifted twice, and that in truth, Parasar had really allowed the second gifting only in the case of a daughter who had been previously betrothed to some other man and not that of a married woman. In his *Vidabha Vivaha Nishedh* (Widow Marriages Prohibited), Pitambar Sen observed that the term 'Vidhaba' (widow) did not at all occur in Parasar, and wondered just what rites had to be followed when marrying widows since the *shastra*s had left no clues on the subject. Widowhood, it was further argued, followed from karmic blemishes. and while one may empathise with the fate of the widow, there was no way in which a preordained event could be overturned by human will or effort. The argument that enjoyed rapidly increasing popularity was that which challenged the legal intervention of an alien State. There was also a technical aspect attached to the argument that could not be easily brushed aside. Kashiprosad Ghosh, for instance, argued that even in British jurisprudence, usage constituted the basis of law, and that widow marriages had not been in vogue for a long time was beyond doubt. Over time, the argument against social legislation also acquired some political dimensions, with the act of law-making itself being connected to the right of self-determination by a people. People voicing such sentiments were not in principle opposed to the proposed law; what they resented was the way the process of law-making ignored their legitimate political rights and ambitions.

Vidyasagar himself continued to be opposed and slandered in the press and on platforms well after the Act had been passed and widow marriages solemnised. In May–June 1880, an essay in the journal *Bongodarshan* argued that the hardships allegedly faced by widows were grossly exaggerated by the pro-reform party. Doubts were expressed over whether Kalimati Devi, the first widow to be married under the Act in December 1856, was indeed a widow, and allegations made about Vidyasagar unscrupulously and secretly bribing willing parties. On 7 November 1886, the *Dacca Prakash* accused him of corrupting the youth. The biographer Biharilal Sarkar was to make the unkind and grossly unjust insinuation that the Sanskrit pundits in favour of the Bill, such as Taranath Tarkavachaspati, Girishchandra Vidyaratna, and Bharatchandra Shiromani, happened to be colleagues and subordinates of Vidyasagar in the Sanskrit College. In the meantime, reports continued to pour in of young widows being touted for a life of prostitution in the city of Calcutta, or how a widowed girl's father and brothers had opted to secure for her a paramour rather than seek marriage. In villages, the pro-reform party had also to put up with persecution by local potentates and zamindars, almost all of whom opposed the idea of widow marriages. At the Jehanabad sub-division in district Hooghly, the local landlord, Sibnarayan Ray, ordered that men abetting a widow marriage be publicly beaten with shoes. It was also reported that the concerned Deputy Magistrate prevented the people so assaulted from filing a complaint for as many as four successive days. Matters had reached such a depressing state that the journal *Bharat Sanskarak*, on 2 October 1874, was constrained to remark that the abolition of sati had actually worsened the plight of Hindu widows. Arguably, there was greater dignity in even self-immolation than spending a lifetime in depravity and under duress.

The position of the ruling classes on the issue, however, was very different. In 1856, the State was not interested in drawing connections between eschatological faith and law; it was more interested in social equity. Also, barring the earlier prohibition of sati in 1829, Act XV of 1856 was the first piece of social legislation designed to assuage the moral courage of the British, as well as that of Indian reformers. The government's position, as clearly enunciated by John Peter Grant, was that it did not seek to determine which of the interpretations offered in the heat of controversy was correct; it simply wished to enact a law that would merely enable the willing widow to marry. And yet, a good part of the problems faced by the State was created by its failure to place custom on a statutory footing in the case of Bengal. By 1876, this had been enforced in the Punjab, Madras, and Oudh.

There is no reliable list of widow marriages held in Bengal immediately after 1856, and perhaps such a list would have been difficult to compile given some obvious constraints. In any case, the number was nowhere near the figure of 300 that Ranade claimed was true of Maharashtra between 1856 and 1900. On the other hand, we must also concede that the prohibition on widow marriages among upper castes in pre-colonial Maharashtra and Gujarat does not appear to have been as strictly enforced as it was in Bengal. In Maharashtra, the Peshwas are known to have permitted this and even collect taxes on this account.

In ethnic Bengal, the first widow marriage to be solemnised on 7 December 1856 between Srishchandra Vidyaratna and Kalimati Devi, both Brahmins, was something of a sensation. From reports that appeared in the press, we hear that on the particular evening, the streets were literally choked by a gathering of curious and excited onlookers that included schoolboys, housewives, and people of all descriptions. For the sake of safety and convenience, the marriage itself was held in premises belonging to Vidyasagar's friend, Rajkrishna Bandopadhyay. Reportedly, English soldiers were kept on alert close by so as to prevent any untoward occurrence. An estimated Rs 10,000 were spent on this occasion, mostly by Vidyasagar himself. By 1867, his expenses on account of such marriages amounted to Rs 82,000, of which only about half had been met by way of donations. For a long time, the onus of finding suitable marriage partners as well as meeting the bulk of the expenses rested on Vidyasagar, until there came a time when he had to specifically warn parties intending to marry that he would not commit himself financially beyond a point. For example, families arriving in Calcutta from outlying areas had soon to be disabused of the notion that widow marriages held in the city fetched ornaments and handsome gifts for the willing bride.

There were three significant features of the first widow marriage that need to be noted here. First, the groom, Srishchandra, once a student at Sanskrit College, developed cold feet as the day of marriage approached, and somewhat reluctantly agreed to the arrangements after *The Englishman* of 27 November 1856 harshly rebuked him for backtracking. Second, on the day of the marriage, the daughter had to be given away by the mother, herself a widow, and contrary to convention, as no male relative agreed to be present. By one account, she was later made an outcast. Third, after his wife Kalimati died prematurely, Srishchandra had to undergo a series of expiations in order to be accepted back into his community.

Given below is a list of a few widow marriages that took place in Bengal for a little over a decade following 1856, which can be authenticated by available records. In some cases, the identities of the marrying parties are also known:

1. 7 December 1856: Srishchandra Vidyaratna, Judge Pandit at Murshidabad, and Kalimati Devi.
2. 25 Aghrayan 1263 bs (December 1856): Madammohan Ghosh of Presidency College, Calcutta, and Thakomani Dasi, aged twelve.
3. 11 Phalgun 1263 bs (21 February 1857): Durgacharan Basu, cousin of Rajnarayan Basu, and Gobindamani Dasi, aged fourteen.
4. 26 Phalgun 1263 bs (8 March 1857): Madanmohan Basu, brother of Rajnarayan Basu, and Nityakali Dasi. The marriage had to be arranged secretly while Rajnarayan's mother was away on pilgrimage. Vidyasagar pledged a monthly sum of Rs 10 to Nityakali.

5. Aghrayan 1264 bs (November–December 1857): Jadunath Chattopadhyay of Sanskrit College and Lakhimani Devi, aged thirteen.
6. Ashad–Sravan 1265 (July–August 1858): Fifteen widow marriages were held in Jehanabad sub-division, as reported by Deputy Magistrate Maulavi Abdul Latif Khan.
7. 10 Phalgun 1270 bs (February–March 1864): Brahmin widow married.
8. 11 Magh 1271 bs (January–February 1864): Baidya widow married.
9. 1868: Jogendranath Vidyabhushan, literary figure, married a widow with the help of Sivanath Sastri.
10. 19 November 1868: The marriage of Nabakumar and Bhuvanmoyee Devi in Dacca, as reported by *Amrit Bazar Patrika*.
11. 1869: Muchiram Bandopadhyay and Manmohini Devi at Birsingha; an incident that led to Vidyasagar severing his links with his native village.
12. 22 Sravan 1277 (August 1870): Narayanchandra Bandopadhyay, son of Vidyasagar, with Bhavasundari Devi.
13. June 1890: Durgamohan Das and Hemantasashi Sen, daughter of Kalinarayan Gupta.

It is reasonable to conclude that there could not have been more than sixty to seventy widow marriages in Bengal in Vidyasagar's lifetime. This list excludes widow marriages among Brahmos, the first of which occurred in 1864, involving Gurucharan Mahalonobis (1833–1916), the grandfather of Prasantachandra Mahalonobis (1893–1972). Reportedly, there were eight more such marriages held in the next five years. Durgamohan Das (1841–97) of Barisal created quite a sensation by getting his young but widowed step-mother married. In June 1890, he himself married Hemantasashi, the widowed mother of Atulprosad Sen (1871–1934), the well-known songwriter and musician. With respect to widow marriages, the Brahmos appear to have a complex history. Brahmo missionaries like Sivanath Sastri, Sasipada Banerjee, and Durgamohan Das contributed greatly towards rescuing stranded widows and rehabilitating them subsequently. Between them, Das and Banerjee sheltered about thirty-five widows at Barahanagar itself. Das even had his widowed step-mother married to a friend. On the other hand, we also know of Sasipada's son, who impregnated a widow by the name of Tara at the Barahnagar Home but refused to marry her. The woman had eventually to be married to another Brahmo by the name of Kunja Bihari Sen, who turned out to be a wife-beater. On 17 April 1891, the *Education Gazette O Saptahik Vartavaha* reported the murder of a widowed Brahmo girl by one Ambica Charan Basu, allegedly a desperately frustrated lover. The severely mutilated body of the girl was left at the doors of the Sadharan Brahmo Samaj office. This particular episode later inspired a novel (*Murala*, 1892) by Deviprasanna Raychaudhuri (1854–1920), a man who arranged for his widowed sister to be married according to Brahmo rites. For a time, it would seem that the Brahmos also had the additional problem of which marriage rites to follow, those used in Hindu marriages or the reformed rites initiated by Debendranath Tagore. Rajnarayan Basu himself consulted Vidyasagar on this question when it came to the marriage of his daughter, but did not obtain any clear directions (see Appendix IV).

That the question of widow marriage was still alive and being publicly debated in Bengal even in the 1870s is evident from the Tagore Law lectures of 1879 (published in 1881), delivered by one Trailokyanath Mitra. In this lecture, Mitra takes a very critical view of Vidyasagar and of his *modus operandi*, raising a number of legal anomalies, whether actual or potential. I list below certain qualifying notes that the *Parasar Samhita* itself and Mitra's work have encouraged me to prepare:

1. That Parasar is the sole authority for Kaliyuga is apparently not supported by other legal texts either preceding or

succeeding it. Rammohun himself relied on Manu and took the view that Manu alone was applicable for all ages. Did Rammohun not know of the *Parasar Smriti* and of its special status? His texts do not mention the text of Parasar, although it mentions many others. The point, though, is that even if he had known of it, Parasar could not have been of any use to him since it sanctions *sahamarana*, which Rammohun was personally fighting. Interestingly, Parasar himself does not appear to believe that his text could override earlier texts, Manu in particular. Manu is classed as 'the only omniscient authority that possesses knowledge of all shastras' (IX.51). Further, Parasar places some of his own precepts under those of Manu.

2. Did Vidyasagar not display some haste in resting his case on Parasar alone? In a detailed note on the 'Vedic Authorities for Widow Marriage' (1887?), Ranade found as many as eight *smriti* works that also supported widow marriages. As early as 1855, Pearychand Mitra, citing Arthur Steele's *Summary of the Laws and Customs of the Hindu Castes* (1827), had expressed doubts about Parasar being the only authority in Kaliyug. Benoy Ghose refers to a *Kulapanji* (genealogical table) belonging to the seventeenth century which refers to a Kulin Brahmin male, Rajnarayan, marrying the widowed daughter of one Ramjeebon Ray, apparently without any reference to Parasar. Madhva, the commentator on Parasar, disagreed with the claim that the text was specific to Kali which, of course, Vidyasagar disputed. This at once raises the question: What takes precedence, a *smriti* text or a commentary on it?
3. Assuming that the taboo on widow marriages preceded Parasar, it would have to be admitted that customary practices against widow marriages had the power to overtake scriptural sanctions. In case the taboos followed Parasar, it would also have to be admitted that in effect,

custom had the power to override the sanction of legal texts.

4. It is quite ironic how the *Parasar Smriti*, on which Vidyasagar rested his case, curses those guilty of ritual violations with prolonged widowhood!
5. In Jimutavahana's *Dayabhaga* (Chapter XI, Section ii), the legal code that was traditionally applicable to Bengal, the rules of inheritance excluded childless widows and barren daughters. Based on this, it is possible to argue that had widow marriages been in vogue in Jimutavahana's time, there could have been no reason to deny inheritance to childless daughters since they could procreate on their being married a second time.

Admittedly, Vidyasagar felt increasingly isolated over the widow marriage question. A closer scrutiny will reveal that even his supporters were not united in themselves. His support came essentially from two quarters: first, the older generation of liberal, Western-educated individuals, and second, the radical youth. The first, although in genuine sympathy with Vidyasagar, were guilty of vacillation and dragging their feet interminably; the young, on the other hand, were numerically too insignificant to make a difference. For widow marriages to succeed in both form and spirit, traditional notions of Hindu conjugality itself had also to undergo certain meaningful changes, which they declined to do at the time. That being said, it has also to be admitted that the limits to Vidyasagar's widow marriage campaign were partly set by Vidyasagar himself. For one, the man was reluctant to support godless marriages, which did not go by any religious or customary rites. To the Brahmo Gurucharan Mahalonobis, he promised help in marrying a young widow from Vikrampur, Kumudini Devi, provided he settled on Hindu marriage rites, which Mahalonobis refused to do. He never encouraged widows marrying under Act III of 1872; in this instance, what irked him was the declaration required of the marrying parties that they did not belong to any established religion. Reportedly, Vidyasagar found this 'bizarre'. It is also somewhat surprising that he never brought up the issue of legally abolishing premature marriages, even when this had a great bearing on his other social campaigns. Undoubtedly, when attempting to popularise widow marriages, his social constituency was limited to upper and middle-class women. Ironically enough, as established by the Census of 1891, several intermediary artisanal and agricultural castes like Sadgops, Sunris, Mahisyas, Telis, and Moiras had begun to turn away from the prospects of promoting widow marriages in their respective communities, where no such embargo might previously have existed. James Wise, writing in the early 1880s, noted as many as twelve *jatis* in eastern Bengal which approved of widow marriages. He also makes the startling claim that in neighbouring Kamrup, even Vaidik Brahmins were known to get their widows married. On 19 August 1876, a paper with a good circulation in rural Bengal, the *Gramvarta Prakashika*, reported that widow marriages, if promoted among lower castes, too, would have helped the dwindling population of the *dhopa* (washeman), *napit* (barber), and *tantubay* (weaver) castes.

And yet, it is very unlikely that Vidyasagar's project was fully complicit in the upper-caste patriarchal move to control female sexuality, in particular the potentially dangerous non-wife, as some feminist authors have made this out to be. In contemporary Bengal, and speaking from a patriarchal perspective, it would have to be granted that when compared to the widow, the Hindu wife herself posed no less of a threat. This was precisely the remark that the writer of the 1880 *Bongodarshan* essay had made, and his purpose here was to assuage widespread fears of widows being especially vulnerable to temptations of the flesh. When Sri Ramakrishna spoke of the threat from the 'Kamini', his reference was not to the age or marital status of the woman, but to the alluring and innate female sexuality *per se* that men were expected to vigilantly guard against. Contrary to claims sometimes made, Vidyasagar's feelings for the persecuted woman were not born of some condescension and paternalistic empathy; they were simply generated by kindliness and a sense of social justice in favour of a class that was just beginning to find its voice. Rather than Vidyasagar himself, it was the colonial State that ultimately appeased the orthodoxy by taking away the inheritance rights of the marrying widow.

Although the attempt to promote the marriage of Hindu widows failed to receive the public support that Pundit Iswarchandra might have expected, the government itself attached great importance to it. In 1877, when conferring Vidyasagar with the title of CIE, Sir Richard Temple, the then Lt. Governor of Bengal, especially praised his work as the undisputed 'leader' of the entire campaign.

Some interesting facts related to widow marriages in Bengal need to be mentioned here, if only in passing. First, the controversy around the issue did not die down for a long time even after the Act was passed. I have found references to some Bengali-language tracts that were produced well beyond the 1920s, and in areas outside ethnic Bengal. Two of these were published from Gauhati and Tippera, respectively, in 1924–25. Also of some interest are two successive pro-reform tracts authored by a woman, Kumudini Ghosh Jaya, from Sirjagunj (Pabna) between 1924 and 1926. In the 1920s, we also hear of the Namasudras seriously debating the issue of widow marriages, and of a body called the *Hindu Vidhaba Vivaha Sahayak Sabha* (Organisation Supporting the Marriage of Hindu Widows) founded in Dhaka. Also interesting is the fact that it was another rebellious Brahmin, Digindranarayan Bhattacharya (b. 1884), who seriously agitated for the relaxation of dietary restrictions traditionally enforced on the widow. His *Bidhabar Nirjala Ekadashi* (1926, 2e) strongly pleaded for the removal of taboos on consuming food and drink on certain days of the lunar month. Even some pundits took to expressing their liberality through works of fiction. In the Pous 1321 bs (January 1915) issue of the Bengali journal *Bharatvarsha*, Mahamahopadhyay Jadeveswar Tarkaratna (1843–1924) authored a story titled 'Ekadashitattwa', in which a Hindu widow is seen to consume milk and fruit even on Ekadashi day (the eleventh day of the lunar month, considered ritually auspicious in the Hindu calendar). Predictably, this drew opposition from Pundit Panchanan Tarkaratna (1866–1940), a scholar once associated with the *Bangabasi Press*, who subsequently gave up his honorific title awarded by the government in protest against the framing of the Sarada Bill.[1]

Also visible is the connection that was increasingly drawn between the unpopularity of widow marriages and certain demographic anxieties involving the Hindus. This was quite emphatically argued by the well-known journalist Prafullakumar Sarkar (1884–1944) in his work *Khayishnu Hindu* (Degenerating Hindus, 1940). In the film *Vidyasagar*, released in 1956 under the M. P. Productions banner, we are also given to understand that the motive behind Vidyasagar's campaign to popularise widow marriages was a growing concern that Hindus would eventually be outnumbered by Muslims and Christians, following their successful attempts at converting the former. We do not know for certain whether Vidyasagar had heard of the efforts of Baba Padmanji (1831–1906) and his collaborator, Dadaji Pandurang Tarkhadkar (1819–82), in promoting widow marriages in Maharashtra. Padmanji produced the first novel in the Marathi language, *Yamuna Paryatan* (1857), in which the main protagonist is a woman by the name of Yamuna, who escapes the hard life of a Hindu widow by embracing Christianity. Padmanji's novel, coming so close on the heels of the widow marriage campaign in Bengal, could not have been entirely unaffected by it. On the other hand, what sets it apart is the blatantly propagandist tone. In the hands of Padmanji, the advocacy of widow marriage becomes only incidental to the larger question of proclaiming the superiority of Christianity over Hinduism. Ironically enough, even such a tendentious project did not preclude the use of a conventional, *Shastra*-based argument, much in the manner of Vidyasagar himself. Padmanji persuaded the Bombay reformer, Dadaji Pandurang, to author a Sanskrit tract (*Vidhavasumarjana*) favouring widow marriages, which was then appended to the printed copies of the novel. Whether Vidyasagar too perceived conversion as eventually posing a demographic threat to the Hindus is a question that must be left unanswered, given the present state of our knowledge. However, it is clear from the way he treated the case of Gurucharan Mahalonobis that for him, radicalism in the social sphere and the cultural could not be joined in any practical sense.

The Excesses of Kulinism

Multiple marriages among men have for long been a pan-Indian practice. However, in Bengal, the practice had certain distinctive historical roots going back to the twelfth–thirteenth century CE. Kulin polygamy was not simply a form of polygamy, but had acquired certain unique characteristics that do not appear to have been replicated elsewhere in India, at least not to the same degree or with comparable consequences. Primarily, Kulin polygamy denotes marital practices associated with Brahmins, which were later extended to Kayasthas as well. In the other upper-bracket caste of the Baidyas, notions of Kulinism appear to have arrived relatively later and with less rigour. The word Kulin commonly refers to social pedigree defined by the ritual and social purity of marital alliances, but its origins may lie in a more general attempt to reorganise and grade the Brahmin community by determining how closely they followed the Vedic praxis. The commonplace belief about a certain king by the name of Adisur organising an exodus of Brahmin and Kayastha families from Kanauj to re-Brahminise Bengal is more legend than history, and yet this does indicate a long entrenched cultural memory indicative of important social changes. Quite possibly, such changes came in the wake of an internally generated reform movement set to restore the decline of orthodox norms. This coincided with the coming to power (in the early twelfth century CE) of the Sena dynasty, which had displaced the Pala kings who had patronised Buddhism. Ballal Sen of this dynasty is usually credited with the creation of the Kulin system, by virtue of which Brahmins were expected to follow certain rules of conduct and exhibit certain ideal qualities. Reportedly, this system became hereditary under his successor, Laxman Sen, the last of the Sena kings in Hindu Bengal.

By this time, there had also arisen a special class of Brahmins called Ghataks, who generally supervised the quality of everyday Brahminical life. One of them, by the name of Devivar, introduced rigidity and complexity within the system by creating *mel*s or closed sub-classes within Brahmins. The *mel*s worked on the principles of endogamy, which is to say that each *mel* had a corresponding social group into which they could marry. This practically amounted to the closure of the system earlier known as *sarvadwari*, by which an exchange of Brahmin daughters could take place across ranks. Devivar also arranged the *mel*s hierarchically, going by the degree of ritual impurity incurred by each. There is a popular story to the effect that a ruler could easily judge the relative purity of a Kulin Brahmin by the length of time it took for him to report to the court when summoned. The presumption here was that the Kulin who dutifully observed every small rite or ritual required of him would naturally be the last to report! This was the very obverse of what Ballal had himself attempted.

Under Ballal's scheme, the marriage of a daughter into a good Kulin family appreciably raised the social status of the father. However, what followed was a demographic shift, whereby it became increasingly difficult to procure an unexceptionable husband, and even Kulin fathers were forced to give away their daughters in marriage to *Gauna*, *Srotriya*, and *Saptasati* families, sub-categories considered inferior in rank. Devivar's new classification had been confined to the Kulins alone, who were now divided into three grades of *Svabhaba* or natural Kulins, *Bhanga* or those who had somehow violated ritual proprieties in marriage, and *Vansaja*, who were guilty of worse violations. In a situation where many *mels* simply died out and where demographically, the number of Kulin families never matched those of the relatively inferior grades, there progressively developed a crisis, leading to the numerical increase of the *Bhanga* and *Vansaja* sub-orders. The demographic imbalance and the anxiety to upgrade one's family in public estimation combined to make polygamy among Kulins prescriptive. Boys of Kulin families were now obliged to marry not only a girl belonging to their own *mel*, but also those from the *Vansaja*, *Bhanga*, or *Srotriya*. The *mel* system, when fully implemented, also led to bizarre developments. Let us imagine a situation wherein family A was obliged to marry into family B. Now, if family A had only one son and family B, say, five daughters, the boy was compelled to marry all five, or else the daughters would remain unmarried all their lives. The pecuniary value of this culture of competition was great, and many Kulins could live simply by the wages of polygamy. But the opposite, too, occurred quite commonly. Kulin girls lived and died unmarried, victims of their father's inability to pay up *pon* or a marriage fee carefully calculated by the groom himself and by touts, who were also known as *ghataks*. A Kulin father had to either pay a prospective groom handsomely or, if he were too poor to do so, fix the marriage of his daughter who had just come of age to an octogenarian already married to several wives.

In her autobiographical fragment, Nistarini Devi (1825–1915) tells us that she was married at the age of eight or nine to a man of about twenty-five, who had already married about twenty-five women. Quite typically, she was never united with her husband or sent over to her husband's family, and virtually lived the life of a widow for the rest of her days. And yet, her family had to undertake to pay the groom's family a sum of Rs 5 every month. There were many instances where the husband would feed and clothe his wife only so long as the expenses were met by her own family, failing which she would be summarily turned out of the house, penniless and without any protection. Rashbihari Mukhopadhyay (1826–95), himself a Kulin and the man instrumental in popularising the drive against polygamy in east Bengal, confessed to have married eight times by the time he was in his teens, simply to overcome the grinding poverty that affected families such as his. Ethnographic reports of the period reveal that the practice of taking multiple wives was most common among *Bhanga* Kulin males. A *Bhanga* Kulin was usually one who, despite originally belonging to an upper strata of Kulins, had ritually disgraced himself by marrying the daughter(s) of a Brahmin of a rank inferior to his. Vidyasagar's own teacher in village Birsingha, Kalikanta Chattopadhyay, was a Bhanga Kulin who had married several times.

There could be two explanations for this. First, it is possible that this class was more numerous; second, as a class that had already fallen in ritual standing, as their very name suggests, they may have also enjoyed a competitive advantage. A *Bhanga* Kulin was probably more affordable for a father with several daughters of marriageable age. Finally, to put matters in a lighter vein, just as a criminal could not be punished twice for the same offence, *Bhanga* Kulins too came to realise that no matter how many more marriages they contracted, they could not sink any further down the ritual scale than they already had!

The evils of Kulinism were public knowledge as early as 1805, and appeared in Claudius Buchanan's *Memoirs of the Expediency of an Ecclesiastical Establishment for British India* (reprinted in 1812). Some twenty-four years later, this was also the subject of reports appearing in the *Calcutta Christian Observer*, and a work of 1822 by Rammohun also refers to the case of one Madho Singh, Raja of Tirhut, who had reportedly moved the government against the practice. In 1835, women writing to the *Samachar Darpan*, published from Serampore, persuasively argued against polygamy. About seven years later, the *Vidyadarshan*, a journal run by Vidyasagar's friend Akshaykumar Dutta, published heart-rending accounts authored by women themselves. One of these, a prostitute from Santipur, narrated how she had chanced upon as many as twenty of her childhood playmates in Calcutta brothels. Dutta himself narrated another incident: a Kulin passing through a village met a young boy who introduced himself as the man's son. The Kulin gentleman was astounded, to say the least, since he had never stepped into that village after the wedding night! Such scandalous stories were greatly in circulation in the contemporary Bengali press.

A serious move to draw official attention to the problem was made in 1855 when Vidyasagar submitted to the government a petition to legally end the practice. The petition carried the signatures of 25,000 Hindus, including that of the Maharaja of Burdwan. Kissorychand Mitra, representing the Young Bengal group, also submitted a petition on behalf of his reformist body, the Samaj Unnati Bidhayani Suhrid Samiti. By 1857, thirty-two petitions had been submitted in all, one of them drafted by Ramanath Roy, the son of Rammohun. Others who tried to move the government included the ruling houses of Nadia, Bhukailash, and Dinajpur. A petition submitted in 1856 by one Rajmohan Roy, a zamindar of Dhaka, carried the signatures of several Sanskrit scholars and pundits. A play titled *Kulin Kul Sarvasya Natak,* authored in 1854 by the dramatist Ramnarayan Tarkaratna (1822–86), was staged in 1856 at the house of one Ramjay Basak.

At this point, the events of 1857 intervened and the motion had to be stalled, to be revived only about nine years later, in 1866. That year, Vidyasagar submitted a fresh petition, again signed by several members of the royalty. On 19 March 1866, a deputation comprising some distinguished gentlemen of Calcutta, including Dwarkanath Mitra, Pearycharan Sarkar, and Pundit Bharatchandra Shiromani, called on the then Lt. Governor, Cecil Beadon, to earnestly request him to intervene in the matter. Beadon was both positive and hopeful and would have happily accepted the idea of even confining the proposed legislation to the province of Bengal. On 5 April 1866, the Bengal government wrote to the Government of India: '... it seems far better that the practice of unlimited polygamy should at once be restricted to Bengal where it pervades to an extent unknown elsewhere.' On 8 August, the Government of India wrote back to say that polygamy was a social and religious institution of the Hindus, and acknowledged 'the great difficulty of dealing with the subject'. This stalled the move for some time. Spirits were temporarily revived when, in 1867, a Special Committee was appointed to examine the issue in greater detail. It had two European members and five Indians, including Vidyasagar. The Committee submitted its report on 7 February 1867 and its verdict was somewhat confused and divided. The majority opinion on the issue amounted to saying that legally prohibiting polygamy on the basis of extant Hindu law would prove to be a difficult task since the *shastras* did allow a man to take several wives on grounds that might well seem frivolous and untenable under English law. More importantly, most members also felt that the evils of Kulinism had been exaggerated and that the declining incidence of such marriages in Bengal warranted the hope that it would soon go out of vogue. The Committee thus came to the conclusion that under the circumstances, a declaratory law against the practice ought not to be passed. Vidyasagar himself offered a note of dissent against this opinion, refuting each of the arguments made by his fellow Committee members. Reformist efforts also suffered a setback from a dispatch coming from the Secretary of State in London, which suggested that even in Bengal, Kulinism was too isolated a practice to merit the enactment of some sweeping prohibitory law. The Secretary of State had reason to add that his office was not even sure if the majority of people in the province of Bengal were decidedly against the practice of polygamy.

In hindsight, it would seem as though in relation to his widow marriage campaign, Vidyasagar used a different set of tactics for the anti-polygamy issue. In the earlier campaign, his tracts had eventually led to legislation; in this instance, having met with a rebuff, both from some of his countrymen and the government, and with the chances of a declaratory law visibly receding, he decided to take his efforts forward by producing texts addressed to the general public. In July 1871 and March 1872, the Pundit produced two papers on the subject under the title *Bahuvibaha Rahit Howa Uchit Kina Etadvishayak Prostab* (A Proposal Examining Whether or not the Practice of Polygamy

Should Cease). His arguments were supported by detailed inventories from select districts in Bengal of people who had entered into multiple marriages. Such lists were obviously based on meticulous personal inquiries since they identified people by name, residence, and the number of marriages each had contracted. In district Hooghly, for example, a certain Ramratna Mukhopadhyay, aged seventeen years, already had forty-eight wives, and another by the name of Dharmadas Mukhopadhyay, aged only five, as many as thirty-five. In his texts, Vidyasagar questioned not so much the issue of the Kulin's right to flaunt his social pedigree as the moral justification of it all.

As in the case of the widow marriage campaign, the first of the two tracts that Vidyasagar produced stated his case while the second proved to be extraordinarily polemical, personalised, and combative. In the second book, as many as 160 pages of a total length of 256 pages were spent in refuting the arguments of his erstwhile colleague from Sanskrit College, Pundit Taranath Tarkavachaspati. This polemic did not rest there but went on to produce anonymous pamphlets from both sides, which used language that was shockingly shallow and indecorous for men of learning. It has been claimed by some that Vidyasagar's engagement with Taranath was actually no more than a sentimental bid to vindicate himself and his scholarship. A closer examination reveals something refreshingly different. Vidyasagar faulted Taranath for grammatical irregularities, but more tellingly, was able to establish the claim that the pundit had actually made false claims and misled the public in the course of their exchanges. Incidentally, he was able to establish this only after much painstaking effort that required comparing Taranath's claims with the manuscript text he claimed to have cited in his support.

What arguments did Vidyasagar offer by way of urging the abolition of polygamy? Predictably, these too were based on *shastras*. In substance, the Pundit made the following points:

1. As per Hindu law, there could be two kinds of marriages, one that was dictated by *sanskar/vidhi* or the obligation

on the part of every Hindu male to fulfil certain ritual requirements, and the other, unions following from sexual passion (*kamya vivaha*).

2. Traditionally, the first was in the interests of progeny, and here, a man was to marry into his own *jati*. In the second case, he could marry both within and outside his *jati*. Vidyasagar's personal interpretation changed this to read that *kamya* marriages could take place only outside one's *jati*.
3. Further, since in Kaliyuga inter-caste marriages were prohibited, a man could not but limit his marriage to his first wife from his own *jati*. In effect, therefore, this was the only marriage that was valid in the eyes of the law.
4. The *shastras*, however, did allow certain exceptions to this rule, and a man could indeed take a second wife under certain contingencies, such as infertility in the wife, her death, or the death of a son born to the couple.

Here, it may be reasonably presumed that in the case of *kamya* marriages, the *Dharmashastras* would have prescribed only an *anuloma* marriage, that is, a marriage in which the *jati* or *varna* standing of the man would be higher than that of his wife. Going by Vidyasagar's interpretation, this was bound to create a problem for the Sudra male. Who would he marry within the *varna* hierarchy if and when driven by sexual passion alone?

Both in Pundit Iswarchandra's time and thereafter, objections were raised to these proposals. As early as 1 January 1866, a protest meeting of Kulin Brahmins was held under the leadership of Radhakanta Deb at the Hindu Metropolitan College, Calcutta, although the *Friend of India* was quick to notice that the opposition was not as formidable as had been feared by some. Several pundits of Nadia, it was observed, had voiced their concern at the continuing ill-effects of Kulinism. Even some orthodox Hindu bodies like the Sanatan Dharmarakhini Sabha of Jessore (now in Bangladesh) pleaded for the discontinuance of polygamous marriages. In the early 1870s and thereafter, some could even draw attention to certain anomalies in Pundit Iswarchandra's proposal. The most important of these came from Bankimchandra's review of Vidyasagar's tracts, published in the *Bongodarshan* in 1873. We now know that this so upset the Pundit that Bankim did not think of reprinting it until after the Pandit's death in 1891, and then in a modified form. Bankim conceded that the evils of polygamy had to go, but also felt that these evils had been somewhat exaggerated. Realistically speaking, he argued, Kulinism would cease to exist with time and with the progressive spread of education and the right social and moral values. Bankim also believed that the Pundit was using the *shastras* rather selectively, and even doubted the accuracy of his lists of polygamous Brahmins. One of his observations that still has a bearing on the question of a uniform system of personal law was whether it would be justifiable on the part of the British government to pass a law applicable to Hindus alone, excluding Muslims.

Vidyasagar's biographer Biharilal observed that the Pundit's argument about inter-caste marriage being barred in Kaliyuga had not been established convincingly, and the *Education Gazette* of 9 May 1873 pointed to the sharply conflicting interpretations of the relevant passages from Manu that Vidyasagar himself and his opponents had offered on a man's entitlement to take more than one wife. Arguably, Vidyasagar's error lay in assuming that Brahmin males entered into multiple marriages only because they were driven by sexual passion. In the case of Kulinism, however, genesis of this practice lay in poverty and certain perceived social needs. But what is more disconcerting, especially to modern sensibilities, are the exceptions permitted by the *shastras*, and which Vidyasagar fully endorsed. When, in 1871, Dwarkanath Vidyabhushan (1819–86), editor of the popular newspaper *Somprakash*, suggested that the government levy a stiff penalty on men intending to marry outside their first marriage, Vidyasagar opposed the move, stating that this would deny men the opportunity to rightfully contract a second marriage as per the ruling of the *shastras*, and what is more, this would also interfere with the religious practices of the Hindus. These exceptions that Vidyasagar accepted were based on two passages from Manu, which permitted a Hindu to enter into a second marriage if the wife gave birth to only daughters, showed malice, used foul language, or proved disobedient to him. The matter does not stop at that. When his critics pointed out to Vidyasagar that the royalty and aristocrats in India were known to freely marry a number of wives, the Pundit offered a reply that appears astonishing for a man of his learning and perspicacity. In his rejoinder, Vidyasagar defended such marriages with the argument that the ways of the royalty or of the gods could not possibly be emulated by ordinary men! In the 1870s, papers like the *Somprakash* and *Bharat Samskarak* also suggested that the matter of infertility in a woman was best determined through a medical examination, and that, after all, the fault may equally lie with the husband himself. To this, Vidyasagar shot back with the answer that the *shastras* had prescribed a waiting period of eight years, after which it was immaterial where the fault lay. In this instance, his continuing to rely on *shastras* pushed Vidyasagar to positions that were regressive even for his time.

It is also noticeable that in his second book, Vidyasagar modified his argument somewhat. It was now his plea that although the *shastras* did permit *kamya vivaha*, this was subject to the consent of the first wife, who could not be wronged or insulted under any circumstances. Vidyasagar strongly supported the institution of monogamy as well as the wife's fidelity to the husband. Both are evident in his *Star Banabas* (1860). But accompanying this is also his innate empathy for the fate that often befell women. The work ends with the following lines:

> Perhaps it was to impart the right lessons to humanity on the wife's fidelity to the husband (*pativratadharma*) that God created the character of Sita. It is doubtful if a woman as accomplished in every respect was ever born on this earth or if, having been joined to a husband as exemplary

in every respect as Ramchandra, a woman was subjected to such misery and unhappiness as she was. (Translated from *Sitar Banabas*)

The Raucous Cry over the Age of Consent

In 1890–91, many parts of India in general, but Bengal in particular, were rocked by a state of near revolt, with deeply agitated men and women taking to the streets amidst cries of 'religion in danger'. At times, they were even joined by young schoolboys. In the history of British India, neither before nor since 1891 has the Hindu orthodox camp displayed the remarkable unity of interest that was witnessed that year. This vociferous protest not only embarrassed the government, but also virtually defeated the prospects of enacting further social legislation for several years to come. Paradoxically, the controversy of 1890–91 marks both the summit and the dramatic defeat of orthodox Hindu sentiments.

'Age of Consent' may be legally defined as the minimum age fixed by statute below which sexual cohabitation with a girl would amount to rape, and hence invite punishment under law. In the 1890s, as per the provisions of the Indian Penal Code, the age of consent stood at ten and it was proposed that this be raised to twelve. In Vidyasagar's time, most reformers had associated the age of consent with the question of infant marriages, albeit somewhat mistakenly. It was often argued that raising the age of consent would also inhibit child marriages. The orthodox position, on the other hand, somewhat contrary to commonplace perceptions, was not to advocate an absurdly low age of marriage for girls as insist on the timely observance of the *garbhadhan* ceremony. Early marriages did not necessarily lead to a premature consummation of marriage, as it was customary for the married girl to be sent to her husband's home not immediately after marriage, but after she showed signs of attaining puberty. In both Hindu law and custom, it was mandatory that the father get the daughter wedded before she went into menses. We have earlier noted how Parasar himself condemned to hell the Brahmin who unwittingly married a girl already in her menses, and the prospects of hell were no less for the father who failed to comply with this requirement. Medhatithi, commenting on Manu II.45, had ruled that the husband was obligated to sexually cohabit with his wife within four days of her first going into the menstrual cycle. The orthodox did not insist on an early age for the marriage of boys; on the contrary, some of them recommended a fairly advanced age. Chandranath Basu (1844–1910), a spokesperson for the orthodox camp in the 1880s, suggested that the age of the groom be thrice as much as that of the bride. However, this was clearly in the interests of protecting patriarchy. As Bankimchandra himself was to write in his work *Dharmatattwa* (Principles of Dharma, 1888), the wife had to venerate the husband just as much the student the teacher, and the son, his parents. However, the reform party, especially comprising those who chose to go by medical opinion, wondered if early marriage itself and its cultural ramifications did not induce premature physiological changes in the girl. They were quite right in assuming that this served to reinforce the depressed state of the female population. Through much of the 1880s, various voluntary agencies worked towards fighting early marriages and ensuring a better conjugal life for a couple that otherwise appeared so incompatible, both physically and intellectually.

Hitherto, the State had remained a passive player and was quite reluctant to be drawn into the heat of the battle engaging the pro-reform and anti-reform parties. However, between 1887 and 1889 there occurred two remarkable incidents that forced the State to sit up and take fresh stock of the situation. In 1887, a woman named Rukmabai caused a flutter by spiritedly refusing to live on the same premises as her husband Bhikaji, on grounds of ill-treatment. The husband duly filed a suit and under the existing laws, the courts were forced to order the restitution of his conjugal rights. Although the case ended in a victory for the plaintiff, what it also revealed was a serious legal anomaly. Under the law, while the husband could enforce his marital rights over a minor wife, the wife herself was left unprotected, unaware of the implications of the law and a poor victim to irrational and oppressive custom. More importantly, this led to the realisation that an anomaly in law could be redressed by the law alone, and not any form of social agitation. The latter emerged with even greater starkness when, in 1889, the press reported the death of a 10-year-old girl, Phulmoni, from forced intercourse by her husband, her senior in age by several years. For both the State and legalists, this settled the need for a legal remedy for which there was no alternative to official intervention. As Ranade saw it, this also called for ensuring legal parity between offences that produced comparable results. While in some cases (Sections 361 and 371 of the Indian Penal Code [IPC]) the existing law gave protection to girls of fourteen and sixteen, in this instance it had failed to protect a girl of barely ten. Accordingly, a draft bill increasing the age of consent from ten to twelve was submitted before the Viceroy's Council on 9 January 1891, and produced a spate of protest pamphlets and meetings. By one estimate, as many as thirty-four protest meetings were held between 17 January and 25 February 1891 in the city of Calcutta alone, involving several lakhs of aggrieved people.

Roughly a month prior to its passing the bill (19 March 1891), the government sought Vidyasagar's opinion on the bill, as it had on many previous occasions. On 16 February 1891, the Pundit wrote back to the government, expressing his reservations on the bill. His letter did not oppose the bill in principle, but the manner in which it had been framed and its future implications. In 1933, Jogendrakumar Chattopadhyay, the editor of *Hitavadi*, produced a fairly long essay on his memories of Vidyasagar, which was published in the Sravan (July–August) issue of the journal *Bangasree.* In this essay, Jogendrakumar also reminiscences about the conversation he had with Vidyasagar, then recuperating at French Chandannagar (district Hooghly), on the question of determining a propitious age of consent A free translation of the relevant passage is produced below:

> At the time, many gentlemen called on him with curiosity in their minds, but Vidyasagar never ever expressed his opinion on the bill that was then being debated. One day, on persistent queries made by a gentleman, he said the following with some obvious irritation in his voice: 'What can be said of these people? They remind me of two groups of apes who were constantly snarling and baring their teeth at one another. The Hindu orthodox feel that they were easing their own path to heaven by virtually trampling upon infant girls and if anyone tried to stop them, they simply go up in chorus, crying: Oh! our religion is being ruined! On the other hand, what can I say of those who are so excitedly trying to get the bill passed! Under the provisions of the proposed bill, they may well be able to protect their girls up to the age of twelve, but what thereafter? One day the girl will attain the age of twelve. Who will protect them then? Is it not foolishness to bring about such changes in society through recourse to law? I am appalled at how people simply do not realise the implications of what they are doing. Once education advances in our society, the evils of polygamy or early marriages will by themselves cease to exist. At this time, you cannot but notice the deep anxiety in the parents of a marriageable girl who is about to attain the age of twelve. But should you live long enough, you will come to realise how people will simply stop considering marriage for a daughter who is only twelve or thirteen years of age. No father will seek a groom for his daughter until she is about fifteen or sixteen. Sadly, no one bothers to see which way our society is heading; they simply shut their eyes and cry hoarse! Oh! what a gathering of foolish apes!'[2]

It is quite striking that in the above passage, social change is seen to be derived not from *shastra*, but from progressive behavioural changes occurring in society. *Prima facie*, this strengthens the case for believing, as some biographers have always believed, that with Vidyasagar, the use of *shastra* was only a tactical ploy. It is equally possible, though, that the Pundit had visualised working over two successive stages; the first beginning with a short-term plan on the use of the *shastras*, and the second, a long-term strategy that further built upon what had been achieved in the short run. Effecting social legislation through a consensus built on expanding levels of education was not a plan that could have been realised in his lifetime, and quite appropriately, Vidyasagar did not begin with such a plan. Also, as I have hinted above, we cannot be entirely remiss of his bid to wrest social leadership using the offices of the Brahmin.

Interestingly, Vidyasagar's thoughts on the Age of Consent Bill produced two radically different sets of reactions. Right-conservative biographers like Biharilal and Subal Mira would have us believe that by expressing his reservations about the bill, Vidyasagar was only atoning for his past mistakes: in Biharilal's words, his 'besetting sins' in offending Hindu sentimentality over the widow marriage campaign. On the contrary, biographers like Benoy Ghose have taken this to indicate a backtracking in the man. There emerges, therefore, an 'early' Vidyasagar and a 'later' one; one was a social crusader, while the other deserted the cause of woman-related reform. Ghose also insinuated that by opposing the Age of Consent Bill, the Pundit had seriously compromised his support to the campaign to end premature marriages of girls. Both these readings, however, are faulty to the core. Vidyasagar never gave up his support for widow marriages, pledging financial support towards the very end of his life to a Sylhet-based organisation that was trying to promote such marriages, and he seriously tried to get one of his grandsons married to a widow. Ghose's critique may be more simply answered by pointing to the fact that the Age of Consent Bill controversy was only tangentially related to the age of marriage; an upward revision in the minimum age of marriage for Hindus occurred only as late as 1929. The bill of 1891 was essentially a move to amend the Penal Code, an eventuality that could be undertaken only by the State.

Notes

1. The substance of the debate between Pundits Jadaveswar and Panchanan on the propriety of the observance of Ekadashi by widows is available in the Ashad 1327 (June–July 1920) issue of the journal *Bharatvarsha*.

2. Translated from Jogendrakumar Chattopadhyay, *Vidyasagar Kotha* (Reminiscences of Vidyasagar). Originally published in *Bangashri* Sravan 1340 bs (July–August 1933).

Postscript

Was Vidyasagar an Atheist?

The question of Vidyasagar's relation to religion has long assumed a political and polemical character. Over time, it has also become somewhat personalised, with mutual criticism from rival camps being sometimes cloaked in snide, underhand sarcasm. Biographers have obviously viewed this question differently, and not always on the basis of established fact. In some cases, this difference stems from a hurried reading of a previous biographer and the tendency to accept older arguments uncritically, if only because, *prima facie*, these appear to agree with certain ideological presuppositions. As we have noticed earlier, Chandicharan Bandopadhyay misled many biographers by claiming that Vidyasagar had been persuaded to include thoughts on God and religion in his school textbook *Bodhodoy* by the Brahmo missionary, Bejoykrishna Goswami, whereas previously no such discussion had been included. Bandopadhyay is known to have learnt this from Bejoykrishna himself, quite possibly at the time of his writing the biography. Now Bejoykrishna passed away in 1899, four years after Chandicharan's biography was published, and presumably therefore any lapse of memory on the part of the biographer could have been corrected in time. The explanation, as now offered by modern researchers, is that *Bodhodoy* underwent several revisions in the course of its publishing history, which in itself poses the question: Did Vidyasagar then have a settled or an evolving view of religion?

Writing in 1984, the scholar Paramesh Acharya demonstrated that references to God and religion occurred in the very first edition of *Bodhodoy* in 1851. In current editions of the work, reprinted apparently from the 1867 edition, God does stage a comeback as both a creator God and as the moral Governor of the universe. But we also find evidence of a creator God in other works by Vidyasagar, such as the *Akhyanmanjari* (1863). Hence, it is reasonable to conclude that sometime between 1852 and 1867, these references were first taken out and eventually restored. Acharya found such references missing in the fifth edition of 1857, but this possibly may have occurred even earlier. Given our present state of knowledge, it is only possible to say that such references were back in place by 1867, albeit in a modified form. Thus, whereas the first edition of *Bodhodoy* described God as a 'Formless, Pure Consciousness' (*nirakar chaitanyaswarup*), this description does not appear in subsequent editions. Also removed permanently were the following lines: 'Hence, it is our duty to be devoted to God, to sing his praise and pay Him our respect' (translation mine).

However, such changes in the text, as I shall presently argue, do not dispute the very existence of God. Also, as indicated above, it is a moot question if Vidyasagar had a settled opinion on God and religion. His close friend and co-worker, Akshay Kumar Dutta, who can be said to have held comparable views on God and religion, also reveals an inner inconsistency that belies any general characterisation. Dutta, as is only too well-known, was a deist and a man of science; he took human productivity to be an independent value by itself, with no relation to prayers or soliciting divine intercession in routine human activities. In a formulaic presentation that has now become almost an adage, Dutta once argued that a farmer would be blessed by a bountiful crop just as much on the strength of his own hard labour alone as he would with the benefit of his prayers being granted by

God. Here, the sense of Akshay Kumar's argument is clear, but it misses out on logical consistency. Dutta's argument would certainly have been more acceptable had he only told us that the quantum of production was the same in both cases. Since he does not categorically state this, there remains a certain ambiguity in his argument. In an essay written for the *Tattwabodhini Patrika* in 1846, Dutta also bemoaned, in a manner quite reminiscent of Rammohun himself, the spread of godlessness and atheism among the contemporary youth. He was also to express unhappiness at the declining power and prestige of unscrupulous Brahmins, who would not hesitate to accept even Sudras at the head of some religious organisations. This seems to be more consistent with the fact that notwithstanding his overtures to deism, Dutta accepted formal initiation as a Brahmo under Ramchandra Vidyabagish (along with Debendranath Tagore and some others) in the year 1841. An equally surprising fact appears in the autobiography of Maharshi Debendranath. When commenting on his appointment of Dutta as the editor of the newly launched *Tattwabodhini Patrika* (founded in 1843), the Maharshi praised the elegance and simplicity of his Bengali compositions, but expressed disappointment at the fact that the author had also spoken approvingly of the Hindu *sanyasi*, typically with matted hair and body smeared with ashes, camped under the shade of a tree.

Vidyasagar, too, as we now know, was in many ways an idiosyncratic Brahmin, but he fully believed in the power and sanctity of Brahmanism. In 1864, he joined those who were resisting the government's attempts to introduce an electric[1] crematorium at Nimtala in north Calcutta. In 1876, while performing obituary rites for his departed father at Kashi, he personally washed the feet of the Brahmins gathered by way of paying respect. Like Rammohun, he never thought of discarding the sacred thread of the Brahmin. His non-conformism never approached the level of dissent identified with members of the Young Bengal group, who sometimes especially took it upon themselves to deliberately offend orthodox sentiments.

The first reference to an 'atheist' Vidyasagar occurs in the testimony of Krishnakamal Bhattacharya, who had known Vidyasagar for a long time and leaves us with some interesting and insightful vignettes from his life. Similar claims have been made ever since, albeit in somewhat muted and modified forms. Chandicharan Bandopadhyay argued that while he believed in God, the Pundit had virtually no faith in the daily religious rites or usages of the orthodox Hindu, and some biographers relate the story about the severe beating he once received from his father, Thakurdas, for neglecting to perform the ritual oblations at dusk (*sandhya*), which are traditionally obligatory for the Brahmin. Once, in the presence of Lalitmohan Chattopadhyay, a great-grandson of Rammohun, he is known to have mocked the very notion of an afterlife. At the time, there was also a story in circulation concerning his open ridicule of religious preachers, whether Hindu, Brahmo or Christian by persuasion. On reaching the gates of heaven, as Vidyasagar once narrated before an amused audience, a man was caned by gatekeepers for practising false religious beliefs. However, when it became known that he had been led to believe these by a certain religious teacher, the gatekeepers were ordered to deliver extra lashings on the preacher himself. The moral of the story was clearly that a preacher had no right to sermonise on God and religion, since he did not have any real understanding of such matters himself. Vidyasagar once told the conservative Hindu leader, Pandit Sasadhar Tarkachudamani (1851–1928), that young students of his college (The Metropolitan College) were unlikely to turn to vegetarianism even after hearing his lectures on propitious food and drink for Hindus. Upon catching sight of Christian evangelists trying to impress upon some young men the religious virtues of Christianity, he mockingly advised them to spare their young and innocent souls and settle on a senile and 'sinful' man like himself! On another occasion, he ridiculed the practice among Brahmos of the New Dispensation Church of imagining themselves as being in a personalised communion with religious figures from the past, like Moses and Chaitanya, reminding them that the latter had long since turned into ghosts! At no stage in his life did Vidyasagar reveal a theological interest or personally observe religious customs or festivities on a daily basis. His will omits any reference to charity bestowed on a religious institution. At Kashi, he even offended local Brahmins by refusing to pay obeisance at the famous Viswanath temple, arguing that for him, his parents themselves were gods descended on earth.

On the observance of caste rules, Vidyasagar reveals a perplexing ambiguity. Mahamopadhyay Haraprasad Sastri (1853–1931) recalled how the ladies of his family were devastated to hear that even as a Brahmin, Vidysagar had not hesitated to share food with the Kayastha Amrit Lal Mitra. It was also rumoured that at the Sanskrit College Hostel, too, he and his students would eat out of the same dish. This was later strongly contested by his brother Sambhchandra, who claimed that his elder brother would agree to this only in the case of his parents. We have had occasion to see how his attitude towards admitting non-Brahmin students to the Sanskrit College was a mixture of liberality and prudent realism. Understandably, it was easier for him to extend admission to boys of the Kayastha caste than it was to extend it to the ritually defiled Suvarnabaniks. It is a tribute to his liberality, though, that in his own lifetime, not only were Suvarnabanik students admitted to the Sanskrit College, but the College also recruited a teacher from that caste.

Some of his biographers have been inclined to think that he was indeed a God-fearing man, if not overtly religious. The scholar Ramakrishna Bhattacharya has aptly pointed out that none of the early biographies have really reckoned with the criticism directed at him by the scholar and evangelist, John Murdoch (1819–1904). Although he initially admired the quality of his primers, Murdoch turned into a strong critic by the 1870s. Thereafter, it was his mission to expose Vidyasagar as a 'rank materialist' and 'secularist' who thoughtlessly propagated a godless education among gullible schoolboys. Murdoch's criticism was focused on three of Vidyasagar's works—the

Bodhodoy, *Kathamala* and *Barnaparichay*—and in substance, his allegations were also three-fold in nature. In the first place, he pointed to the 'low miserable morality' in the *Barnaparichay*, which took lying or the use of foul language as acts that were merely socially reprehensible and not a rebellion against God. Second, he also took exception to Vidyasagar's eliminating all references to the Bible and to the soul and afterlife in Chamber's *Rudiments of Knowledge*, on which the *Bodhodoy* was based. Finally, he strongly disapproved of the Pundit's contention that our personal judgement in everyday matters was based on sense perceptions and worldly experience. This, in his opinion, was an open rebuttal of the Divine Will and mandates, and had no place in a system that hoped to disseminate sound education to young minds. It is interesting that in this enterprise, Murdoch failed to enlist the support of fellow evangelists; in 1872, the Christian Vernacular Education Society admitted that its own textbooks could not stand competition from those by Vidyasagar, and hence there was no question of replacing them. The Society also disagreed with the view that the Pundit's books were 'secular' in nature or spirit. Although seemingly 'un-Christian', they still taught the right moral lessons to students, the Society felt. Such lessons, then, did not necessarily have to be additionally supported with reference to the Bible. In hindsight, it would appear as though on this issue, the authorities in charge of missionary schools took a pragmatic view of the situation. They were quite alive to the fact that after 1854, the government policy on education encouraged a secular education, and that an added emphasis on a 'Christian' education ran the risk of antagonising middle-class parents. Hindu society of Calcutta in the 1870s had to be perceptibly different from that in the 1820s, when a man like Rammohun would readily agree to Hindu boys turning to the Bible to discover for themselves the 'truths' they had been taught.

In recent times, the charges of atheism in Vidyasagar have been repeated by Radharaman Mitra, the historian of urban Calcutta, in his work *Kolikatay Vidyasagar* (Vidyasagar in Calcutta,1982). In support of his claim, Mitra drew upon two sources: the testimony of Krishnakamal Bhattacharya and the letter of 7 September 1853 addressed to the Council of Education, discovered by Brajendranath Bandopadhyay, in which Vidyasagar dismissed both Vedanta and Samkhya as 'false systems of philosophy'.

In the 1960s, Benoy Ghose, who somewhat uncritically framed his study of Vidyasagar within the notion of a 'Renaissance Bengal', found it unlikely that the Pundit's 'modernism', 'realism', and 'humanism' could co-exist with the palpable belief in a Creator God. Ghose's contention was that Vidyasagar's moral pedagogy could not come to terms with a discussion on God and religion, and when this did happen, he first took care to posit 'matter' before 'God'. Echoing these sentiments, Badruddin Umar argued that if Vidyasagar had accepted God as a substantive and credible category, and especially given his knowledge of Nyaya philosophy, this reversal of priorities could not have occurred in some fit of absentmindedness. Gopal Haldar, also emphasising the 'secular' and 'realist' credentials of Vidyasagar, suggested that the Pundit was in all probability pushed to include the subject of God in keeping with the government's educational policy, which made a distinction between 'godless education' and education that was partial to any religions tradition.

Each of these arguments, however, may be effectively met with a counter-argument. First, a survey of the educational policy in mid-nineteenth century India would reveal a penchant for promoting secular education, especially by virtue of Wood's Dispatch of 1854. The Dispatch itself may have reflected educational thought in contemporary England, which, without going to the extreme of pushing for a godless education, was anxious to ensure that State funding of mass education was directed more along non-religious lines than the religious. Second, Vidyasagar's atheism will not stand purely on the strength of a personal testimony since there are also testimonies from people who knew Vidyasagar rather well, but who lead us to an opposite conclusion. That Vedanta and Samkhya were 'false' systems of philosophy was an extremely daring thing to say and may have contributed to Vidyasagar's unpopularity in the 1850s. Even in 1927, when Brajandranath Bandopadhyay published the 1853 letter for the first time in the *Modern Review*, he was constrained to conclude with the following remark: 'In his zeal for practical ends, Vidyasagar could not find anything useful in the Indian system of philosophy...he lacked the breadth and vision of Rammohun Roy who understood both the Eastern and Western standpoints.' However, there is also an interesting similarity between Rammohun and Vidyasagar with respect to the Vedanta. Both were convinced of its unsuitability as a course of study in modern educational institutions and yet would not dissociate from it altogether. Rammohun was to open a Vedanta College in Calcutta even after he had appealed to Governor-General Amherst not to invest state funds in furthering traditional Hindu education, and Vidyasagar, as we know, would not agree to the scheme mooted by his successor in office, E. B. Cowell, to discontinue the teaching of Smriti and Vedanta in the Sanskrit College.

In retrospect, Vidyasagar's labelling Vedanta and Samkhya as 'false systems of philosophy' appears to have argumentative flaws that are apparently hidden from us. For one, it is questionable to club together idealistic Vedanta and materialistic Samkhya. Could both be 'false' at the same time? Second, Pundit Iswarchandra does not clarify which school of Vedanta he was referring to. Assuming that he was referring to Advaita Vedanta, it stands to reason that he was guilty of confusing the subjective idealism of Berkeley with the monistic idealism of Advaita. Third, contrary to Vidyasagar's claim, Samkhya has very little in common with Berkeley. Fourth, the rejection of Samkhya and Vedanta as systems of philosophy does not by itself preclude a belief in God. The presumption that it was only with time that Vidyasagar's innate rationalism and materialism pushed him to sequentially place the category of 'matter' before that of God is also indefensible, since this arrangement occurred even in the first edition of *Bodhodoy* in 1851. Apparently, then, on this particular question, the Pundit's views do not appear to have changed. But this also begets another interesting question. By taking matter to precede God Himself, was Vidyasagar hinting at the idea of a Constructor God rather than a Creator? If yes, we will be forced to acknowledge a certain irony here since a Constructor God as different from a Creator God was a foundational principle among practitioners of Advaita Vedanta. The clubbing of Vedanta and Samkhya is understandable from one perspective alone. Going by Ramkrishna Bhattacharya's argument, this begins to make sense if, by 'Samkhya', our reference is to the later Samkhya which, in alliance with Yoga, turned quite speculative and theistic. Pundit Iswarchandra, as we now know, was not given to metaphysical speculation, and the passive, quietistic role of a yogi would have ill-suited him.

Finally, quite contrary to what Haldar suggests, Vidyasagar may have been led to revise his texts precisely because of the changes in educational policy occurring after 1854. There may also have been some social pressure at work. The concept of God as a formless abstraction (*nirakar chaitanyaswarup*), one imagines, would not have gone down well with the Hindus. Swami Vivekananda was to express some displeasure at this, but even to others, this would have appeared far too close to the Brahmo conception of God, which accepted the idea of a God endowed with attributes (*saguna*) but not with form (*sakara*). We have noted elsewhere how, for a man known to have no pronounced religious leanings or even an intellectual interest in religion, Vidyasagar's personal library included a wide variety of texts, one of which was a compilation of seventeen discourses on Brahmodharma by Acharya Ramchandra Vidyabagish (*Parameswarer Upasana Bishoye Prathamabdhi Saptadash Byakhyan*). Chandicharan Bandopadhyay suggests that Vidyasagar was once associated with the faction of the Brahmo Saṃaj (Adi Brahmo Samaj) led by Maharshi Debendranath, but gradually pulled himself away from it after recurring petty squabbles between various members turned matters rather unpleasant.

A closer scrutiny, however, would suggest that Vidyasagar remained sceptical about the theodicy of the Brahmos. In truth, one of the arguments consistently articulated by him against the idea of a God and Providence was that the commonplace perpetration of evil and injustice on earth was quite inconsistent with the idea of a just and merciful God. Debendranath Tagore was once constrained to comment quite unhappily about how some *nastiks* (atheists) present among his co-workers were ruining his reputation by refusing to publish a pious lecture on religion by the veteran Brahmo leader, Rajnarain Basu (1826–99). Here, his reference was clearly to Akshaykumar Dutta and Vidyasagar, who were both members of the Paper Committee which vetted papers submitted to the *Tattwabodhini Patrika* for publication. It is also on record that Vidyasagar removed himself from this position once the Maharshi formally merged the Tattwabodhini Sabha with the Brahmo Samaj in 1859.

However, in the much-debated *Bodhodoy* itself, Vidyasagar not only grants the existence of God, but also endows Him with several qualities: omniscience, omnipotence, and omnipresence. God is seen to be Compassionate, a benevolent Protector. and one who provides the means of sustenance to all forms of life on earth. It would not be unreasonable to draw comparisons between this conception of God and that of the Brahmos, who repudiated the idea of a God endowed with form (*sakar*), but endowed Him with some human qualities (*saguna*). In both instances, God is also the sole source of life and consciousness in all living beings. In the world of living creatures, as Vidyasagar also argues, each life form has been bestowed with properties which are functionally consistent with its very existence and lifecycle. *Prima facie*, this would underscore a belief in some Providential Design and seem consistent with a tale that he included in his *Akhyanmanjari* Part II, titled 'Aishik Vyabasthay Biswas' (Faith in Divine Arrangements). In this story, a despondent boy struggling to survive in a hostile world still believed that Providence had assigned to him a certain place and role in the world, and the issue at hand, therefore, was really for the boy to discover this for himself. On one level, creation was a mystery for Vidyasagar and whether directly or indirectly, this is a perception that he articulated on several occasions. In the first place, as I have suggested above, the idea of a merciful and compassionate God seemed incompatible with the oppression and brutality perpetrated by the strong upon the weak, or the innocent being wantonly made to suffer. Vidyasagar was devastated to hear of the sinking of the ship *Sir John Lawrence* off the coast of Odisha on 25 May 1887, in which accident all the passengers drowned. Mahendranath Gupta narrated how, to illustrate the incongruity of it all, Vidyasagar would cite the parable of Chengez Khan, who allegedly ordered that all his enemies held captive in war be mercilessly slaughtered.

Even when speaking from the perspective of a devout Hindu, the world would still have remained a mystery for Vidyasagar. The Pundit once told Mahendranath Gupta the following:

> Our Hindu philosophers have been unable to satisfactorily explain what they sought to do. There is no way in which we could comprehend the ways of God. What, then, is our duty? In my view, our sole aim should be work towards self-improvement and make this world of ours a better place.[2]

As a man of action, Vidyasagar revealed an aversion to metaphysics, but also responded to it appreciatively when put forth with a certain eloquence and originality. On 5 August 1882, Sri Ramakrishna called on Vidyasagar at his Badur bagan residence and stayed back until about 9 pm. On that occasion, among several other things that the saint said was a remark that reportedly struck Vidyasagar with some force. The ineffable Brahman/Reality/Absolute, Ramakrishna had observed, could not be ritually polluted by word of mouth (*ucchistha*) since It could not be described in human language at all. Pundit

Iswarchandra reportedly admitted that there was a Power behind the working of the world, although he knew not just how to understand that Power or make it a matter of human cognition. The Brahmo journal *Unity and the Minister* (n.d.) put this very well in the following words:

> Although he [Vidyasagar] was not a religious man in the general sense of the term and his beliefs and insights not so definite as one would expect, he had an unostentatious and natural faith and dependence upon the Being who is Absolute, which, whosoever closely watched him must admit.

Both Biharilal Sarkar and Subalchandra Mitra concur in calling Vidyasagar 'a man of his age', but they also used this epithet in a pejorative sense, critiquing someone whom they considered to have been swept away by the rushing tide of faithlessness and scepticism. Of the two, Mitra even chose to end on a mystical note:

> Vidyasagar was a man of the age; he followed the course indicated by it. No doubt this course has brought on a greater mischief to the real Hindu, has materially injured Hindu religion, has propelled the Hindu society with great force in the direction of disorganisation, but Vidyasagar ought not to be blamed for it. God alone, who made him with such materials, knows why he did so.

Here, I propose to take a cue from such characterisation, but invert the intention with which it was previously said. To me, Vidyasagar does appear to represent the new intelligentsia in colonial Bengal, but in a special sense. It is my feeling that he belonged to a new class which neither forsook tradition, nor was prepared to slavishly follow it. Over time, this class had developed new notions of religion and morality, rejecting both the hedonism, the laxness, and promiscuity of Babu culture in early nineteenth-century Calcutta and the reactive and reckless radicalism of Young Bengal that followed it. Vidyasagar himself had a deep-seated sense of religion, but one that was thickly enmeshed with notions of personal virtue, an honest calling, and a pressing sense of public duty. It is interesting that unlike some of his eminent contemporaries, as for instance Bankimchandra, Krishnakamal Bhattacharya, and Dwarkanath Mitter, he was never drawn to Auguste Comte and Positivism. A godless religion did not appeal to him, even though he never volunteered to express an opinion on the nature or functions of God with any degree of conviction. There is apparently a hidden paradox in the fact that while he attached little meaning to ritual observances, rites and rituals in their social form were undoubtedly important. We may aptly recall his dissatisfaction with civil marriages in general and his insistence that Gurucharan Mahalanobis take to Hindu marriage rites when marrying a widow. Religion in its collective, ceremonial or highly abstract forms did not attract him, and it was thus that he stayed away from the two major currents of Hindu religiosity that influenced contemporary Bengal: the abstract monotheism of the Brahmos and the neo-puranic devotional cultures, perhaps best exemplified in the life and work of both Bankimchandra and Sri Ramakrishna.

Like most people, Vidyasagar was affected by mood swings, and there were connections that he would then draw between the inscrutable, unpredictable, unstable rhythms of everyday life and thoughts on the ineffable and the transcendent. It was precisely at these moments that he turned inwards, sometimes listening with rapt attention to the esoteric and mystical *dehatattwa* songs rendered by the Muslim Baul singer, Akhiluddin, or else to Shyamasangit (devotional songs evoking the goddess Kali) from Jagatdurlabh Chattopadhyay, father-in-law to one of his daughters. The first he liked because of the way it brought forth the utter helplessness of man before the forces beyond his control and conception; the second because it evoked memories of the careful nurturing and tenderness that he would have received at the hands of his mother and from women in general. It was thus that he joined heaven to earth, the surreal to the real, a sense of transcendence to a firm commitment to this world.

Notes

1. It is unclear if this was, indeed, an electric crematorium, although this is what one would normally expect.

2. From the *Sri Sri Ramakrishna Kathamrita* by Mahendranath Gupta.

Appendix I

Iswarchandra Vidyasagar: A Historical Chronology

1820 (26 September) Birth at Birsingha village (then in district Hooghly, later made a part of district Midnapore) to Thakurdas Bandopadhyay and Bhagavati Devi

1825–28 Student at village *pathshala* under Kalilkanta Chattopadhyay for three years

1828 Leaves for Kolkata accompanied by Thakurdas; hosted by Jagatdurlabh Singha; instruction at local *pathshala* under Swarupchandra Das

1829 (1 June) Admitted to Sanskrit College

1830–31 Wins monthly scholarship of Rs 5; passes examination with distinction; Upanayan ceremony performed at age eleven

1834 Married to Dinamayee, daughter of Shatrughna Bhattaharya of village Khirpai

1835 At Sanskrit College, studies Sanskrit literature (Sahitya) under Pundit Jaygopal Tarkalankar; rhetoric (Alankar) under Pundit Premchand Tarkabagish; English classes in Sanskrit College discontinued

1836–38 Studies Vedanta under Pundit Sambhuchandra Vidyavachaspati; *smriti*

	under Pundits Harachandra Bhattacharya and Haranath Tarkabhushan
1839 (22 April)	Passes examination conducted by the Hindu Law Committee
1839 (16 May)	The title 'Vidyasagar' is mentioned in his Certificate of Merit of the Hindu Law Committee Examination; studies Nyaya under Pundit Nimaichand Shiromani
1840–41	Further studies in Nyaya under Pandit Jaynarayan Tarkapanchannan
1841	After completing his studies (a period of twelve years and five months in all), appointed Seristidar/Head Pandit at Fort William College, Calcutta, at a salary of Rs 50 per month; starts learning English and Hindi privately with assistance from Durgacharan Bandopadhyay, Neelmadhav Mukhopadhyay, Rajnarayan Basu, and Ananda Krishna Basu; composes *Basudev Charit* based on the *Bhagavat Purana*, but fails to publish due to the disapproval of the authorities at the Fort William College
1843	Appointed member of the Paper Committee of the *Tattvabodhini Patrika* along with Akshaykumar Dutta; Prelude (*Upakramanika*) to the *Mahabharata* published in the *Tattvabodhini Patrika*
1844	Governor-General Henry Hardinge establishes 101 schools at various places in Bengal, Bihar, and Odisha; Vidyasagar and G. T. Marshal, Secretary to Fort William College, entrusted with the selection of teachers
1846 (6 April)	Resigns from the post of Head Pundit at Fort William College

6 August	Appointed Assistant Secretary to Sanskrit College on a salary of Rs 50 per month
1 September	Submits report, 'Notes on the Sanskrit College', to Secretary, Rosomoy Dutta; Secretary disapproves of the reform measures suggested and refuses to forward the report to the Council of Education; Vidyasagar resigns post of Assistant Secretary, handing over charge to Pundit Taranath Tarkavachaspati
1847	Establishes Sanskrit Press and Sanskrit Book Depository in partnership with Pundit Madanmohan Tarkalankar; publishes *Betal Panchabimsati* at the request of G. T. Marshal; Bharatchandra's *Annadamangal* published by Sanskrit Press; Fort William College purchases 100 copies at Rs 6 each; this helps to clear the loan of Rs 600 used to buy the printing machine; dispute with Principal Kerr of Hindu College
1848	Publishes *Banglar Itihas-Part II*, adapted from the last nine chapters of Marshman's *History of Bengal*
1849 (1 March)	Appointed Head Writer and Treasurer of Fort William College on a salary of Rs 80 per month; publishes *Jeebon Charit*, based on biographical sketches of European men by Robert and William Chambers Fifth brother, Harish Chandra, dies at age eight; son Narayan Chandra born on 14 November
1850	Starts *Sarvashubhakari Patrika*; first issue includes anonymous essay on the ills of early marriages (*Balyavivaher Dosh*), now taken to be authored by Vidyasagar

4–5 December	Resigns a second time from Fort William College; appointed Professor of Sahitya at Sanskrit College on a salary of Rs 90 per month Submits report on the reorganisation of the Sanskrit College; appointed Honorary Secretary of Bethune Girls School; severs relations with friend and business partner, Madanmohan Tarkalankar
1851 (5 January)	Posts of Assistant Secretary and Secretary to Sanskrit College abolished; Vidyasagar appointed first Principal of Sanskrit College on a salary of Rs 150 per month
6 April	Publishes primer *Bodhodoy*, compiled from various English readers, originally called *Shishushikha-Part IV*; publishes *Sanskrit Vyakaraner Upakramanika* and *Rijupath*, Parts 1–3
9 July	Kayastha students admitted to Sanskrit College; Sundays declared a holiday; holidays no longer based on the Hindu calendar
12 August	Bemoans the death of his friend, J. D. Bethune
November	*Upakramanika* and *Rijupath* replace *Mughdabodh* in the teaching of Sanskrit grammar; daughter Hemlata born
1852 (April)	Another 'Note on Sanskrit College' submitted
28 August	Sanskrit College students charged an admission fee of Rs 2; publishes *Rijupath-Part II* and an edited version of the Hindi *Betal Pacchisi*
1853	English made compulsory in the Sanskrit College curriculum; five new teachers appointed, of whom Prasannakumar

	Sarvadhikari teaches English; publishes *Sanskrit Bhasha O Sanskrtit Sahitya Bishayak Prastab*; publishes *Vyakaran Kaumudi-Parts 1 and II*; publishes edited versions of *Kiratarjuniya* and *Raghuvamsam;* modern algebra texts replace *Beejganit* and *Lilavati*
1853–54	Establishes, free schools, night schools and charitable dispensaries at his native village, Birsingha
1853–58	Asiatic Society publishes an edited version of *Sarvadarshansamgraha*, edited by Vidyasagar
1854 (January)	Fort William College ceases to exist; appointed Member, Board of Examiners for civilian examinees; salary at Sanskrit College enhanced to Rs 300 per month
February	Recommends to Lt. Governor Halliday the pressing need for teaching through the vernacular
June	Monthly tuition fees of Rs 1 introduced at Sanskrit College
July	Vidyasagar dispatches Educational Report to Lt. Governor Halliday
December	Caste rules for admission to Sanskrit College further relaxed; publishes *Vyakaran Kaumudi-Part III*; publishes Bengali adaptation of Kalidas' *Abhigyana Sakuntalam*
1855 (24 January)	Publishes tract, *Vidavabibaha Prachalita Howa Uchit Kina-I,* amidst huge controversy; appointed member of Committee to examine the question of establishing modern universities in India
13 April	Publishes *Barnoporichoy-I*

1 May	Given the additional charge of Assistant Inspector of Schools for South Bengal (districts of Hooghly, Nadia, Burdwan, and Midnapore) on an additional salary of Rs 200 per month
14 June	Publishes *Barnoporichoy-II*
17 July	Model school founded in Sanskrit College to train teachers; Akshaykumar Dutta appointed Headmaster of the senior section
4 October	Issues public appeal in favour of widow marriages; appeal signed by nearly 1,000 men submitted to the Legislative Council; the tract *Vidabhavivaha Prachalita Howa Uchit Kina–II* published
21 November	Writes to DPI, Gordon Young, disapproving admission of Suvarnabanik students to Sanskrit College
27 December	Appeals to Legislative Council for prohibition of Hindu polygamous marriages; about 200 Model Vernacular schools opened in four districts of Bengal by this time
1856, 16 July	Widow Remarriage Act passed
August	Appointed Secretary of Bethune Girls School; designation changed to Special Inspector of Schools for South Bengal
7 December	First widow marriage under the Act of 1856 celebrated at the residence of Rajkrishna Bandopadhyay, Sukea Street; publishes *Charitabali* and *Kathamala* (adapted from *Aesop's Fables*); second daughter Kumudini born
1857	Calcutta University holds its first Senate meeting; Vidyasagar appointed Member of Arts Faculty; appointed Examiner

	for Sanskrit, Bengali, Hindi, and Oriya languages by Calcutta University; publishes edited version of *Shishupal Bodh;* Army occupies the Sanskrit College and turns it into a clinic for wounded soldiers; College shifts to rented premises in Bowbazar; returns to old premises in January 1860
1857–58	Sets up thirty-five girls' schools in the four districts under his charge: twenty in Hooghly, eleven in Burdwan, three in Midnapore, and one in Nadia
1858	Watched the staging of the plays *Kulin Kulsarvasya* and *Ratnavali* by Ramnarayan Tarkaratna
July	Resigns his posts of Principal, Sanskrit College and Special Inspector of Schools
15 November	Collaborates with Dwarkanath Vidyabhushan to start the paper *Somprakash*
1859	Vidyasagar watches the staging of Umeshchandra Mitra's *Vidabavivaha Nataka* at Metropolitan Theatre; resigns from *Tattvabodhini Sabha*
1860	Publishes introductory chapters of the *Mahabharata* in Bengali translation; publishes *Sitar Bonobas* and an edited version of *Valmiki Ramayan*
1861 (April)	Appointed Secretary to Calcutta Training School; takes over the management of the paper *Hindoo Patriot* following the death of Harish Chandra Mookerjee; publishes an edited version of Kalidas's *Kumarsambhava*
1862	Appoints Krishna Das Pal as editor of *Hindoo Patriot*; publishes *Vayakaran*

	Kaumudi–IV and an edited version of Bana Bhatta's *Kadambari*
1863	Appointed Inspector of Ward's Institution; elected Corresponding Member of German Oriental Society; publishes *Akhyanmanjari*
1864	Elected Member of Royal Asiatic Society of Great Britain; lends Rs 1,500 to Madhusudan Dutt; Calcutta Training School named Hindu Metropolitan Institution and subsequently renamed Metropolitan Institution; publishes Bengali dictionary, *Sabdamanjari*
1865	Authors two reports on Ward's Institution and subsequently resigns his post at the Institution
1866	Takes over Metropolitan Institution; directs second appeal to the Legislative Council on the subject of Hindu polygamous marriages
May–June	Sets up relief kitchens at Birsingha following acute famine conditions in Bengal and Odisha; called '*dayar sagar*' (ocean of compassion)
16 December	Meets with serious road accident when returning from Uttarpara, seriously impairs his health
1867	Eldest daughter married to Gopal Chandra Samajpati; publishes revised and enlarged version of *Akhyanmanjari*
1869	Resigns his post as Secretary, Bethune Girls School, publishes Kalidas's *Meghdootam*; severs ties with extended family at Birsingha, vows never to return; sells 1/3 share each of the Sanskrit Press Depository to Rajkrishna Bandopadhyay

	and Kalicharan Ghosh; raises Rs 8,000 in this manner, which clears outstanding debts; donates Sanskrit Book Depository to Brojonath Mukhopadhyay; publishes *Bhrantivilas* based on Shakespeare's *Comedy of Errors*
1870	Donates Rs 1,000 to Mahndralal Sarkar's Indian Association for the Cultivation of Science; mother Bhagavati Devi dies at Benares; son Narayanchandra marries widowed Bhavasundari, much to the delight of Vidyasagar; publishes *Uttaracharitam*
1871 (8 August)	Tract on Hindu polygamy published; published an edited version of Kalidas's *Abhigyanasakuntalam*; purchases property at Karmatar and retreats there to regain his heath
1872	Establishes Hindu Annuity Fund for the benefit of Hindu widows; appointed Trustee of the aforesaid body; second daughter Kumudini married to Aghorenath Chattopadhyay
1873	Establishes Metropolitan College; eldest daughter Hemlata widowed; tract on Hindu polygamy goes into second edition
16 August	Vidyasagar resigns from the Managing Committee of the Bengal Theatre on account of prostitutes being engaged as actors
1874 (28 January)	Denied entry into Asiatic Society Museum on account of 'improper' dress; the poet Bharatendu Harsichchandra accompanying him also turns back, severs ties with son Narayan Chandra

1875 (31 May)	Revises will, denying Narayan Chandra any share in the property; third daughter Binodini married to Surya Kumar Adhikari
1876	Appoints Surendranath Banerjee as Professor of English literature at Metropolitan College on a salary of Rs 200 per month; dissociates himself from Hindu Annuity Fund following differences of opinion; builds private residence at Badurbagan, Kolkata; father Thakurdas dies in Benares; Vidyasagar present at deathbed
1877	On the occasion of the Delhi Durbar, Sir Richard Temple, Lt. Governor of Bengal, confers Certificate of Honour on Vidyasagar; youngest daughter Sharatkumari married to Kartik Chandra Chattopadhyay
1880	C.I.E. conferred on Vidyasagar
1882 (5 August)	Ramakrishna Paramhamsa visits Vidyasagar at his Badurbagan residence
1883	Nominated Fellow of Punjab University; publishes Bana Bhatta's *Harshcharitam*
1884	Vidyasagar gifts Cassell's *Illustrated Works of Shakespeare* to Chandramukhi Basu of Bethune College, the first Indian woman to pass M.A. examination; visits Kanpur to regain his health
1885	Sells his remaining shares of Sanskrit Press Depository to Rajkrishna Bandopadhyay for Rs 5,000
1887	Declines to accept the title of Mahamahopadhyay conferred on him by the Government of India

1888	Wife Dinamoyee dies; publishes *Akhyanmanjari–II*, *Niskritilabhprayas*, and an anthology of poems, *Padyasamgraha–I*
1889	Publishes *Sanskrit Rachana* (anthology of early Sanskrit compositions)
1890	Publishes *Slokamanjari*, *Padyasangraha–II*; republishes *Anandamangal* of Bharatchandra; Bhagavati Memorial Vidyalaya opened at Birsingha
1891 (16 February)	Vidyasagar expresses his reservations on the Bill proposing amendment in the Indian Penal Code and Criminal. Procedure Code for raising the age of consent from ten to twelve; Bill passed nevertheless on 19 March 1891 as Act X of 1891
29 July	Dies at his Badurbagan residence at 2.18 in the morning; cause of death diagnosed as cancer of the liver

Appendix II

Works of Iswarchandra Vidyasagar

A. Works Written or Compiled in the Bengali and Sanskrit Languages

1. *Banglar Itihas,* 1848
2. *Jeebon Charit,* September 1849
3. *Bodhodoy* (Shishushikha-IV), April 1851
4. *Sanskrit Vyakaraner Upakramanilka,* November 1851
5. *Rijupath: Part I,* November 1851; *Part II,* March 1852; *Part III,* December 1851
6. *Sanskrit Bhasha O Sanskrit Sahitya Bishayak Prastab,* March 1853
7. *Vyakaran Kaumudi: Part I,* 1853; *Part II,* 1853; *Part III,* 1854; *Part IV,* 1855
8. *Sakuntala,* December 1854
9. *Vidhabavivaha Prachalita Howa Uchit Kina. Etadbishayak Prastab,* Book I, January 1855; Book II, October 1856. Select portions of Book I published in the *Tattwabodhini Patrika,* January 1855. Part translation of the two tracts into English by Vidyasagar, titled *Marriage of Hindu Widows;* English translation subsequently translated into Marathi by Vishnu Parasuram Shastri in January 1865
10. *Barnoparichay: Part I,* April 1855; *Part II,* June 1855
11. *Kathamala,* February 1856
12. *Charitabali,* July 1856

13. *Mahabharater Upakramanika*. First serially published in the *Tatwabodhini Patrika* between 1849–53; published as a book in January 1860
14. *Pathmala*, 1859
15. *Sitar Bonobas*, April 1860
16. *Akhyanmanjari*, November 1863, enlarged edition published in 1868
17. *Sabdamanjari* (Bengali Dictionary), 1864
18. *Bhrativilas*, 16 December 1869
19. *Bahuvibaha Rahit Howa Uchit Kina Etadbishayak Vichar*, Book I: 10 August 1871; Book II, 1 April 1873
20. *Vamanakhyam*, 1873
21. *Nishkritilabh Prayas*, April 1888
22. *Padyasangraha, Part I*: 2 July 1888; *Part II*: 1889
23. *Sanskrit Rachana*, November 1889
24. *Slokamanjari*, May 1890

B. Works Published Anonymously but Attributed to Vidyasagar

1. *Ati Olpo Hoilo*, 5 May 1873
2. *Abar Oto Olpo Hoilo*, 7 September 1873
3. *Brojovilas*, 3 November 1884
4. *Vidhabavivaha O Jessore Dharmarakhini Sabha*, 11 November 1884; renamed *Vinay Patrika* in the second edition
5. *Ratnaparikha*, 19 August 1886

C. Edited Works in Bengali and in Languages other than Bengali

1. *Annadamangal* of Bharatchandra, 2 Vols, 1847[1]
2. *Betal Pacchisi*, January 1852
3. *Raghuvamsam* of Kalidas, June 1853
4. *Kirataarjuniyam* of Bharavi, 1853
5. *Sarvdarsanasamgraha* of Madvacharya, 1853–58
6. *Shishupal Vadha* of Magha, 1857
7. *Kumarsambhava* of Kalidas, 1861
8. *Kadambari* of Bana Bhatta, 1862
9. *Meghadootam* of Kalidas, April 1869
10. *Utaararamacharitam* of Bhavabhuti, April 1869

11. *Avhigyanasakuntalam* of Kalidas, June 1871
12. *Harshacharitam* of Bana Bhatta, March 1883

D. Posthumously Published Works

1. *Vidyasagar Charit* (Autobiographical Fragment), September 1891
2. *Bhugolkhagolvarnanam*, 1892
3. *Prabhavatisambhashanam*, originally published in the Bengali journal *Sahitya* in 1892
4. *Matribhakti* (Essay on George Washington), 1892
5. *Chagoler Buddhi*, published in the Bengali journal *Sakha* in 1894

E. Unpublished Work

1. *Vasudev Charit* (composed sometime between 1842 and 1847)

Note

Vidyasagar partly authored the *Nitibodh*, leaving Rajkrishna Bandopadhya to complete it in 1851. There are references to his also editing the following works, which cannot be verified:

a. *Selections from the Works of Goldsmith* (n.d.)
b. *Poetical Selections from English Literature* (n.d.)

This list adds up to forty-nine works if the above two works are also included. If the two parts each of the Widow Marriage and Polygamy tracts are counted separately, the number increases to fifty-one, which is very close to the number fifty-two indicated by Chandicharan Banopadhyay.

Selected Works of Vidyasagar were first edited and published by his son, Narayanchandra, in 1895. Subsequently, Sunit Kumar Chatterjee, Sajani Kanta Das, and Brajendranath Bandopadhyay edited and published the entire corpus of his writings in three volumes between 1937 and 1939 under the auspices of the Midnapore Vidyasagar Memorial Society. This edition was published by Ranjan Publishing House of Kolkata. Standard editions of his *Sakuntala* and *Sitar Bonobas* were also published independently by the Bangiya Sahitya Parishat in 1945 and 1948, respectively.

Note

1. Printed by the Sanskrit Press; however, there is reason to believe that this work was actually edited by Madanmohan Tarkalankar.

Appendix III

Miscellaneous Information Related to the Number and Social Composition of Students at the Calcutta Sanskrit College, Metropolitan Institution, and Bethune School

A. Number of Students at the Government Sanskrit College: 1824–51

Year	Number
1824	115
1825	104
1826	142
1827	172
1828	186
1829	142
1830	156
1831	148
1832	185
1833	190
1834	181
1835	135
1836	121
1837	120

(Contd)

(Contd)

Year	Number
1838	140
1839	111
1840	117
1841	126
1842	164
1843	140
1844	182
1845	188
1846	262
1847	226
1848	273
1849	268
1850	288
1851	299

B. Tabular Statement on Brahmin and Non-Brahmin Students in Sanskrit College: 1863–73

Year	Brahmin	Non-Brahmin
1863	64	36
1864	57	43
1865	59	41
1866	65	35
1867	61	39
1868	62	38
1869	64	36
1870	60	40
1871	63	37
1872	66	34
1873	67	33

C. Relative Student Strength of Leading Colleges in Calcutta: 1882–91

Year (→) College (↓)	1882	1883	1886	1888	1889	1890	1891
Presidency	374	383	180	333	399	423	479
General Assembly	484	402	304	415	348	329	353
Metropolitan	341	406	556	837	862	706	689
City College	52	85	174	269	290	317	327
Ripon College	–	–	149	274	430	525	457

D. Annual Expenditure Incurred by Select Colleges in Calcutta: 1888–89

College	Total Expenditure (in Rupees)	Annual Expenditure on Each Student (in Rupees-Anna-Paisa)
Metropolitan	33,077	27–12–1
City College	13,122	46–14–1
Ripon College	16,354	42–4–1
Presidency College	1,32,781	312–6–9
General Assembly	43,347	123–13–6

E. Relative Academic Performance of Students from Select Colleges of Calcutta: 1888

College	Candidates Sent Up	1st Class Honours	2nd Class Honours	Without Honours
Presidency College	92	12	16	20
Metropolitan	168	1	14	65
City College	69	1	6	23
Ripon College	77	–	5	20

F. Tabular Statement on the Number of Girls Admitted, Withdrawn, and Remaining on the Rolls of Bethune School at the End of the Year

Year	No. Admitted	No. Withdrawn	No. Remaining on the Rolls
1849	54	29	25
1850	40	21	44
1851	11	27	28
1852	10	0	38
1853	30	25	43
1854	20	21	42
1855	19	16	45
1856	26	16	55
1857	23	27	51
1858	25	26	40
1859	43	37	56
1860	43	27	72
1861	40	33	79
1862	33	19	93

G. Caste Identity of 79 Girl Students at the Bethune School for the Year 1861

Caste	Number
Brahmin	9
Baidya	3
Kayastha	14
Sadgop	5
Karmakar	5
Teli	15
Tanti	16
Modak	3
Subarna Banik	9

Source: Arabinda Guha (ed.), *Unpublished Letters of Vidyasagar*. Calcutta. Ananda Publishers, 1971, 23, 41, 42, 77.

Shatabarsha Smaranika, Vidyasagar College, 1872–1972. Kolkata. Vidyasagar College Smarak Grantha Samiti, 2019. Chief Editor: Ramakanta Chatavarti, 407–15.

Appendix IV

Three Letters from Vidyasagar in Translation on the Issues of Marriage and Conjugality

A.

To the Editor, *Somprakash*[1]

Dear Editor,

The *Somprakash* of 6th Bhadra, 1278 bs had put the following question before its readers: '(To) those who are attempting to legally put an end to multiple marriages in men ... [we ask] should such an unjust act be at all enacted on the strength of a royal statute? And if indeed this comes to pass, will the ruler himself not be liable to take part of the blame?'[2]

Your question may lead people to assume that the provision allowing a man to take a second wife in case the first was found barren was hitherto unknown in this country and was now being enacted as a new law. This is far from the truth and had you only more carefully examined the arguments of the pro-reform party, you would not have raised such questions.

The *shastras* permit a man to remarry in case his first wife proves to be barren or unchaste. Many men have been known to take a second wife under such enabling provisions. But even outside these, the tendency to marry at will has gained considerable ground. Those who seek to change this through recourse to law have only one objective in mind: to put an end to such shameful, loathsome, unpleasant, immoral, self-seeking instances of polygamous marriages. And finding no other way to effectively do away with this evil practice, they have been forced to seek the intervention of the State. The kind of remedy that they seek has been appended to the tract on 'An examination of the question on whether or not polygamous marriages should be ended'. The purport of this tract is essentially to establish the fact that unless the first wife be proven to be barren, an outcaste, perpetually ill, unchaste or somehow unfit for marriage, her husband will not be able to remarry in her lifetime. The underlying merit of the proposal is that, while on the one hand it disallows a man to marry at will, it permits him to take another wife as per special provisions traditionally sanctioned in the *shastras*. In this way, the prescriptive power and the dignity of the *shastras* are maintained. The authors of these *shastras* allow a man to remarry even in the lifetime of the wife should she be proven to be a barren woman. They have also taken care to fix the propitious time for this to be carried out. They have ruled that a woman may be declared barren should she fail to conceive within eight years from the time she goes into menses. They have left no room for determining whether it was the husband or the wife who was at fault.

It is clear that those who advocate putting a stop to polygamous marriages do not wish to contest the longstanding rule, sanctioned by our *shastras* in certain given circumstances. Hence, it would be redundant on the part of those agitating the issue to claim that a husband was indeed entitled to take a second wife in case the first proved to be barren. And if, going by their proposal, a new rule is indeed put in place and if a man, despite being impotent himself, takes another wife if the first wife failed to give birth to a son within the aforesaid eight years, how is the ruler to be blamed? After all, the ruler is not enacting a new law; he is simply endorsing the people's will to abide by the rules of the *shastras*. In any case, it does appear quite unjust on your part to accuse those who seek to put an end to polygamous marriages through a royal fiat.

You do concede that great wrongdoing attaches to those marrying at will and you do also grant that the evil of polygamous marriages must be promptly put to an end. The only matter on which you disagree is the propriety of approaching the ruler for a suitable remedy, since that amounts to the ruler wantonly interfering in the social practices of our community. And yet, surprisingly, you propose that a deterrent tax be imposed on those undertaking multiple marriages. Apparently, you also take this to be a reasonable and effective method of discouraging polygamous marriages. But we are still constrained to ask: 'Does the imposition of such a tax also not amount to State interference?' If only you were to examine this more carefully, you would discover that the proposal will amount to interference in religious matters, too, since the *shastras* have mandated that a man take a second wife should the first prove to be barren or suffering from any other disqualification. If a tax such as the one you propose were to be imposed, will this not obstruct the fulfilment of a religious duty or ensuring a progeny? Frankly, this proposal of yours has not been given adequate attention. If only you were to weigh matters more carefully you will no doubt realise that to legally put a stop to the practice of polygamy will have a far more salutary effect on the community life of the Hindus than attempting this through a prohibitory tax. If such a tax were indeed imposed, rather than put a stop to this evil practice, it will only sully the good name of our English rulers in the eyes of every civilised race.

Kashipur,
8th Bhadra 1278 bs — Sri Iswarchandra Sharma
(23 August 1871)

Source: *Vidyasagar Rachanavali* (Collected Works of Vidyasagar), Sahityam Edition, Vol. II. Kolkata, 2006, 1383–85; translation mine.

B.

To Rajnarain Basu,[3]

Warm Greetings.
Your letter reached me a few days ago, but several engagements kept me from answering it promptly. Please do not be offended.

I have reflected at length on the issue of your daughter's marriage, but cannot make up my mind as to what appropriate advice I might offer to you. It is not at all easy to offer advice on matters as complex or as delicate as this one. First, you happen to be a Brahmo. Considering the great respect in which you hold the Brahmo Samaj, it would be only appropriate for you to adopt the reformed marriage rites that Devendranath Tagore had adopted when solemnising the marriage of his daughter. I am assuming that you hold these rites to be consistent with the ideals and beliefs of the Brahmo Samaj. On the other hand, should you prefer to go by the older and established marriage rites of the Hindus, there is bound to arise certain difficulties in the way of popularising Brahmo marriages. Also, it cannot be said with any certainty if the adoption of Brahmo marriage rites will lead to the marriage being counted as legally valid. It is for such reasons that I feel both reluctant and incapable of offering you any specific advice on this issue. The only advice that I can give you at this stage is not to rush into any decision.

On the present question, it is also my understanding that it would be injudicious to seek someone else's view. In this case, it is best to act according to the dictates of one's own conscience. Each person you ask is bound to have a different opinion on the subject and will advise you accordingly; they are less likely to take into consideration what is good for you.

Under the circumstances, it is best to go by your own judgement in this matter ....

Dated the 6th Aswin (?)

Source: *Vidyasagar Rachanavali* (Collected Works of Vidyasagar), Sahityam Edition, Vol. II. Kolkata, 2006, 1374–75; translation mine.

C.

To:

Dear Babu Durgamohan Das,[4] with my greetings and good wishes,

... being preoccupied with several matters of late, I simply could not find the time to write back to you. Please do not be offended.

I cannot adequately express my pain and anguish upon learning that you have failed to overcome the hurdles that have come your way in accomplishing your desired objective. However, I can easily feel the distress and exasperation that this might have caused you; it would be indeed hard to wipe these clean off your mind. In everyday life, it is but an unspoken rule that *bona fide* acts carrying good intentions behind them do not always come to fruition. 'Shreyamshi Bahuvignani', as they say in Sanskrit; there are numerous obstacles on the path of performing good deeds. Ever since news of your sincere and continuing efforts (to seek a groom for your widowed stepmother) had reached me, I feared that these would be frustrated once your elder brother was apprised of them. And what I had feared all along has now come to be realised. All the same, just because this attempt of yours has failed, you should not turn despondent and give up all hopes of succeeding in the future. We keep working in so many different directions and with sundry aims, but not all of these efforts succeed. The main reason for this is that the people working with good and laudable intentions in mind are but small in number, whereas countless are those who are only eager to frustrate and defeat these intentions. Under such circumstances, we must feel happy and fortunate to have achieved what little we do achieve. The respect and praise that I would have showered on you had you succeeded in your enterprise I would not hesitate to bring forth despite your failure. Regardless of whether or not you have succeeded in achieving what you set out to do, I now have ample knowledge of your resolve, the strength of your convictions and the nobility of mind. And it is equally clear to me that so long as you remain in control of your work, success is bound to come to you. I am inclined to believe that very few among us would have ventured to take up the difficult task that you had taken up for yourself. This establishes my faith in your manliness. I pray that you have a long life and that many of us benefit from your continued presence.

I have often reliably learnt of your exemplary qualities and have come to accept you as a man noted for his geniality, modesty, fearlessness, and accommodative spirit, a philanthropic soul always eager to work for the welfare of others ....

(no date given)

Sincerely,
Sri Iswarchandra Sharma

Source: *Vidyasagar Rachanavali* (Collected Works of Vidyasagar), Sahityam Edition, Vol. II. Kolkata, 2006, 1375–76; translation mine.

Notes

1. Dwarkanath Vidyabhushan (1819–86), an alumni of the Sanskrit College who also served on the faculty of the College for some time. The weekly *Somprakash* was founded in 1858 with support from Vidyasagar. It proved to be a leading newspaper of the time.

2. The *Somprakash* of 6th Bhadra, 1278 bs (21 August 1871) had written thus:

> To those who are attempting to legally end the practice of multiple marriage among men, we are constrained to put the following question: It has been proposed that should a wife prove to be barren, the husband would be free to take a second wife, but will this proposal not be the cause for much unpleasantness and heartburn? After all, it is just as possible that the man himself proves to be impotent and, in any case, the cause for infertility, whether in the case of the man or the woman, cannot be determined without conducting detailed medical tests. If it be the case that the man himself was at fault and not the woman, will it not be an act of gross injustice for

> the man to take another wife? And if this unjust act be enacted on the strength of a royal statute, will the ruler himself not be liable to take part of the blame? (translation mine)

3. Rajnarain Basu (1826–99): An alumnus of the Hindu College, and known for his bohemian habits in early life. He was attracted to Brahmoism and, along with Devendranath Tagore, was one of the pillars of the Adi Brahmo Samaj, the oldest of the three factions within the Brahmo Samaj. He taught English briefly at the Sanskrit College and also served as house-tutor to Rabindranath Tagore for some time. He was the maternal grandfather of Sri Aurobindo.

4. Durgamohan Das (1841–97): A successful advocate and active member of the Sadharan Brahmo Samaj, he was instrumental in popularising Brahmodharma in eastern Bengal. He was also an active worker in the fields of female education and widow marriage. The above correspondence refers to his initial failure to get his young but widowed stepmother married. In this radically courageous enterprise, he was eventually successful. Quite extraordinarily, too, when his first wife, Brahmamayi, passed away in 1876, Durgamohna authored a personal memoir describing her life, a copy of which was sent to Vidyasagar in 1881. In 1890, Durgamohan himself married Hemantasashi Sen, the widowed mother of the poet and musician, Atulprasad Sen (1871–1934). The well-known political leader Chittaranjan Das was his nephew and Abala Bose, married to the scientist Jagadish Bose, his daughter.

Select Bibliography

Acharya, Paramesh. 'Development of Modern Language Text Books and the Social Context in Nineteenth Century Bengal'. *Economic and Political Weekly*, 26 August 1986.

——. 'Is Macaulay Still our Guru?' *Economic and Political Weekly*, 28 May 1988.

——. 'Bengali Bhadralok and Educational Development in Nineteenth Century Bengal'. *Economic and Political Weekly*, 1 April 1995.

——. *Bangali Prabuddha Samajer Seema O Vidyasagar Bitarka*. Calcutta: New Horizon Book Trust, 2002.

——. *Bangalir Shikhhachinta*. Kolkata: Dey's Publishing, 2011.

Adhikari, Santosh Kumar. *Adhunik Manasikata O Vidyasagar*. Calcutta. Vidyasagar Research Centre.

——. *Vidyasagar and the Regeneration of Bengal*. Calcutta: Suvarnarekha, 1980.

Bandyopadhyay, Aparna. 'Hindu Revivalism and "Unchaste" Widows in Colonial Bengal'. *Asian Studies*, Special Issue (Gendered Asia) XXXVI (1&2), January–December 2018.

Bandopadhyay, Brojendranath. *Vidyasagar Prosongo*. Calcutta: Gurudas Chattopadhyay, 1931.

——. *Iswarchandra Vidyasagar, Deenabandhi Mitra*, Sahitya Sadhak Charitramala. Calcutta: Bangiya Sahitya Parishat, 1970.

Bandopadhyay, Chandicharan. *Vidyasagar*. Allahabad: Indian Press, 1909, 3e.

Bandopadhyay, Chittranjan. *Bongo Prosongo*. Calcutta: Ananda Edition, 2001.

Bandopadhyay, Sekhar. 'Caste, Widow Marriage and Reform of Popular Culture'. In Sumit Sarkar and Tanika Sarkar (eds), *Women and Social Reform in Modern India*. New Delhi: Permanent Black, 2011.

Basu, Swapan. *Banglay Nobochetanar Itihas*. Calcutta: Pustak Bipani, 1984.

____. *Samakale Vidyasagar*. Calcutta: Pustak Bipani, 1993.

Bhattacharya, Ramakrishna. *Vidyasagar, Nana Prosongo*. Kolkata: Chirayat Publications, 2011.

Bhattacharya, Sabyasachi (ed.). *Development of Modern Indian Thought and the Social Sciences*. New Delhi. Centre for the Study in Civilzation and Oxford University Press, 2007.

Bhowmik, Shekhar. 'Benche thako Vidyasagar'. *Anandabazar Patrika* (Robibasariya), 22 September 2019.

Capper, John. *The Three Presidencies of India*. London, 1853.

Caroll, Lucy. 'Law, Custom and Statutory Social Reform. The Hindu Widow's Remarrriage Act of 1856'. In Sumit Sarkar and Tanika Sarkar (eds), *Women and Social Reform in Modern India*. New Delhi: Permanent Black, 2011.

Chakravarti, Ramakanta. 'Vidyasagar O Mulyabodh'. In *Bangalir Dharma Samaj O Sanskriti*. Calcutta: Subarnarekha, 2002.

Chattopadhyay, Bankimchandra. 'Bengali Literature'. In Jogesh Chandra Bagal (ed.), *Bankim Rachanavali*, Vol. III. Calcutta: Sahitya Samsad, 1969a.

____. 'The Study of Hindu Philosophy'. In Jogesh Chandra Bagal (ed.), *Bankim Rachanavali*, Vol. III. Calcutta: Sahitya Samsad, 1969b.

____. 'Sankhya Darshan'. In Jogesh Chandra Bagal (ed.), *Bankim Rachanavali*, Vol. II. Kolkata: Sahitya Samsad, 2004a.

____. 'Vahuvibaha'. In Jogesh Chandra Bagal (ed.), *Bankim Rachanavali*, Vol. II. Calcutta: Sahitya Samsad, 2004b.

____. 'Sir William Grey O Sir George Campbell'. In Jogesh Chandra Bagal (ed.), *Bankim Rachanavali*, Vol. II. Kolkata. Sahitya Samsad, 2004c.

Chattopadhyay, Goutam (ed.). *Awakening in Bengal* (Selected Documents), Vol. I. Calcutta: Progressive Publishers, 1965.

Chintamani, C. Y. (ed.). *Indian Social Reform in Four Parts. Being a Collection of Essays, Addresses, Speeches &c with an Appendix*. Madras: Minerva Press, 1901.

Devi, Nistarini. *Sekele Kotha*, Ashok Chattopadhyay (ed.). Kolkata: Chirayat Prakashan, 2011.

Dutta, Bhavatosh. *Bangalir Manavadharma*. Calcutta: Mitra O Ghosh, 2000.

Gidumal, Dayaram. *The Status of Women in India. Or a Handbook for Hindu Social Reformers.* Bombay. 1889.

Ghose, Benoy. *Vidyasagar O Bangali Samaj* (All volumes combined). Hyderabad: Orient Longman, 1984.

Grealia, Shoshun Razel Gordon. 'The Widow Marriage Taboo in Jewish and Hindu and Jewish Law and Lore'. In Theodore Ithamar and Yudit Kornberg (eds), *Dharma and Halacha. Comparative Studies in Hindu-Jewish Philosophy and Religion*. Lanham: Lexington Books, 2018.

Guha, Arabinda (ed.). *Unpublished Letters of Vidyasagar*. Calcutta: Rekha Guha, 1971.

Gupta, Mahendranath. *Sri Sri Ramakrishna Kathamrita*, Vol. I. Calcutta: Kathamrita Bhavan, 1961.

Haldar, Gopal. *Vidyasagar. A Reassessment*. Delhi: PPH, 1972.

Hatcher, Brian A. *Idioms of Improvement. Vidyasagar and the Cultural Encounter in Bengal.* Calcutta: Oxford University Press, 1996.

———. *Iswarchandra Vidyasagar. Hindu Widow Remarriage. A Complete Translation with an Introduction and Critical Notes*. New Delhi: Permanent Black, 2012.

———. *The Life and Afterlife of an Eminent Indian*. New Delhi: Routledge India, 2014.

Mandal, Archana. 'The Ideology and the Interests of the Bengali Intelligentsia. Sir George Campbell's Educational Policy'. *Indian Economic and Social History Review* 12 (1), 1975.

Mitra, Indra. *Karunasagar Vidyasagar*. Calcutta: Ananda, 2012.

Mitra, Subal Chandra. *Iswar Chandra Vidyasagar. Story of His life and Work*. New Delhi. Rupa & Co., 2008.

Mitra, Trailokyanath. *The Law Related to Hindu Widows*, Tagore Law Lecture for 1879. Calcutta: Thacker Spink & Co., 1881.

Mukhopadhyay, Balaichand (Banaphool). *Vidyasagar.* Calcutta: DM Library, 1948.

Mukhopadhya Manik, et al. (eds). *The Golden Book of Vidyasagar.* Calcutta: All Bengal Vidyasagar Death Centenary Committee, 1993.

Murshid, Golam (ed.). *Vidyasagar Smarakgrantha.* Calcutta. Vidyadoy Library, 1960.

Nag, Arnab (ed.). *Iswarchandra Vidyasagat: Byakti O Byaktitwa.* Kolkata: Akshar Prakashan, 2020.

Papers Related to Infant Marriages and Enforced Widowhood in India. Calcutta: Government Printing Press, 1886.

Parasar Samhita, Banganubad Sahit. Calcutta: Kailash Chandra Singha & Sureshchandra Singha, 1886.

Ray, Alok, et al., (eds). *Dusho Bochorer Bangla Probondho Sahitya,* Vol. 1. New Delhi: Sahitya Akademi, 2011.

Ray, Ananta Kumar. *Vidyasagar. The Great Indian Educationist and Philanthropist.* Calcutta: Rohini Kumar Roy, 1921.

Sarkar, Biharilal (compiled). *Vidyasagar Arthat Samalochana Sankalita Iswarchandra Vidyasagarer Jeebon.* Calcutta: Baninath Nandi, 1895.

Sarkar, Sumit. 'Vidyasagar and Brahmanical Society'. In Sumit Sarkar, *Writing Social History.* New Delhi: Oxford University Press, 1997.

Sastri, Sivanath. *Men I Have Seen.* Calcutta: Modern Review Office, 1919.

Sen, Asok. *Iswar Chandra Vidyasagar and His Elusive Milestones.* New Delhi: Permanent Black, 2016.

Shatabarsha Smaranika, Vidyasagar College, 1872–1972 (Chief Editor: Ramakanta Chakrabarty). Kolkata: Vidyasagar College Shatabarsha Smarak Grantha, 2019 [1972].

Singha, Kaloprosnno. *Satik Hutom Pyanchar Naksha,* Arun Nag (ed.). Kolkata: Ananda Publishers, 2010.

Tagore, Rabindranath. 'Vidyasagar Charit'. In Viswabharati (ed.), *Rabindra Rachanavali,* Vol. II. Kolkata, 2002.

Tattvabhushan, Sitanath. *Social Reform in Bengal: A Side Sketch.* Calcutta: The City Book Society, 1904.

Tripathi, Amalesh. *Vidyasagar: The Traditional Moderniser.* Hyderabad: Orient Longman, 1974.

Umar, Badruddin. *Iswarchandra Vidyasagar O Unnish Shataker Bangali Samaj*. Calcutta: Chirayat Prakashan, 1962.
Vaidya, Narayan Keshav (ed.). *A Collection Containing the Proceedings which Led to the Passing of the Act of 1856*. [With an Introduction by M. G. Ranade and an Appendix compiled by Pandit Narayan Keshav Vaidya.] Bombay: Mazagon Printing Press, 1885.
Vidyaratna, Sambhuchandra. *Vidyasagar Jeevancharit O Bhramanirash*. Calcutta: Chirayat Prakashan, 1992.
Vidyasagar Rachanavali, 2 Vols. Kolkata: Sahityam, 2006.

Index